WOODLAND GARDENING

WOODLAND GARDENING

Richard Bird

Line drawings by Duncan Lowe

Souvenir Press

First published 1992 by Souvenir Press Ltd,
43 Great Russell Street, London WC1B 3PA
and simultaneously in Canada

ISBN 0 285 63094 6

Phototypeset by Intype, London

Printed in Great Britain by
Redwood Press Limited,
Melksham, Wiltshire

Contents

List of Illustrations

The white-berried form of *Pernettya mucronata* in dense shade
Liriope muscari, always worth growing for its autumn flowers
The curious *Lysichyton americanum* in damp woodland
Persicaria bistorta, good ground cover for the woodland edge
Polypodium australe 'Wilharris', a well-behaved, low-growing fern
Pleiobastus auricomus, a good, low-growing bamboo
Pulmonaria saccharata, providing colour for late winter and spring
Primula japonica in a damp spot in a woodland garden
Rosa rugosa will grow happily on woodland margins
Sanguinaria canadensis 'Plena', sensational in light woodland
Trillium sessile (now *T. kurabayashii*) with its wonderful red flowers
The tiny yellow flowers of *Viola pensylvanica*

Introduction

The cool simplicity of much of the woodland flora has an appeal that is quite different from that of most of the other garden plants that we grow. The shady situation which such plants enjoy contrasts strikingly with that of the traditional sunny, open flower beds in which people generally grow their plants; indeed, shade is considered by many to be one of the gardener's enemies. However, there is an extraordinary number of plants that can be grown under woodland and shade conditions, and much pleasure can be derived from creating the circumstances in which they will thrive.

Fortunately, the plants that grow in woodland gardens have largely been ignored by the plant breeders, and so have retained the natural simplicity and delicacy of their wild counterparts. Apart from the delights of the individual flowers, *en masse* they lend themselves to various types and styles of gardening. They can be used in a wild woodland setting, in which our normal garden plants would look out of place, and be allowed to seed and spread by themselves, often accompanied by grasses and other 'weeds'; or they can be grown in a more organised fashion, in borders created for them under the trees and shrubs. On the other hand, they are perfectly at home under the ornamental trees and shrubs of a more formal setting that we would normally associate with smaller gardens.

Woodland gardens need not be gloomy places. They are usually full of changing patterns of light and shade, with shafts of sunlight alternating with dappled light filtering through the leaves. The foliage and flowers brighten the scene with variations in their shape, texture and, above all, colour. The last is especially true of leaves, which encompass a tremendous range of greens from sombre to flippant, especially in the variegated forms. Life can be tranquil in a wood, but never dull.

At the turn of the century, when woodland gardens became popular, it was considered more or less essential to have a very big garden in which large areas could be set aside specifically for this purpose. If the owner was lucky, there was already an existing wood that could be used, but often one had to be specially created. This wood might resemble a native woodland or it could be planted with one species, such as hazel (*Corylus avellana*), whose main purpose was to create dappled shade. In fact, it might resemble not a wood but simply a shaded bed – although large, the rectangular nut walk at Sissinghurst Castle in Kent, for example, could never be confused with a wild wood – and this principle can be extended to modern gardens.

In the modern garden there is not the space (nor often the time) to create vast areas of oak wood, but there are many ways of creating areas of shade, large or small, under which woodland conditions can be produced, enabling the gardener to add another dimension to his or her garden. Some gardeners, myself amongst them, are lucky enough to have a natural wood in part of their garden, but it is quite possible to create a shade garden under one tree or under a few shrubs in the lee of a hedge or fence.

Many gardeners find it very difficult to cope with shady areas, and the most common mistake is to try and ignore the absence of sun, treating the shady patch as an ordinary border. Sun-loving plants under these conditions soon become very drawn and weedy-looking, with little or no flower. On the other hand, with a little preparation and the right choice of plants, these areas that are generally considered inhospitable can be turned into one of the most interesting places in the garden.

This interest need not be confined to the spring, when the majority of woodland plants flower, but can be extended over all the seasons. Even in winter there are a few plants, often scented ones, that will flower. And the colour of the bark or the structure and character of the trees add much interest at this time of year, when other borders are dull and lifeless. In high summer quite a number of plants can be found flowering in the woodland garden, but there is also the benefit of the colour of the leaves and their delicate tracery etched against the sky. During this time of year trees can also provide welcome respite from the sun, or temporary protection from the rain.

These pleasures assume that you can stroll and sit under the trees and shrubs, and this is an essential part of the woodland garden; you can actually walk into the border and become part of it. In more conventional borders only those the size of a mouse can enjoy this privilege.

The range of plants that can be grown in woodland conditions is surprisingly large. Many can be obtained from garden centres, but more can be found in the increasing number of old-fashioned nurseries located around the country. Another exciting prospect is that more and more new plants are being introduced from far and wide, in the form of seed, and it is possible for the woodland gardener to discover that he or she is the only person growing a newly introduced plant. Quite humble gardeners can thus find themselves in the position of the rich estate owners of previous centuries who were the first to raise particular species of rhododendron or camellia.

Of course, the easiest way to deal with a woodland condition is to avoid all the work that multiple planting involves and to plant with an all-pervasive ground cover. I think there are two objections to this. The first is that ground cover is not as easy to grow as it is always portrayed, and the second is that it is a wasted opportunity; little aesthetic pleasure or horticultural satisfaction can be achieved by walking along a path lined with a single plant. Having said that, however, if the area involved is vast, then mass planting can have its advantages (and ground cover will find its place later in the book).

Having got as far as purchasing this book indicates that you have an existing area to plant, or wish to create one. Either should provide you with a source of considerable extra interest in your garden. Most woodland plants multiply quite quickly and easily so it need not be an expensive exercise, but you will have to get your hands dirty. In spite of what the Sunday papers are always trying to tell us, gardening is not something that you can do in thirty seconds a week. But then, it should not be so anyway, since a lot of the enjoyment comes in the doing as well as in the looking. If a garden is well prepared in the first place there should be little slog in its maintenance; and weeding, for example, can become a pleasure and not a chore.

In her famous garden at East Lambrook Manor, Somerset, Margery Fish created quite a bit of shade; she once wrote:

If I had to choose between a sunny and a shady garden I would choose the shady one every time, not only for its peace and timelessness but also for the plants that can be grown in it. It seems to me that they are often more interesting and more beautiful than those that like to bask in the sun.*

This seems to sum up the essence of woodland gardening.

This book sets out to tell you how to create a woodland garden and what to plant in it. It will give you all the essential information you need, but the final garden should be yours and not mine. All successful gardens reflect the gardener, so if you come up with your own ideas, use them; let it be your garden, and you will enjoy it all the more.

* From *Gardening in the Shade* by Margery Fish.
Reprinted by permission of Faber & Faber Ltd.

1 Woodland Conditions in the Wild

Before contemplating the creation of a woodland garden, it will be instructive to look at the conditions under which shade-loving plants grow in the wild. To the impatient this may seem unnecessary, but a few moments' study, as with good bed preparation, can make a world of difference to the result and to the subsequent ease of maintenance. Many of the top growers in all aspects of gardening owe a lot of their success to studying how their chosen plants behave in the wild; then, by creating similar conditions in the garden, they give them the optimum chances of performing at their best.

Woods and forests occur all over the planet except where they are restricted by cold, such as at the poles or on the tops of mountains, or where it is too dry, such as in desert areas. The type of woodland depends very much on the climate; here we are talking about temperate gardens, so all the woodlands and forests of the tropics must be omitted. This is a pity in some respects as the flora of these regions is very exciting and colourful, but it calls for different techniques, usually under glass, which are beyond the scope of this book.

Because the woodland plants that are grown in gardens have a very wide native distribution, it is theoretically necessary to consider all the temperate woodlands that can be found in Europe and North America; and, to a certain extent, those that inhabit the cooler mountainsides of Asia are as important as those that can be found down the road from your home. Fortunately, as far as we are concerned, they all follow the same basic principles, and so a stroll through your local wood will be as instructive as an expensive expedition to more remote parts.

Woodlands and forests constitute the climax of the growth of vegetation. If a piece of ground is left to itself, first grass and weeds appear, followed by brambles and low shrubs; then trees begin to push up, in Britain one of the earliest being birch (*Betula*). As these trees rapidly develop, slower-growing ones such as oak (*Quercus*) are following along behind. These gradually overtake and overpower the first-comers, their leafy canopy cutting out sunlight and shedding the rain around the trees' margins, so that the brambles and weeds are suppressed and only grow in clearings where there is still light and moisture.

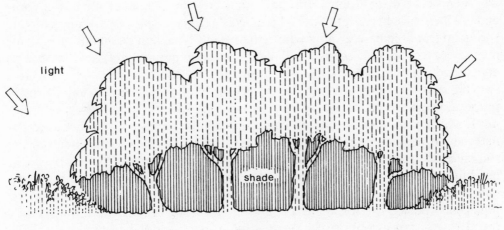

Figure 1.

Eventually the wood reaches its climax and is fully grown. Occasionally trees die or are blown over, and the succession starts again in the space that is formed, but basically the wood will go on for ever unless climatic change or man interferes.

Let us first approach the wood from the south in high summer. One of the first things you notice is that you cannot see the wood for the trees, as the saying goes. All that can be seen is the first row of trees and a tangle of vegetation under them (Figure 1). A tree in the inside of the wood will normally receive its light from above, and so when all the trees are tightly packed together most of the foliage is at the top of the tree where it can capitalise on this light. The trees at the edge of the wood also receive light from one side, and are thus able to have branches of foliage right down to the ground. Some light manages to get under these branches, and so there is a tangled mass of grasses, herbaceous flowers and shrubs growing under the trees on the margin of the wood. Pushing through this undergrowth, the explorer comes into the wood proper. If the trees' tops are all touching, such as in a thick oak wood, then the going immediately becomes much easier because the gloom caused by the thick canopy of leaves means that little can grow beneath it. The floor is carpeted with leaves and the remains of other dead vegetation. In older woods this can be quite springy with the accumulation of generations of leaves – and, as we will see, this thick carpet is of key importance in any wood. Occasionally where the light manages to penetrate there may be an odd clump of grass, a bramble or even an herbaceous flowering plant of some sort.

Sometimes one comes across a small clearing where a tree has blown over or has been struck by lightning. Here the sun is now able to penetrate to the floor, and all hell has been let loose. Foxgloves (*Digitalis purpurea*) immediately spring up from the bare ground where their seeds have lain dormant for perhaps many years. Foxglove seeds need light for germination, and so the sudden appearance of the light breaks the dormancy and before long the glade is a swaying mass of stems carrying the typical purple flowers. Similar tall spires of purple flowers are produced by the rosebay willowherb (*Epilobium angustifolium*), which is another of the first colonising plants. Grasses also quickly germinate, as do the brambles (*Rubus*), the seeds of which have either been in the soil since the last time the wood was cleared or have been dropped by birds, perching above, when they were eating the fruit. The sequence follows the one described earlier: birch quickly appear, followed, at a leisurely pace, by replacement oaks. Birch is a great coloniser. Its seed is very light and will easily travel vast distances on a soft breeze, so that most woodland areas are usually generously supplied. The oak will have originated from the acorns supplied by the remaining trees around the glade, or possibly from the last crop of the toppled tree. Acorns do not stay viable for very long, and usually must have germinated by the spring after they have fallen.

Passing through the wood, we come to a stream wending its way between the trunks. Here the vegetation is a bit thicker. There are odd clumps of carex and ferns, as well as more shrubs and grasses. The canopy has not opened up appreciably, but there is a lot more moisture available and other plants are able to compete successfully for their share.

A forester's ride is the next feature to break through into the wood. Here it is like the edge of the wood, with the trees reaching down to the ground, and more herbaceous plants, grasses and shrubs spilling out from underneath the lowest branches. A little way out from the trees, where the ground receives sun for part of the day, is a much greater range of flowering plants, the ranker vegetation such as the grasses and shrubs being kept at bay by the ride being cut once or twice a year. Growing up through the trees is a number of climbing plants such as honeysuckle (*Lonicera periclymenum*), and wild roses (*Rosa arvensis*). These have very little except stems in the lower part of the trees, but once they burst through the canopy into the sunlight they are a mass of leaves and flowers. The glory of these flowers can best be seen from some vantage point above the wood, but fortunately many grow on the edges of the rides and margins, where their flowers form a cascade of colour through the branches of their supporting trees and shrubs.

Briefly back into the wood, then as we leave it by its northern margins the vegetation again grows thick as the light is able to penetrate to the ground. But here it is only light, not sunlight, so the growth is not quite so luxuriant but more drawn, and there are not so many flowering plants.

Let us repeat this pleasant stroll, but this time in the spring before the leaves
have appeared on the trees. Now as we approach the wood it is possible to see
well into it, as there is nothing to break the view. The branches of the outside
trees still sweep low, but not so low as in summer when they are weighed down
with leaves. The grasses have not yet started to grow and the other rank
vegetation is still below ground or, in the case of shrubs, without leaves. But
there is plenty of other vegetation to see. The remains of a drift of wild daffodils
can be seen disappearing into the interior. Following it, the eye sees large areas
of flowers under the trees, sometimes drifts of one type, sometimes several
together.

Contrasting with the daffodil is a patch of the blue-flowered lungwort (*Pulmonaria officinalis*). Wood anemones (*Anemone nemorosa*) wave daintily in the
wind, earning their other vernacular name, windflowers; they cover a large area,
with their spreading rootstock running through the soft leafmould. Little wood
sorrel (*Oxalis acetosella*) appears in odd clumps here and there. As we cross
the stream we see tufts of primroses (*Primula vulgaris*) dotting the banks
amongst the remains of the lesser celandines (*Ranunculus ficaria*) that have
already finished flowering. A damp dell beside the stream is filled with the
hundreds of garlic-smelling ramsons (*Allium ursinum*), which carpet the ground.
On the far side of the ride is another carpet, this one a great sheet of blue
disappearing in a haze towards the edge of the wood. This is caused by millions
of bluebells (*Hyacinthoides non-scripta*). A wonderful contrast at the edge of
the ride is the pink of the red campion (*Silene dioica*), which merges with the
bluebells as they disappear under the trees. There are many other spring flowers
to be seen, both under the trees and along the margins of the clearings and
rides. The only completely bare places are under the evergreen hollies (*Ilex
aquifolium*), at the edge of the wood.

Two views of a wood, which at first sight have little to do with the creation
of a small shade bed in the corner of a garden – but within these two scenarios
there is a lot of important information for the shade gardener.

SHADE

The first thing to note is that the density of shade is of paramount importance.
During the summer very few plants will grow under the trees, where there is
little light; more will grow on the margins, and even more just outside the trees
where the sun will reach the ground for a short period each day. During the
late winter and early spring when there are no leaves on the trees the sun will
reach the ground throughout the wood, and consequently there are flowers
everywhere. By the time the trees have leaves these spring flowers are over,
have seeded and have died back underground, so that when we went for our

summer stroll there was virtually no sign of their existence, except a few brown stems here and there.

In other words, the woodland flora is making the most of the early part of the growing season, before the trees have got going. Although there are many plants for later in the season, the majority of woodland ground plants flower in the spring when conditions are best for them. For the woodland gardener this means that spring is going to be the height of the year.

On the edge of the wood where the trees have capitalised on their location and their branches almost reach the ground, a certain amount of vegetation will continue into the summer; but in clearings caused by fallen or felled trees, the surrounding trees will not have had time to develop new low branches or foliage and so, for a time at least, the sun and light will penetrate further, allowing for ground plants to grow beneath them. This indicates to the gardener that if the tree canopy is kept high, light will be able to get under it and the flowering season can be extended. As we will see later, this can be done in several ways, but it can affect the choice of trees to create the shade. It should be remembered that trees with heavy leaves and fruit tend to have branches that sag lower as the season progresses.

One particular group of plants that has adapted successfully to woodland conditions is the climbers, which clamber their way out of the dark, up into the light. Unfortunately, unless viewed from a higher vantage point, little can be seen of their flowers – but it does, once more, emphasise the importance of sunlight.

Light is needed for photosynthesis, the process by which plants use the sun's energy that strikes the leaves to convert the carbon dioxide and water into sugars, thus providing, in turn, energy for the growing plant. If this light is denied, a plant becomes very drawn as it searches vainly for the light. Cover a patch of grass with a bucket so that no light can enter and lift it after a couple of days, and you will see that the covered blades of grass have grown more rapidly than those surrounding them as they have tried unsuccessfully to reach the light, and that they are much paler as they have been unable to manufacture chlorophyll. (This is the green pigment in all plants, except saprophytic ones that use the help of fungi to supply their needs, which absorbs the sun's energy to fuel the conversion process.)

From our imaginary walk it can be seen that different plants grow in different degrees of shade. In dense shade under evergreen trees, and under some trees that have a very close canopy of overlapping leaves, such as beech (*Fagus sylvatica*), very little will grow. Under a lighter, dappled shade such as provided by ash (*Fraxinus excelsior*), a few more plants are likely to grow because a certain amount of light filters down between the leaflets of the pinnate (compound) leaves. It is a light that moves, not only as the tree moves in the wind but also as the sun moves across the sky. This type of shade is one that many growers like to create, and there is a number of trees and shrubs that will provide it. The same kind of shading is created to screen glasshouses and cold-frames, where a slatted wooden screen or a plastic screening net is used to the same purpose as the leaves on the tree – namely, to allow a certain amount of light to filter through, but not concentrated or constant enough to burn the plants below.

A third type of shade is partial shade. This is typified by the woodland ride, where the sun may reach the ground for an hour or two each day; in other words, the ground may receive quite a lot of light, but only a limited amount of sunlight. In the garden this is most applicable to north sides of buildings, walls or fences, where there is no overhanging shade but where the sun may penetrate for only a short while in the morning or evening. This kind of light also applies to beds under trees that have had their lower branches removed so that plenty of ambient light is present during the hours of daylight, and just occasional periods of sunlight.

Nature makes use of most of its resources, and plants that have adapted themselves to differing degrees of shade enjoy the benefit of less competition than those out in the open. Most of them have adapted their leaves to less light and to the close conditions found under trees and shrubs, so that if they are planted outside in full sunlight they quickly wilt. It is possible, though, to grow some of these shade-lovers in full sun (and this will be dealt with in the next section, on moisture).

Many plants that would normally grow outside in full sun are capable of growing in a certain amount of partial or light shade, but this is usually at the sacrifice of flowers. It would seem that all the energy they can muster is required to keep the plant alive and growing towards the light; there is very little left over for creating flowers and seed. Seed production is very expensive in terms of energy, much more so than alternative vegetative methods of reproduction, and it is interesting that while most woodland plants do produce seed, many also propagate themselves by running underground or by producing offsets.

There is a trend in modern gardening books to use symbols to indicate the properties of various plants, and sun and shade are often represented by an outline of a sun and a filled-in black sun, respectively. The shade symbols are often sprinkled liberally about without much care or thought, and are rarely a true indication of a plant's ability. Many may well be able to grow in partial shade – in fact, most plants will – but the miserable amount of flower that is produced from those that are basically sun-lovers really does not justify the bother of planting them.

Another aspect of the blanketing effect of leaves can be observed after they have fallen. Large leaves such as those of sweet chestnut (*Castanea sativa*) or sycamore (*Acer pseudoplatanus*) tend to form a thick wet blanket over every-thing, smothering any seedlings or small ground plants. Starved of light and in a wet atmosphere, the weakened plants are ready to succumb to rots and other diseases. Smaller leaves such as oak tend to cause less of a problem, with the result that any woodland-floor plants can continue growing through them.

MOISTURE

Whilst light is probably the most important factor regarding woodland plants, moisture is also high on the list of things to consider. Trees use up copious amounts of water every day. Constantly transpiring, they pour forth masses of water from their leaves in the form of vapour. The root systems of trees are extremely vigorous in their search for moisture, and will often travel vast distances to look for it. Under the bench in my alpine house I have some pots of seed that are plunged into gravel on top of a polythene sheet. Any ungermi-nated pots are usually left two or three years in case there is any late germi-nation. Picking up some pots that I considered unlikely to produce anything, I was surprised to find that they were anchored to the gravel plunge. On investi-gation I discovered that roots were not coming from the pots, but going into them. The roots of an ash tree, some distance away, had come up under the alpine house, found their way through minute holes in the polythene and then had entered the seed pots through the drainage holes, in search of the moisture that was regularly applied to them. Many readers will be familiar with the more severe problems caused by roots searching for moisture below foundations and breaking into drain pipes.

With competition of this sort, it is difficult for herbaceous plants to hold their own against trees. One way of coping is for the plants to take advantage of the period when the trees are using very little water – namely, when they are not in leaf – and here we discover another reason why woodland plants flower in spring: it is a time when they can make the most of the available moisture. They also make use of any available nutrients that have accumulated from rotting vegetation and other sources during the autumn and winter, before the trees hungrily grab them all.

During the winter, rainfall is evenly spread over a wood as there is little to obstruct its progress through the leafless branches, but once the dense canopies of leaves have been formed then the distribution becomes more erratic, often depending on the type of tree. Those with thick leaf cover, such as beech, are likely to shed the rain to the outside of the tree as the water trickles progressively from one leaf to the next (Figure 2). In trees with a more open canopy or with leaves that do not form such a continuous cover, some rain will penetrate and fall to the ground within the circle of the tree's branches. Most trees will have a certain amount running down their branches and eventually down the trunks, sometimes forming small rivulets running away from the base of the tree. These trickles of water tend to follow the same lines unless the ground is disturbed, and vegetation may be found growing in the same pattern, making use of the extra moisture. More rain is likely to fall on one side of the tree than the other (Figure 3). This is determined by the prevailing winds, and in Britain, for example, it tends to be the south-west side. These various factors are well worth bearing in mind when planting up a shady area, as they will indicate where plants are likely to receive the most moisture.

HUMIDITY

The atmosphere under the trees is usually moister than in open areas. The leafmould on the woodland floor is like a wet sponge gently releasing water vapour. This is enhanced by that given off by the lower foliage, and is entrapped by the canopy itself. An additional factor is that the trees tend to limit the passage of air through the wood; the air here is more stagnant than outside, and, of course, the wind is drastically reduced. All these factors mean that the air is much more turgid. Where streams pass through woods the air is even more moist, and the vegetation can become quite luxuriant.

If plants that normally grow under the shade of trees are planted in the open ground they tend to transpire much more quickly than they normally would. This means that unless they have adequate moisture reserves at their roots they are likely to flag and wilt. Many woodland plants can be grown in the open as long as they have a moisture-retentive soil that never dries out. Primroses (*Primula vulgaris*) do better under shady conditions, but can be grown in open borders if they have quite a lot of organic material incorporated around them so that they remain moist throughout the year. They will not tolerate dry, hot conditions and will quickly turn up their toes.

TEMPERATURE

The temperature inside woods is less prone to wild fluctuations than in the outside world. It is usually cooler in summer and warmer in winter. Even the presence of a single deciduous shrub, for example, is often sufficient to prevent the frost from reaching the ground, and spring-flowering plants that will suffer in open ground are likely to come through the mild frosts of spring unscathed if they have this light cover. Similarly, the trees and shrubs are likely to break the chilling winds that can be more damaging than the frosts. Leafmould also acts as a thermal blanket and helps keep the ground warm. However, after a cold spell it will have the reverse effect and take longer to thaw out; but then,

wet   dry   dry   wet

Figure 2.

wet   dry   wet

Figure 3.

this can be an advantage, because plants are often more adversely affected by rapid fluctuations in temperature than by the temperature itself.

SOIL

Woods and forests will grow on virtually any type of soil as long as it is not too dry or waterlogged, so there is little reason why nearly all gardens should not be able to grow a few trees or shrubs to create a shade garden of some sort. There are certain limitations that some gardeners find inhibiting, particularly if they live on a chalky soil. Here it is impossible to grow rhododendrons, for example, which is often one of the main desires of woodland gardeners; but there are usually many other plants that can be grown successfully under these circumstances, so no one should mourn the loss of just a handful of lime-haters.

Many woods grow on rocky slopes. Here the ground will not support veg-etation, except in the cracks and crevices between the rocks. The trees them-selves are often further apart because of the lack of suitable footholds and, since quite a lot of light gets in because of this wider spacing, the wood is able to support an interesting flora, some of which grow in the spaces between the rocks, while others grow in the accumulations of debris that form in hollows and crevices. I have never been able to garden under such circumstances as the county in which I live is not a particularly rocky one, but I would dearly like to try – I am certain that many exciting plants could be grown on rocky ground.

As one would expect, a more typical cover than rocks for the floor of a wood is leafmould (it is, of course, also present in rocky woods, but usually in pockets). This leafmould is vital to the condition of the woods, both for the trees and for the lower-growing plants. Leafmould is the fibrous material created by the partial rotting down of fallen leaves. It is a recycling process, in that a lot of the nutrients that have been taken up by the tree will pass back into the soil with these rotting leaves, ready for the roots of the tree to reabsorb. The worms and other minute animals present help to mix the leafmould with the top few inches of soil, creating what is known as leafsoil. This is nutritious and, being fibrous, it holds a good amount of moisture. It also acts as a mulch and helps prevent the soil beneath from drying out. Over the years the leafsoil in a wood can build up to quite an impressive depth.

It is in this leafsoil and leafmould that the ground plants grow. Many of them, the wood anemone (*Anemone nemorosa*), for example, have rhizomatous roots that run around in this loose, friable top layer. It provides them with everything they need and prevents them from totally drying out in their dormant period.

Many gardeners have traditionally used leafmould where many now employ peat. However, with the garden use of peat now having a stigma attached to it, many more are turning to leafmould as a cheap alternative. There is a problem here in that many woods are being stripped, for garden use, of their carpet of leaves and, worse still, of the layer of leafsoil that has taken many generations to build up. This is worse vandalism than stripping areas of peat, as it threatens the very existence of our woods by breaking the nutrition cycle and impoverishing them; soon trees will start dying out, leaving a disaster on our hands. As we will see later, it is possible to make your own leafmould, and all gardeners are strongly urged to do so, leaving that of the woods where it belongs.

2   Creating a Shade Garden

So far shade has been considered in terms of woods, but it should be made clear that here woods and shade gardens are being defined in a somewhat liberal manner. If you are lucky enough to have an acre or more of woodland or can plant such an area, then you should learn a lot from this book. But size is not important – because if, on the other hand, you have a very small garden, then there is still a great deal that can be achieved by just planting one tree or even a single shrub and creating a small shade garden under it. In other cases it may be that there is an existing shady area created by a wall or hedge, and that this can be used to house a collection of woodland plants.

There are two possibilities that we must consider in this chapter. First, that there is an existing area of shade that needs transforming into a profitable garden area; or, second, that the shade has to be created as well as the border. The first is easier in some respects, and certainly quicker, but the conditions may well be dictated by which trees and shrubs are already there. The second is obviously slower, as the trees have to establish themselves, but at least there is the advantage that you can choose their types and positions.

SOIL

Starting with the basics, let us first look at the soil. As we have already seen, woods can grow on any type of soil, and it follows that a shade garden can be created on a similar wide variety. However, the better the quality of the soil, the better the chances of success. It must be borne in mind that trees and bushes become a permanent feature, and only a limited amount of work can be undertaken on the soil once they are established; so good ground preparation is necessary before any planting can take place.

The first essential, as with any form of gardening – even wild gardening – is to rid the soil of perennial weeds. If the soil is a light one then it is possible to do this entirely by hand, digging it over several times and removing the weeds and any broken-off pieces of root as you go. Inevitably some pieces will remain in the soil, but these can usually be removed as soon as they throw up their first leaves. I have cleared ground on many occasions like this, but, then, I have a light soil. Anyone with a sticky clay has a much more difficult task, as the pieces of root become embedded in the clay and are difficult to remove.

The only real way of coping with this is to use a chemical weedkiller. Many people are now reluctant to use chemicals in the garden, and I have a certain amount of sympathy with them. However, if the weeds are killed off properly there will be no need to use weedkillers again; it should be a one-off operation, thus leaving no chance of a build-up of chemicals in the soil. Many of the modern weedkillers become inert as soon as they touch the soil and are much safer than the older residual ones. As far as personal safety is concerned, there should be no danger as long as the instructions on the packet or bottle are followed. Since it is the permanent weeds one is attacking, any weedkiller used should be one that kills the roots and does not simply burn off the leaves. One based on glyphosate, which is not persistent, is probably one of the best to use. It takes two or three weeks before all parts of the weeds are killed, but it does cope with most perennial problems.

One way of cleaning the ground without chemicals that is often advocated is to cover it with a black polythene sheet. This does work, but it takes at least a year to get effective results and there must not be even the slightest hole in the plastic, or the weeds will discover it and push through sufficient foliage to sustain growth below ground. During the year or so that the polythene is on the ground the garden will look somewhat untidy.

Having cleaned the soil, your next task is to drain it, if it so requires. Again, it cannot be stressed enough that if such attention is called for, the problem should be dealt with before trees and shrubs put down roots and become a permanent obstacle to undertaking any major modification.

While most woodland plants enjoy moist conditions, very few will tolerate stagnant water, so it is important to ensure that no water lies in the area that has been earmarked. Perhaps too much stress is laid on this in books, as very few gardens need to have drainage systems installed, but in a heavy clay a hole dug for a tree can turn into a sump that collects water, and it may be necessary to dig a drainage channel away from it. (This will be dealt with later, when tree-planting is considered.) Most woodland-floor plants are surface rooters and so, as long as there is no water lying on the surface or the soil does not remain waterlogged, there is probably nothing to worry about. But if there is a permanent threat of stagnant water then a drainage system employing clay, plastic pipes or gravel should be used.

What is most important is to improve the soil, as this will not only provide more nutritious conditions for the plants but will also improve the drainage around their roots. The ideal is a rich, humusy loam that emulates the leafsoil of the woodland floor. Some gardeners will be lucky and have this already;

others will have to create it. When solid, sticky yellow clay is dug over for the first time it seems impossible that this could ever be converted into a good life-sustaining soil, but it can.

Surprisingly, one of the best things for it is grit or gravel, which breaks up the clay and allows it to drain. Grit is a useful ingredient of a leaf soil in other respects, too. In any compost that is likely to retain too much water, grit is invaluable: the humus content retains sufficient moisture for the plants, and the grit allows any excess to drain away. It also has the reverse effect. When peat dries out it is very difficult to re-wet; the water just runs off the surface. The presence of grit, however, opens up the soil, allowing the water to enter and soak the peat.

An alternative in helping to break up a clay soil is to use ash. We are told these days that we should waste no organic material but should compost it all. While I agree almost entirely with this, I do have some old-fashioned feelings about it too. When weed is burnt on a bonfire, the soil on the roots is burnt as well. As it is lightly fired, this becomes hard – almost like pottery in consistency. This is important, as it means that the clay cannot be broken down again into a sticky mass, and when the particles of this semi-fired clay are returned to the soil they help to break it up. The garden in which I grew up was a new one created out of the heaviest Wealden clay, and yet now it can be dug in midwinter with a fork. This is due in part to the bonfire ash and in part to the compost.

The addition of compost or humus is another way of breaking down the soil. As will be discussed in a moment, farmyard manure, leafmould, hop waste and a lot of other materials, as well as garden compost, can be used.

Very dry, sandy soils can also present a problem. Here the aim is to make the soil moisture- and nutrient-retentive. Again, humus is the key. Unfortuntely this kind of soil can be very hungry and, unless bulky, the organic material soon disappears. Fine peat, in particular, is useless in this context. One often hears people bemoaning the fact that they have poured bales of peat into the soil and it has just disappeared – no wonder there is a peat problem! Any of the materials mentioned at the end of the previous paragraph will do.

Although I occasionally make bonfires of some of the more pernicious weeds, as much to get the ash (as described above) as to get rid of the pests, most of the organic waste from my garden is composted. The addition of humus to the soil is a vital part of any gardening. As we have already seen, in a natural woodland there is always a natural cycle in which the leaves fall to the ground and rot, producing food for the tree to produce more leaves. In the garden there is not normally sufficient concentration of trees and shrubs to allow this to happen; the wind blows the leaves away, or the over-zealous gardener tidies them away. Another factor is that the garden will possibly be planted with more plants than would be usual in natural conditions, and all these plants need feeding – especially if, again, the gardener tidies away all the spent vegetation in autumn. It is essential, then, over and above any need to improve the soil, for the gardener to step in and provide this part of the cycle.

To do this, you must dig as much humus into the top layer as possible. Once the bed has become established it is essential to continue adding a top-dressing each year. It will probably be impossible (because of roots) as well as undesirable (because of the need to avoid root disturbance) to dig this in, but if it is simply put on the surface as a mulch then the worms and other organisms will gradually work it into the top layer – as, indeed, happens in natural woodland.

If you dig into a woodland floor you will often find that the rich humusy layer extends only a few inches down. This is sufficient for most woodland-floor plants, while the grosser feeders are happy to push their roots well below this layer in search of moisture and nutrients that have been leached out of the upper layer. In theory a layer of organic material is sufficient to feed both the upper and the lower levels of vegetation, but there is one problem. If the material is not fully rotted, it will carry on breaking down. To do this it requires nitrogen, and it will abstract it from the soil. In a wood with not much growing under the trees this is no problem, but in our situation, where we are trying to grow as much as possible under the trees, it can mean that instead of a surplus of nutrients there is a deficiency, at least while the humus is breaking down. It is therefore quite common practice to scatter some inorganic fertiliser – either a general-purpose one, such as Growmore, or one with a higher nitrogen content – before putting down the layer of shredded bark or whatever it might be. For those who dislike using inorganics, their use can be obviated by making certain that any humus added to the soil has broken down completely. An alternative would be to add a thin layer of well-rotted farmyard manure to the soil before spreading the bark.

ORGANIC MATERIALS

It is no good continually referring to organic material and humus without going into a bit more detail as to what it is and how it can be obtained. Basically, it is any vegetable matter that has rotted down or is in the process of rotting down. It can be purchased at a price from the local garden centre, or in bulk at a lesser price; sometimes it can be free for the asking, especially horse manure, or it can be made from organic waste.

Shredded bark   Until recently, bark removed from any timber cut in this country was burnt or just left in heaps in the woods. Fortunately, it was finally realised that here was a valuable asset that could be returned to the soil for the benefit of all. Bark comes in several different forms and grades. It can be just shredded bark, in which case it requires to be stacked for several months – preferably at least a year, so that any resin present can evaporate or be leached out. This will also allow it to start decomposing. The grades vary between coarse, which takes a long time to break down, and fine, which will be incorporated into the soil more quickly.

Manufacturers are never content with a simple product, and bark can now be bought in several other (expensive) forms such as composted – that is, pre-rotted – or enriched, which incorporates an inorganic fertiliser. Bought by the bag, bark is relatively expensive; by the lorry-load, it works out much cheaper. As with so many products, it is the transport that costs money, and if you live near an area of tree production it may be possible to fetch your own bark direct from the woodyard at a fraction of the cost.

As to which to buy, it is really up to your preference. Although the finer grades tend to incorporate into the soil more quickly, they need constant renewal. The coarser ones last longer, acting as a valuable mulch rather than adding much to the soil itself. These are not so aesthetically pleasing, particularly if they consist of strips of bark rather than chips. Either way, buy in bulk if you can, and you can store it if it is freshly stripped from the trees.

Shredded garden materials　Until recently anything that would not rot, such as hedge-clippings or cabbage stalks, was burnt. With the advent of the garden shredder it has become possible to cut up even quite thick branches and to turn them into valuable compost. I am not too keen on gadgets in the garden, but I make exceptions for machines which undertake tasks that cannot normally be done by hand. So, for example, the lawn-mower is permitted – indeed, it is welcomed! And the shredder, in spite of its noise, fulfils a function that would otherwise not be undertaken, so the job it does of converting materials that would in the past have been burnt, into a valuable mulch and compost, earns it a place in the tool-shed.

Literally any organic garden waste can be shredded, but it is normally the material that cannot easily be composted, such as woody stems, that are put through the machine. Once they have been shredded, the resulting pellets should be stacked in a heap for six months, and turned occasionally to let in the air, before they are put on to the garden.

Leafmould　This is one of the best and most natural materials to add to a woodland garden. All that is required is a wire-netting cage in which to place the leaves, and the patience to wait for them to rot. The cage can easily be home-made and need not be to any specific design, its purpose being simply to prevent the leaves from blowing away. Leaves can equally well be composted by stacking them in a heap, if it is positioned in a sheltered place. Gather them from the garden during the autumn, and place them in the cage. To ease collection, you can place low wire-netting fences in strategic positions to catch the leaves in drifts as they blow past. This may seem an elaborate and unnecessary procedure, but in a large garden where there are a lot of leaves to clear up it can save valuable time.

Unfortunately leaves take a long time to rot down, but if they are collected every year this becomes unimportant, because a cycle will be established and a new batch for spreading will be available annually. Freshly stacked leaves are deceptive as to the ultimate amount of leafmould that will be available. A huge mound will be reduced to a few inches by the time they have rotted, so collect as much material as possible. In urban areas local authorities can often be persuaded to let you have leaves that they have swept up from pavements or parks, but you must be prepared to sift through them and remove any rubbish, such as polythene bags and tins. Non-gardening friends often burn piles of leaves or take them down to the local rubbish tip and, doubtless, would be grateful for your taking them away.

Under no circumstances should you go down to the local wood and remove the leafmould or leaves, as this is a valuable part of the wood's natural cycle and removal will impoverish them to the detriment of the trees.

Composted garden waste A great deal of waste material is produced in the garden each year. Under natural circumstances it would be recycled where it falls, but in a garden this is normally deemed to be too untidy, so most gardeners remove old flowering stems and cut the grass before it becomes rank and flops to the ground. All the waste from most gardening procedures, such as weeding, mowing the lawn and dead-heading, can be used. It can be stacked neatly either in compost bins made from slats of wood or in containers specially bought for the purpose. Having been brought up in the country, I tend to follow the old cottage garden practice of simply stacking the waste up in a neat heap; the only attention that it gets is my turning it perhaps once or twice a year if I have the time. There is always plenty available, so I do not have to try and convert the weeds and other material into compost in record-breaking time.

In a small garden it may be more sensible to use recommended containers and to cover the waste with polythene or some other waterproof material to keep out excessive moisture and to keep in the heat. A chemical accelerator will help speed up the process of breaking down (the directions on the packet should be followed). These can be purchased from garden centres or shops. Compost seems to rot down more easily if the different ingredients are mixed up, not heaped in separate thick layers. There is not generally a problem unless thick layers of grass cuttings smother the whole heap. Turning occasionally with a fork helps reduce any concentration.

Although almost anything can be composted, there is a problem with weeds that contain seeds. It is often stated in print that the heat of the compost heap will kill off any seeds. But this is wishful thinking rather than experience talking, and most compost, unless it is made from seed-free material in the first place, will produce a crop of seedlings when spread on the ground. Perennial weeds such as couch grass and ground elder can survive in a compost heap.

Farmyard manure The incredible increase in the number of horses in recent years has brought with it, naturally, a vast increase in the amount of manure to be disposed of. To many stables and to private individuals keeping horses, dung heaps are becoming an embarrassing problem, and many are more than willing to let gardeners have as much as they want as long as they remove it. Again, transport is the expensive thing, but if you are able to move it there is a lot of good-quality manure waiting to be had for free. Manure should never be used fresh but should be stacked until it has rotted. Unexpectedly to people unused to handling it, well rotted farmyard manure is odourless and not in the least offensive. It is, however, rich in nutrients, especially nitrogen, and can cause lush growth if used too heavily. It is best used in combination with, for example, shredded bark, where excess nitrogen will be taken up by the rotting bark.

Farmyard manure can contain quite a lot of weed seed, particularly if the animals have been fed hay or have been bedded on straw. Often the bedding is wood shavings, though, or a similar inert material which is weed-free. There are several other types of manure from other farmyard animals, including cattle, pigs, sheep and chickens.

Mushroom compost Mushroom growers regularly change the material on which they grow their mushrooms. This is usually a mixture of chopped bracken, straw or similar material laced with horse manure. In some areas it can be acquired very cheaply; it is well worth buying as it is a marvellous material for conditioning soil. Its one disadvantage is that it usually has chalk added to it. This will obviously have an effect on the soil, making it impossible to grow ericaceous plants, such as rhododendrons, but this need not cause difficulties – simply restrict this type of compost to areas of the garden in which calcifuges (lime-haters) are not grown.

Other materials There are often other locally available materials that are good for adding to the soil. Hop waste is a good example. This is the spent hops after they have gone through the brewing process, and such waste can often be obtained from breweries or from firms that have bought it. There are other organic wastes that are by-products of manufacturing processes – cocoa-bean shells are another recent product to appear on the market, but they do have a tendency to turn into an unattractive sticky mass that seems to attract moulds. Experiment carefully with small quantities of this kind of product before you cover the whole of your woodland garden with it.

In woodland areas it is quite possible to simply cover the ground with a thin layer of grass cuttings. These rot down, as would leaves in a natural setting, and are dug into the top layer by the action of worms. Do not pile them too thickly, or the temperature generated will kill off any plants that pass through them. They can form an impenetrable blanket, so stir them occasionally with a fork if the birds have not done it for you.

Similarly, straw can be used as a ground cover which will eventually rot and be carried into the soil. This can be a bit unsightly but is useful in areas such as the back of a border, where the ground cannot be seen. Chopping it up may speed up its assimilation into the ground, but it will then blow around more easily.

* * *

I have dwelt for rather a long time on what might seem an uninteresting aspect of woodland gardening, but it is important to get the soil into the right condition if you hope to have flourishing plants. And you should go to great lengths to make or obtain as much organic material as you can.

CREATING SHADE

Having prepared the soil and added humus, both to condition the soil and to retain moisture, you are in a position to start planting. In an open garden, the first thing to do is to create some shade; there is no point in planting shade-loving plants at this stage if there is no shade to protect them.

We have already seen the conditions under which woodland plants grow in the wild, and it is well worth bearing these in mind when creating your own patch of shade. The principles are the same whether you are planting up an acre or just a small bed. All the same, do not expect to get too much into a small area. In many gardens just one or two trees are sufficient to create shade – any more will produce crowded conditions that will not only look wrong but will make it difficult to grow other plants, because the competition for moisture will be too fierce and the shade too dense.

Types of shade   The ideal shade for any garden is a light, dappled one cast by deciduous plants. This is a moving light that is created by the motion of the leaves and by the passage of the sun overhead. Another good shade is formed by having a high canopy which allows in the morning and evening sun but denies entry to the hot midday rays.

Another form of shade that is worth mentioning but does not really belong in this book, as it is not so much part of a woodland garden, is that cast by a north wall or hedge. Here the sun may reach the ground only during the very early morning or late evening, with, possibly, just a few days around midsummer when the noonday sun manages to peep over the top. Many of the plants that we will consider in a woodland setting will grow under these conditions as long as the soil has been adequately provided for.

Shade cast by trees Trees come in a wide variety of shapes and sizes. One advantage of woodland gardening is that it makes you look at trees with a more critical eye and therefore appreciate their diversity. Tall trees with a single trunk and branches that form an upright cigar shape are typified, for instance, in the deciduous Lombardy poplar (*Populus nigra* var. *italica*), and some of the evergreen conifers. Here the light can get in right up to the trunk beneath the ascending branches, and only a small area of shade is created on the northern side of the tree (Figure 4). These are not particularly good shade-creating plants and should not be used where space is at a premium. On the other hand, in larger plantings where a proper wood is being created, these shapes will offer a pleasing contrast to the more usual rounded ones.

A tree with wider spread will obviously give more shade, but these must be selected carefully as some will create more than others. A large tree such as a beech (*Fagus*), with branches that sweep down to the ground, will allow little light to penetrate to any plants beneath it (Figure 5). The oak (*Quercus*) is an example of a tree that, although often producing branches that reach the ground, can be lopped so that the canopy is high, allowing plenty of light to come in beneath its branches but keeping out the hot midday sun (Figure 6). If you are planting trees that you intend to lop, make certain that you are choosing specimens that will not look mutilated or lose their character when they have lost their lower limbs. For example, a weeping willow (*Salix babylonica*) would look a bit odd if all its lower branches were cut off to allow the light to get beneath it. As well as aesthetic considerations there are also physical ones to take into account. If beeches are too heavily lopped, for example, they become top-heavy and their brittle trunks are likely to snap.

Trees do not have to be tall, and in the smaller garden shorter specimens with the same proportions, such as the rowan (*Sorbus*), provide a relatively high canopy and are ideal for creating a light shade. Multiple-stemmed trees are, in a way, like very large shrubs. They are not as satisfactory as trees with a single trunk, as they tend to block more light because of their spreading nature, especially if they form a thicket (Figure 7). But if they are high and airy (as are some *Eucalyptus*, for example) or if the lower branches can be

Figure 4.

Figure 5.

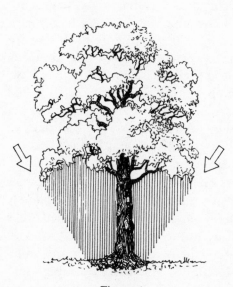

Figure 6.

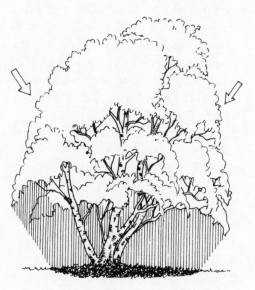

Figure 7.

removed without destroying the shape of the tree, then they generally suit our purpose.

As well as the position of the canopy, another factor is its density. Beech trees have a very dense canopy of rounded leaves that allow very little light through. Oak leaves are more irregular in shape and are not so densely packed on the tree, so some moving light does penetrate. Ash trees (*Fraxinus excelsior*) have a more open structure and pinnate leaves made up of individual leaflets which allow quite a lot of light to filter through. As well as light, moisture, in the form of rain, can be blocked by the leaves. Rain falling on the dense beech will drip from leaf to leaf until it has run to the perimeter of the tree, whereas the ashes' more open leaves will allow the rain to fall to beneath the trees.

Some trees are thirstier than others. This does not matter if their roots are generally well down, such as the oak's, but species such as many willows (*Salix*) and beeches, whose roots can be very close to the surface, can create serious competition for any plants sited under them. Most deciduous trees use little water in the winter and spring before they come into growth, so that plants that flower and die back early, such as bluebells (*Hyacinthoides non-scripta*), have finished their life-cycles before the trees start to have any real effect on the moisture levels.

Problems with trees   The roots of trees will travel a long way in their search for moisture and nutrients. They can be damaging to the foundations of buildings, under which the permanently cool and moist conditions are to their liking. Buildings on heavy clay are the most prone to damage. The clay adjacent to and under the building contracts in dry periods as the tree sucks out the moisture, and then expands again when the rains return. This continual, irregular contraction and expansion is what causes the damage. Without the tree roots the clay would remain uniformly moist, or with only slight variation. Some trees (poplars (*Populus*) being the main culprit) are worse than others and should never be planted near houses on clay; keep them at least 20m (65ft) away. There is not usually a problem in areas where the rainfall is in excess of 75cm (30in) a year or on soils other than clay, as long as there is no clay underlying them. If in doubt, consult a structural engineer before you plant.

Roots can also be invasive of drains and sewage installations. The fine roots can find their way between joints and then shatter or distort the pipes as they grow. So it is sensible to avoid planting your wood on top of the house's drainage system. Another problem is that it is very easy to underestimate a tree's growth. It can be difficult to realise that the small tree purchased in a container could one day reach 25m (80ft) or more. A tree of this size could block out a great deal of light from the windows of a nearby house, even if it was planted at what at the time seemed a reasonable distance away for a 3m (10ft) sapling.

Indeed, when considering all these factors, do not forget that they equally apply to your neighbour's property and that siting a tree on or near a boundary will not only allow the branches to encroach on his or her space but may cause the roots to damage buildings – for which you could be liable.

All these warnings might seem to suggest that the worst things to plant in your garden are trees, and that they should be avoided at all costs. This is far from the truth, and if poplars are avoided on clay soils and sensible precautions taken as to the size and siting of trees, you should encounter no problems.

Choosing trees Given that the above considerations have been taken into account, the choice of trees is very much a personal one. When planting a sizeable wood, many people prefer to choose native trees, to give it a more natural look – though possibly including one or two exotica for interest. The range of native trees in both Britain and America is extensive enough to provide a wood with plenty of variation in shape, colour and texture.

Those who are able to grow on a grand scale may prefer to create an arboretum, in which a large number of specimens are collected together. In some cases the collection may be limited to one group, such as conifers, or to a single genus – *Acer*, for the sake of argument. I suspect many gardeners would love to do this, but it does call for a great deal of space and money. In the smaller garden, where only one or two trees are to be planted, the choice can be more open: as most of the plants in any garden are either aliens or have been derived from introduced plants, non-native trees will not look out of place. In spite of this, the most common trees seem to be native oaks and birch, both of which are suitable for the type of garden we are considering.

The question of the colour of the trees is particularly important. Most trees have foliage that is a shade of green, and these greens generally blend well with one another. A change of emphasis can be created by using trees with a variegated or a purple foliage, but this should not be overdone. Combining a number of variegated trees is very difficult to do successfully. They usually clash and become too busy, creating a restless image quite contrary to the normal tranquil nature of a wood. An overemphasis on purple foliage tends to deaden the landscape: one such tree may glow amongst the greens, but a block of them seems to hang like a lead weight.

All trees produce flowers of some kind, but not all are conspicuous. Some of the most spectacular flowerers are, perhaps, best treated as specimen trees and planted by themselves, although drifts of blossom through a wood can be magical, as can the occasional spire of white climbing above the surrounding green. Unfortunately one of the most spectacular, the horse chestnut (*Aesculus hippocastanum*), is a very hungry and thirsty tree with a dense shade that makes it difficult to underplant successfully. Of course, in a large wood there is no need to have plants under every tree, but it is really not a tree for the small garden.

Autumn colour is a worthwhile bonus provided by many trees, and when all other considerations are equal it is preferable to go for those that provide it. Some will supply decorative fruit as well. Such trees are especially appreciated in smaller gardens, where every one should earn its keep to the maximum. Once the leaves have dropped, the gardener is left for several months looking at bare trunks. Once mature, many trees, such as oaks and sweet chestnut (*Castanea sativa*), have craggy barks which make for interest, but there are many more – the *Acer*, for example – that have decorative barks at all stages of their lives and are well worth acquiring. Trees with decorative bark need to be seen at quite close range (they are also nice to touch), and so there is a good case for planting them near paths from where they can be appreciated. Some, such as silver birch (*Betula pendula*), have a lively bark that will show up at a distance and make a good focal point deep in the wood, especially if three are planted together – odd numbers of plants seem to work better together than even numbers.

Avoid trees that exude excessive honeydew. Limes (*Tilia*) are particularly prone to this, covering plants beneath them with a sticky black coating. This not only inhibits the plants' chances of photosynthesis but will also attract moulds, as well as greenfly which may well introduce virus infections.

Creating shade with shrubs   So far we have only considered trees, which are really most applicable to larger gardens. Shrubs are equally capable of creating the shade that is required by many plants and, of course, their scale makes them eminently suitable for the smaller garden. Their main disadvantage is that, being shorter, less light can penetrate beneath them. This problem is exacerbated by those whose branches come right down to the ground. If they are deciduous it will be possible to grow under them a few winter-flowering plants such as snowdrops (*Galanthus*), but many taller plants will be out of the question. It is better, therefore, to choose taller bushes and shrubs that will allow a certain amount of light to reach under them, or trees like those mentioned earlier, that will not look out of place if some of the lower branches are trimmed off. There are also shrubs that do not have dense canopies of leaves, and these will make an admirable choice.

Of course, it is not just the plants that will find many bushes too low. The advantage of trees is that paths can be created beneath them so that you are able to wander through, working on, or simply admiring and enjoying, the plants. In a shrubby wood paths can still be created, but the gardener will often have his head in the sun.

My earlier comment regarding anticipation of final size applies as much to shrubs as it does to trees. Gardeners often plant shrubs too close together, so that when they mature they are fighting for space and light. This is fine if you are strong enough to cut out a few of them as the wood grows, but many gardeners find it very difficult to steel their hearts sufficiently to remove any shrubs they have planted. Most of the best gardeners are quite ruthless when it comes to sacrificing plants for the overall appearance of the garden. But if you do not want to thin out shrubs, plant them at a distance apart that will allow them the right relationship when they mature, and interspace them with temporary plantings that will die out as the shrubs grow. Heathers (*Erica*), for example, are often used in this context. These quickly spread and fill the gaps between the shrubs, only to die back as the latter grow closer together.

Choosing shrubs   There is a greater diversity of shrubs than of trees, and there is a tendency to use more introduced plants than native ones in gardens. They fit in well with native trees – look how well rhododendrons have adapted themselves to the landscape – and most sit very happily in our gardens. Because of the great variation more care is needed in their groupings than with trees.

The same restrictions apply to shrubs with variegated and coloured foliage as to trees. Do not overdo either. Use them for contrast and relief. Too much can become very restless and will certainly detract from any underplanting that you wish to use. On the whole, purple-foliage plants like to be in a sunny position (they are likely to turn green or at least lose some of their colour in the shade), and therefore they are not very good for underplanting trees or larger shrubs. Some of the yellow- and golden-leaved shrubs, on the other hand, prefer to be out of the scorching sun, and so are good for livening up a dark corner. *Philadelphus coronarius* 'Aureus' and the various golden forms of elder (*Sambucus*) are typical of this type of shrub.

It is useful to mix a few evergreen shrubs along with the deciduous ones, as these will help to create variety, especially in the winter when the visual quality of the garden can wane. Wide, dense bushes are not much use for underplanting with herbaceous plants, but the woodland garden should be balanced, the purpose being to create an overall effect and not just to provide shelter for the plants beneath.

Whereas with most trees flowering is considered an added bonus, with shrubs it is often of paramount importance when choosing between them. The colour of the flowers and their timing are both criteria that must be taken into account. Harmonise colours and, if possible, spread the flowering times over the seasons so that there is not just a concentration in spring. In the autumn shrubs can provide a spectacle in the woodland garden, especially as there are few flowering plants around at that time of year. Some have leaves which exhibit a wonderful range of autumn colours and, of course, in most years there is a fine display of colourful berries and other fruit.

There is a surprising number of shrubs that flower in the winter, so these can be used to supplement evergreen trees and shrubs and those chosen for their attractive bark, to add interest during the bleaker months. There are also some shrubs – *Corylus avellana* 'Contorta', for example – that have curious shapes, with twisted or corkscrew branches, and these are best appreciated in the winter when the leaves are absent. Any shrubs that are planted for winter interest should, if possible, be in a position where they can be readily seen (near a path, for example), as the ground may well be too wet to venture far in search of excitement. Once shrubs have grown to a reasonable size, the woodland garden will provide valuable cut material for the house during the winter. Many of the winter-flowering shrubs are fragrant, which is an added bonus at this time of year.

Shrubs and trees together In any natural woodland, trees and shrubs live together. At the wood's climax many of the shrubs are squeezed out, but they still exist round the margins and in clearings. In a garden wood it is preferable not to plant the trees too close together, so that light can penetrate allowing the shrubs to grow, which in turn will provide light shade for other plants. There is, of course, no need to have any trees at all; there is sufficient diversity in height, shape, colour, leaf density and so on amongst shrubs to provide a more than adequate woodland area in most gardens.

If possible, however, it is a good thing to introduce at least one tree, even if it is only a small sorbus, to add variety, particularly of height, to the scene. A mixture of both not only creates a variety of habitats for the plants but also produces a pleasing visual effect. The contrast in heights and shapes will make the wood an interesting place in its own right, even before any underplanting is taken into consideration. Using both, a false perspective can be created at the edge of the garden by planting trees at the back and shrubs beneath and in front, thereby imitating the edge of a wood and making it appear to stretch well beyond the boundary.

Artificial shade It will be some years before the shade created by the new planting will be sufficient to start underplanting. It is quite likely, in the meantime, that you will be offered or will find plants that you would like to grow, and it seems a pity to let them pass. If there is sufficient space, it is a good idea to create an artificially shaded area by constructing a simple frame over which shade-netting is stretched. Use the type of shade-netting sold for covering greenhouses, which is readily available from most garden centres and stores. The framework can be made of wood, or the metal tubes of an old poly-tunnel that has lost its polythene cover (of which there seems to be a large number around these days).

A more permanent shade house can be created by building a stronger framework and covering it with wooden laths. In larger gardens this can be used as a nursery bed for growing and increasing plants before they are introduced to the woodland area. The bed beneath the shading can be prepared in the same way as the woodland beds. It should contain a good loam, supplemented by humus and, if necessary, grit to help with the drainage. Most plastic shading will stretch, and even break, when it is laden with snow, so it is wise to remove the netting in the autumn. There is no harm in this as far as the plants are concerned and, indeed, it mirrors the pattern of the deciduous trees' habit of dropping their leaves.

As an extension of this idea, there is no reason why a shade area should not be created by erecting a wooden framework and covering it with climbing plants in the form of a pergola. The plants will have to be selected with care as some, such as the Russian vine (*Fallopia baldschuanicum*) or ivies (*Hedera*), will produce too dense a shade, whereas some of the roses (particularly if they have black-spot and drop some of their leaves!) will provide just the right amount. Clematis, if kept pruned, will also make a good cover.

Clearing the site Remove unwanted trees and shrubs before preparing the soil and planting. Check with your local authority before cutting down any trees, as you may need permission. This may not always be forthcoming as, unfortunately, the policy of conserving trees has been too rigidly adhered to in many respects. While some developers have ridden roughshod over the regulations and done a lot of wilful damage without any hindrance, more sensible management schemes have been thwarted by do-gooders who want to preserve all trees without any thought to the future. A continuing policy of renewal, akin to what happens in the wild, rather than hanging on to all trees until the bitter end, is what is required. It was this latter policy that left so many large gaps on our landscape after the 1987 hurricane struck the south-east of England. Many of the very old trees that should have been gradually replaced over the past forty years were left for sentimental reasons, only to be wiped out in one night. If a renewal policy had been implemented there is no doubt that, although the damage would have still been severe, it would not have been so catastrophic.

If you have an existing wood that you wish to use, it is likely that you will have to remove the ranker growth. This is best done by hand. It is hard work, but by doing it this way you will be certain that only the plants that you want removed are removed, and you will gain an intimate knowledge of your wood that no amount of wandering through it will achieve. It is possible to use brushwood-killers, but you are likely to accidentally remove some shrubs or young trees that you would rather have kept. Thin out the trees as well, so that a dappled light shade can reach the woodland floor. If the wood is large enough, it is also a good idea to create some glades.

Since trees are more difficult to extract than shrubs, you may need professional help, especially as you will need to get them down without harming the surrounding trees. If you do cut them down yourself, be certain to wear the correct protective gear.

Planting trees and shrubs   Trees and shrubs purchased in containers can be planted at any time of the year as long as it is not too hot, too cold or too windy. Bare-rooted plants (those dug up from nursery beds) should be transplanted only between late autumn and early spring.

Dig a hole that is at least twice the diameter of the root ball to be planted and to such a depth that the neck of the tree or shrub will be at the same level as it was in the pot or nursery bed. Mix some compost or slow-release fertiliser (bonemeal, for example) into the bottom of the hole and into the spoil that will be replaced around the plant. Place the plant in the hole and add a little of the spoil so that it stands upright, firming it under the roots so that there are no air gaps. If support is required (see below), put the stake in while the roots can still be seen, so that there is no chance of damaging them and thus reducing the tree's chance of survival. Refill with the spoil from the hole, gently firming as you go. The tree or shrub should be well watered in. If the plant is bare-rooted, spread out the roots carefully before the hole is filled. Most container plants can be planted as they are, without disturbing the roots, but should they be twisted round and round the inside of the pot it is best to try and gently untangle them and, again, spread them out in the bottom of the hole.

If the soil is a heavy one, it should have been improved as mentioned above (page 16). Drainage is particularly important: it should be remembered that a planting hole dug on a heavy clay soil can turn into a sump into which water drains. If there is any likelihood of this, a trench should be dug and filled with gravel to lead away any water that might otherwise accumulate in the hole.

Most trees should be staked when newly planted. Latest thinking on the subject suggests that they are better staked low down, only 30cm (12in) or so from the ground, so that the top may move in the wind while just the base of the trunk and the roots are held firm. A single stake with a proprietary tree-tie is all that is normally required, although in windy areas two stakes on opposite sides of the tree may be beneficial. In exposed positions some shrubs may need staking, but, again, it should be low down – just sufficient to prevent the roots from moving.

Once planted, the tree or shrub should be mulched with bark chippings or some other organic material to help retain the moisture around the roots, as well as keeping them cool and preventing the growth of weeds which could well slow down the development of the plant. The most difficult time when creating a woodland garden is the initial stages. Once the cover has developed, its very nature will help keep many of the weeds at bay as they will not like the shady conditions, but while the canopy is still open and while there are still patches of bare earth a constant vigilance will be needed in order to thwart unwanted weeds. This can be achieved either by regular hand-weeding or hoeing, or by covering the ground with a shredded bark mulch. This is only effective if it is about 10cm (4in) deep. Even with a mulch, a few weeds will appear, and it is important to remove them as they do so.

Obtaining plants   As we will see later (page 33), it is best in a woodland setting if planting can be achieved in drifts. To do this, quite a number of each plant is required. This can become an expensive exercise if you need to buy twenty of each that you wish to grow, so it is worth while considering propagating some of them yourself. Seed can be obtained from seed-merchants, but their range is often restricted to colourful, brash plants for sunny positions. A much better range can be obtained from the seed exchanges that many societies, such as the Hardy Plant Society, run. You have to be a member to use this facility, but it is well worth joining.

Many of the plants are stoloniferous, or creeping, and if one pot is purchased a year or so before planting begins, it is often possible to divide the plant several times, either into other pots or into a nursery bed (under shade), so that a larger number will be available when needed. Some plants spread so rapidly that there is no need to buy more than one or two, which will soon cover the area allotted to them.

Garden centres and stores will be able to supply a few of the basic plants, but for a much wider selection it is better to go to specialist nurseries. These have sprung up all over Britain and America and are usually staffed by enthusiastic plantsmen who enjoy talking about plants as well as growing them, so a lot of good advice can be obtained, as well as good plants.

Underplanting Planting can begin in a garden where the cover is already developed or in a newly planted one where the trees and shrubs have grown sufficiently to provide some shade. The soil that was originally prepared at the time of planting the shade plants should be dug over, and any weeds removed. Extra humus of some sort (see pages 18–22) should be incorporated if the soil looks a bit tired or starved.

The best time for putting in the majority of plants is going to be while there are no leaves on the trees, so that the new plants have a good chance of establishing themselves before the canopy cuts off the light and the trees' roots grab all the available moisture. Do not do it when the ground is frozen or when it is waterlogged from heavy rain. Once they have been planted, water well and, if possible, give the ground a good mulch of bark or leafmould.

Some plants, such as foxgloves (*Digitalis purpurea*), can be sown directly into the ground. Copious amounts of seed can be collected from the wild without in any way harming the local populations, and broadcast in your wood. There will never be any need to replant or sow again, as they will come up year after year in spite of their being biennials.

Design Many aspects of design have already been touched on in preceding sections. However, there are one or two points that are worth emphasising.

The planting of a woodland area should be informal – in fact, the more random it is the more natural it will look. Having said that, I must add some qualifications, because if plants are just dotted around in one glorious mixture the scene will have none of that sense of tranquillity and peace that a wood normally gives.

The main planting of trees should not be in rows or blocks, as this will certainly be far too uniform to give a natural appearance. They can be well mixed as long as they do not contain a large number with variegated foliage (which will appear over-busy): this will give a good undulating effect when the wood is seen from the outside, and will not be really noticeable from the inside. What will be more noticeable will be the trunks and the effect of their barks (see page 27).

In a small garden it is especially important not to plant too many trees of the same variety – indeed, it is important not to plant too many trees at all, as they will look out of scale. As mentioned earlier, it is better to plant only one or two trees to give the shade area height and contrast, and then fill in the rest with shrubs. If you want to grow only shade-loving plants and are not too worried about what plants provide that shade, then one large oak is as good as anything – as long as it already exists, for if it does not then your enthusiasm for gardening may have long since waned by the time the tree is big enough!

The use of different-coloured foliage in the trees and shrubs has already been covered (see pages 26 and 28). With the underplanting it is much better to have drifts of one particular plant, rather than mixing them up. This is not only more restful to the eye and more aesthetically satisfying, but, in most cases, more natural, as a lot of woodland plants have a creeping tendency, forming large mats or colonies. Do not plant in geometric blocks, as is often seen with bedding plants. The drifts should be irregular and merge naturally, without a hard line. Some plants can be equally well planted in drifts, or allowed to mix with others.

These are usually the taller slender plants, such as foxgloves or lilies, which naturally sow themselves amongst other plants, cropping up here and there, generally in the lighter areas.

Try not to put plants next to each other that have flowers with colours that clash (unless, of course, they flower at different times of the year). Harmony will give a much more peaceful atmosphere, typical of woodland. Light colours such as white and yellow brighten up the shady areas, whereas deep reds and purples become dull and can disappear. A really cheerful sight, for example, is a drift of yellow Welsh poppies (*Meconopsis cambrica*) in a woodland setting. Pale blues also stand out. A *Campanula persicifolia* sowed itself in my wood in surprisingly dense shade, and yet it has flowered there for many years, shining out like a beacon. This use of light colours, of course, applies to foliage as much as to flowers. Golden and variegated leaves on both herbaceous plants and shrubs create a focal point, frequently for a large part of the year. They are often worth planting some way back in the wood so that they draw the eye into the interior.

As this use of variegated foliage implies, underplanting should not be restricted to plants grown mainly for their flowering ability. Foliage plays a large part in any garden, and is particularly useful during periods when the number of flowering plants is limited. The thought of drifts of hostas or of the wonderful pleated leaves of *Veratrum* will soon make the point. Sometimes foliage can provide a focal point as effective as the colour of flowers. Even though it is as green as its surroundings, a clump of the gigantic leaves of *Gunnera manicata* beside a water feature is certainly eye-catching.

Spread the flowering period of plants over the whole of the wood or shade area, so that interest is maintained throughout the garden over the whole of the year. In larger gardens it may be necessary to plant more than one clump or drift of certain plants in order to ensure this. Thus primroses (*Primula vulgaris*) can be planted in several large drifts amongst plants that flower later in the year. Early-flowering plants can be positioned near paths so that they can be seen without one's having to leave the paths, but bear in mind that this will leave gaps later on. Taller plants such as hellebores (*Helleborus*) will show up over quite a distance, and can be planted further back where they are likely to be masked by other plants once they have finished flowering.

In some cases it is possible to put two plants almost on top of each other so that one grows through the other. This is particularly true of bulbous plants. *Anemone nemorosa* or *A. blanda* grow well with *Cyclamen hederifolium*, as the former flower in spring and then disappear below ground without trace while the latter does not flower until the autumn. Bluebells (*Hyacinthoides non-scripta*) are also good bulbs for underplanting, although these would not be recommended for a small garden as they can spread, rapidly taking on the role of pest.

If the ground to be planted has a natural dip in it this can be used to effect. Taller trees or shrubs can be planted on the higher ground to emphasise the dip, and even if water does not run through the lower part it is possible to increase the amount of moisture-retentive soil here and grow plants that would normally be associated with damper areas – ferns, for example — thus giving the impression of a stream.

In a large woodland garden, space can be afforded for those plants that are generally referred to as ground cover. These can cover large areas, but they should be used with care as they can become boring, especially when not in flower. Vast stretches of bluebells can be breathtaking, but an enormous area of hostas can be quite tedious in its uniformity and these plants should be restricted to smaller drifts. In a small woodland garden or shade area, be even more wary of using ground cover. There is nothing intrinsically wrong with it, but there are so many other, more interesting, plants that you can grow. The other problem is that ground cover plants tend to spread, which is fine in a large area, but in a small patch they can overpower more choice plants unless they are frequently weeded out.

Always allow plenty of access to the wood in the form of paths and stepping stones, possibly even rides in bigger woods. It is also important to provide somewhere to sit and enjoy the surroundings and the wildlife. All these will be dealt with in the next chapter.

3 Special Features

There are one or two features that can be constructed to give the woodland garden extra interest, both in its appearance and to provide it with specialised habitats that will allow more plants to be grown. There are also features that will make access easier, and it is these that we consider first.

PATHS, BRIDGES AND STEPS

It is pointless creating a wood if you do not have access to enjoy it. If you are starting with an existing wood, then paths can be laid out when you are clearing any undergrowth. Be certain that the paths are broad enough for two people to walk side by side without being constantly hindered by low branches. Paths can be carved out in an existing wood, but in a new planting it is difficult to guess how big the trees and shrubs will eventually become, and there may have to be some judicious pruning and thinning out at a later stage. However, if possible try not to plant too densely alongside the paths themselves. This is not only important for comfort, but it will also allow in more light so that interesting plants can be introduced along the lines of the paths, where they can be easily seen.

Do not make straight paths. Let them curve, weaving in and out of some of the larger trees and shrubs. There are two reasons for this, one practical and the other aesthetic. If the paths are straight, then winds can be funnelled down them, gathering speed and doing damage as they go. The second reason is that one of the basic tricks of gardening is to obscure what lies in front. This allows you to concentrate on what is at hand, but at the same time creates anticipation as to what lies round the corner. This is a particularly useful technique in a small garden because it gives the impression of greater size, especially as you are not able to see the boundaries – which as far as the person walking down the path is concerned could be miles away.

On longer stretches of path it can be visually effective to have a focal point at the end. Statuary is the traditional thing to place in this kind of position but it can, of course, become expensive, especially if you need several pieces.

However, a focal point can also be effectively achieved by plants. A white-trunked tree, such as the birch *Betula utilis jacquemontii*, makes a very eye-catching feature and has the advantage of being viewable to good effect from different directions, which makes it ideal to plant at a corner rather than at an end of a path. The same effect can be created by single specimens of a large variety of trees and shrubs that have attractive bark, foliage or flowers.

In larger woodlands the paths can be wide enough to earn the name of 'rides'. Here the sun will be able to penetrate so that the margins, and indeed the path itself, can be planted with wild flowers that will attract butterflies. Because of the availability of sun, these flowering plants need not be restricted to those that require shade, thus adding another dimension to the wood.

The surface of the path can be simply left as bare earth, compacted by the passage of feet. Where the path's edge is not obvious it can be lined with logs or by plants moving away from it in drifts. In lighter areas grass can be grown. The best grass for this is a natural woodland one, wood meadow-grass (*Poa nemoralis*), which can be bought in some lawn mixtures. It can be mown tight in more formal areas, but in larger woods it can be left to grow quite long, with only the occasional cut being given. Where the path passes under trees the grass may well be a little thin, or even non-existent.

A more formal surface might be given to the path, particularly in muddy areas, by covering it with stones or gravel. This can either be allowed to peter out at the edges, or have lengths of wood used as a kerb or retainer so that a neat edge is formed. This type of path can look too formal in a woodland, giving the impression of having been laid by a local authority. Another formal-appearing material, but one that is more in sympathy with the wood, is bark chippings. This can be laid to a few inches' depth between logs or strips of wood. It is soft to walk on, suppresses any weeds, prevents shoes from getting muddy, and yet it fits in well with the atmosphere of the wood. If you are using bark in this quantity, it is best to buy it by the lorry-load; individual bags will prove very expensive.

If there are any really wet areas in the wood through which the path passes, it may be necessary to drain them or to erect duckboards so that visitors can pass over them without getting muddy.

Bridges over streams can be of any material or design that you like or can afford. Some of the old iron bridges of the past were really delightful, but they would cost a fortune to construct today. Wood is a more realistic material. The simplest bridge is one or more planks or logs laid across the stream. Handrails are not always necessary, but if elderly people are likely to use the bridge or if there is an appreciable drop then they should be fitted. Wood can be slippery, so it is a good idea to cover the treads with a piece of small-meshed, galvanised chicken-wire, which will give a good slip-free surface. All wood used in the bridge's construction should be soaked in preservative before it is used so that its life is prolonged for as long as possible.

As an alternative, if the stream is not too deep, stepping-stones can be created. They must have a flat surface on which to stand and must be firmly embedded in the stream so that they do not rock when stood upon. Stepping-stones can also be used as a substitute for paths, especially for secondary paths which are just used as a means of access to the underplantings, for weeding and general maintenance. These can be made from slabs of stone or paving, or from sections of a tree trunk. If wood is used it must have been treated with preservative and, as it will often be slippery, be covered with a piece of small-meshed, galvanised chicken-wire.

In woods on sloping sites it may be necessary to erect steps. Wood, once more, is the most natural of materials, although steps can be sympathetically made of stone or rustic bricks. Again, wood must be treated with preservative. The steps can consist of a riser (the vertical face) made out of one or more logs, stacked one on top of the other and held there by posts driven into the ground in front of them, and then the space behind filled in with rammed-down earth to form the tread. An alternative is to drive some thin logs into the ground so that the risers form a sort of palisade effect. The treads of the steps can be filled with stone or shredded bark, as long as they are not too loosely packed and do not create the possibility of slipping. The treads should be level with the tops of the risers and should be kept topped up if there is a tendency for them to sink.

A further alternative is to create the steps out of old railway sleepers cut into short lengths. These have the advantages of being flat and of having been soaked in tar, which will preserve them for a long time.

If the steps are steep or continue for any distance it may be necessary to build some handrails, especially if they are likely to be used by the elderly. It is advisable to keep the steps free of vegetation, although if they are deep enough and there is enough light they can be grassed over – but remember that they will be difficult to mow.

GLADES AND SITTING AREAS

It is important to remember that the purpose of the woodland garden, or indeed any garden, is enjoyment, and it is a good idea to introduce glades in which you can picnic or just sit. These can be areas left free of trees and shrubs and sown with grass, which can either be cut tight like a lawn or cut only a few times a year, just enough to keep it under control. If the glade is of a reasonable size, the sun will easily reach it and it will be possible to plant the edges with some of the more sun-loving plants. Rather than a formal herbaceous border, it will be more in keeping with the woodland setting to use native wildflowers.

While the young are willing to sit on the grass, older people usually prefer to sit on seats, and so you should provide benches of some sort. The material and design are up to you, but wood and iron are the best-looking for the situation. A popular idea for woodland settings is to create a seat out of a fallen log, but if possible this should be made in such a way as to provide a back. Seating, of course, is not confined to the glades; it can be placed anywhere in the wood where it would be nice to simply it and stare (or even snooze). Typical positions are at the junction of paths or on the edge of the wood facing some view.

A type of seat that always looks good and is generally comfortable is one that is built round the trunk of an ancient tree, the trunk providing the backrest. This kind is often placed at the very centre of the wood – providing that there is a tree there, of course – thus creating a focal point rather like the centre of a maze.

Seating need not be confined to the ground: tree-houses can be an exciting, romantic alternative for children (and even for some adults). This is not the place to go into their construction, but one should be warned of the obvious: they must be well built, and safe. They can be placed in any part of the wood: some may enjoy the seclusion of the centre, while others may prefer the outlook that the edge of the wood provides. Be warned: do not position your favourite plants underneath the tree-house, as they are liable to be trampled on by marauding pirates. Many other types of 'camps' and play areas can be constructed – but I leave this to your imagination.

WATER FEATURES

The concept of tree-houses may be a bit far-fetched for those who are able to plant up only a small area of shade, but the incorporation of a small water feature is not. Water enlivens any part of the garden. If running, its sound is always very relaxing; and either moving or still, it provides reflections that animate the scene. But there is another important factor in incorporating water into a garden: it provides a new series of habitats, allowing a greater number of different types of plants to be grown. Of course, it is not only new habitats for plants that are provided; many forms of wildlife will gladly move in, some, such as frogs and newts, only occasionally being glimpsed, while others – dragon-flies, for example – will give continual joy throughout the summer.

A pond in dense shade is of no use, as it will fill with leaves which will form a festering, stinking black layer at the bottom, allowing nothing to live in it. Any pond or stream must have some light to support life, either in the water or on its banks. The best place for a pond is in a clearing or at the edge of the wood or shade area, both places receiving some sunlight during the course of the day. The ideal situation would be where part of the pond is in permanent sunshine, although this is not imperative.

A stream can flow through any part of the wood. Under the densest shade little will grow, but as it passes through lighter areas more opportunities are presented for planting along its banks and in the stream itself. On the margins of both pond and stream bog gardens can be developed; these should have a reasonable amount of light, although it is not essential to have them in full sun.

Lucky is the person who has natural water, especially running water, in his or her garden. Most of us have to work hard to acquire such a facility, and even harder to make it look natural. There are several ways of creating a pond. The old-fashioned way is to dig a hole and puddle it with clay. This is hard work – as I know, since I have created one in this manner – but the result is a pond that looks more natural than most of those using modern liners. The one big advantage is that you can plant directly into it without fear of splitting the lining.

The lining of the hole, then, is a thick layer of gooey clay. If you are lucky (or unlucky, depending on your viewpoint) you may find it in your garden. In my case the topsoil is a good loam, but once you get down several feet into the subsoil you find the material that the best ponds are made of. This has allowed me to line the hole with a good thick layer of clay dug from its bottom. I cannot remember having such fun since childhood, stamping and punching the wet clay into position. It should not be allowed to dry out before the water is put in, or it will crack. It is likely that the pond will not be entirely sealed at first, but any small leaks will eventually clog up. Bigger leaks may require it to be emptied and resealed. The water will at first be cloudy, but it will clear. To start with the pond will look very stark, but it will soon blend in with its surroundings and after a couple of years it will look as though it has been there for much longer.

A more conventional material to use is one of the specialist ones such as butyl that can be purchased from garden centres. First, you dig the hole and line it with sand to prevent stones or other sharp objects puncturing the butyl. Then stretch the liner across the hole and slowly fill it with water. As it fills it sinks and assumes the shape of the hole. The edges of the butyl can be covered with rocks or buried in the bank below water level. The latter method not only hides the liner but provides a rim of wet soil in which you can position marginal plants. This kind of pool is immediate, with clear water and no leaks right from the start. Take care not to pierce the liner, especially round the margins where it is below ground and thus vulnerable to accidentally being spiked with a fork.

The third type of pond has a rigid liner which you buy premoulded. Dig a hole of similar shape and slip the mould in place. The size of this kind of pond is restricted and, unfortunately, it rarely looks other than what it is – a plastic pond. The last type is one lined with concrete. The techniques are too involved to go into in this book, and, besides, the regular outlines of such a pond are usually too stark for a woodland setting. With concrete, regular shapes are easier to construct than the more flowing lines that can be followed with other materials.

The water in a pond can be static or flowing. In either case, unless fed by a natural stream, it will need topping up from time to time. This can be done either from the mains water supply, or, better still, by relaying all the rain-water from roofs or from patios and drives into the pond.

Movement of the water can be achieved by using a fountain or (better in a woodland setting) by creating a stream or 'spring' trickling into it. Pumps can be installed in or beside the pond (the latter types are the most powerful) which will push the water uphill to allow it to trickle down an artificial stream bed, or to well up out of rocks beside the pond. Pumps will require electricity, and it must be remembered that electricity and water can make a lethal combination if not handled properly; so if you do make an installation, employ a qualified person if you have any doubts about your own ability in this field.

Streams are more difficult to construct. Puddling is not a practical proposition. Strips of butyl liner can be used, but these are very difficult to disguise, except possibly if the watercourse is dead straight, as creases inevitably form and will show unless care is taken. A concrete stream bed is an easier possibility, but involves a lot of work. To prevent it cracking, lay a good layer of hardcore as a foundation. The stream will look rather harsh to start with, but with time and the judicious use of rocks and plants it will soon begin to look natural, particu-larly if you keep it reasonably full of water. To keep the water flowing, you can use pumps to lift it from a pool at the bottom end of the stream to another at the top. The descent need not be too steep, but if the movement is sluggish or non-existent the water will soon become foetid and rather unappealing.

There is quite a number of flowering plants that will tolerate being grown in damp positions in a light shade. Ponds offer three different types of habitat for this kind of plant: floating in the water, in the shallow water round the margins, or in the damp soil at the edge of the pond or stream.

In a puddled pond pieces of floating plant which usually grow very easily from cuttings can be anchored to the bottom of the pond with something heavy such as strips of lead. These will soon grow away. Plants in the margins can, likewise, be planted directly into the pond, but take care not to dig too deep a hole – otherwise the clay liner may be punctured. It might be better to build up soil around a plant to stabilise it, rather than burying it, and allow it to put its own roots down into the clay. Plants for the damp soil, as with any other soil, can be planted directly into it. Clay forms an impenetrable barrier to water, and it is often found that the soil immediately next to this kind of pond is bone-dry in spite of water being only a short distance away. Boggy areas can be created by making a bowl of clay next to the pond and, by lowering the bank at that point, allowing the water to flood over into it. This will fill only when the pond itself is full so that it will not be permanently under water but, on the other hand, if sufficient humus has been added to the soil, it should never dry out.

Lined ponds, with either a flexible or a rigid liner, need different techniques, as there is no soil in which to plant. In recent times special pots have been designed for ponds. These have lattice sides which allow easy penetration by the water and an equally easy way out for the roots, which can then spread across the pond floor searching out any pockets of nutrients that they can find. Such pots are easily obtainable from most garden centres. The plants should be planted in a soilless compost, in the same manner that you would pot up any plant. Then lower the container to the floor of the pond. To get plants into the centre of the pond, two long pieces of string can be threaded through the top lattices of the pot and the ends of each piece held by two people standing on either side of the pond with the pot suspended in the centre. The plant is then lowered and the strings withdrawn. Flat ledges can be constructed around the edge when the pond is dug, so that plants requiring shallow water can be stood upon them in their lattice pots. The rigid liners usually have these ledges built into them.

You can create a bog garden by extending a flexible liner well beyond the edge of the pond to cover a shallow depression, which you then fill with a humusy soil. Not all damp-loving plants like to have their toes permanently in water, so if possible arrange it so that water flows into this area only when the pond is overflowing. Holes can be made in the liner so that excess water passes through, leaving behind just enough in the organic material in the soil to provide a damp environment. In periods of drought your bog garden will need watering, unless the pond is regularly filled up by hand to overflowing. A wide range of flowering plants can be grown in these boggy areas – from water-loving irises, to kingcups (*Caltha palustris*), to many of the candelabra primulas. Foliage plants such as reeds and bulrushes can also be included. In chapter 7, on perennial plants for shade, a number will be mentioned in detail.

The margins of a stream can be planted in the same way and with the same range of plants. In denser shade streams can be lined with ferns, which will enjoy the cool, moist atmosphere. Some woodland plants prefer a moister situation, and large drifts of plants such as ramsons (*Allium ursinum*) can be planted – if you can stand the smell of garlic.

Wildlife will naturally be attracted to the water, and so there is no reason to import any. Fish are an exception, and although I suspect that they would eventually arrive as eggs on the feet of ducks, it would be more expeditious to introduce them yourself. I prefer to see native species in a natural pond but many gardeners love to have more exotic foreign fish which can be obtained from special aquatic centres, often attached to garden centres. Do not introduce them until the pond has been provided with oxygenating plants as well as other plants that offer shelter from sun and marauding birds. Some sunlight should reach the pond, if fish are to be kept.

It is amazing how quickly other forms of wildlife colonise a new pond. Less than an hour after starting to fill mine a pond skater appeared on the surface, and within six months, before I had started planting the pond myself, colonies of rushes (*Juncus*) and reedmace (*Typha angustifolia*) had started developing.

PEAT BEDS

Peat beds are special borders for growing a wide range of plants that like a moist peaty condition and, usually (but not always), shade. Although they are known as peat beds they do not necessarily incorporate peat: leafmould, as we shall see in a moment, is a perfectly acceptable alternative. There is not a world of difference between a peat bed and a woodland garden, except that many of the plants grown in a peat bed would be less capable of standing the hurly-burly of a woodland setting; they need just that extra bit of attention. It is a bed for a plantsman who wishes to grow choice plants and is prepared to look after them, rather than letting them fend for themselves.

Traditionally the soil of a peat bed has been a mixture of one part (by volume) good loam, two parts coarse peat and one part grit. The recent campaign against the use of peat in the garden has had its effect, with many gardeners now reluctant to use so much peat, and so this has been replaced by either one part peat and one part leafmould or two parts of leafmould. The peat has a tendency to give the soil an acid pH, which, of course, is preferred by ericaceous plants such as rhododendrons. Leafmould can be acidic but is generally more neutral, which is not necessarily a bad thing. When leafmould breaks down it is more nutritious than peat and is therefore more valuable in the soil.

The grit is added to the soil to ensure good drainage. The organic content (peat or leafmould) holds sufficient moisture for the plants' needs, and the grit allows any surplus to drain away. The loam, of course, provides the bulk and the nutritional elements to the compost.

Peat beds are normally constructed in a shady area, either under trees or against a north wall. There are some plants that like this type of soil but prefer to be in the sun, so it is quite common practice to build the bed so that part sticks out to catch most of the day's sun. It can be constructed flat on the ground or raised up in tiers, a little in the manner of a rock garden. The latter is more common.

The beds are supported either by peat walls or by logs. Just before the campaign against using peat started, peat blocks were once more becoming widely available. These are solid blocks of peat about twice the size of a building brick. They are used in the same fashion, each layer overlapping, with the occasional one turned sideways back into the soil to act as an anchor. The blocks are soaked in water for a couple of days before they are used, and should never be allowed to dry out as they are extremely difficult to re-wet. The walls are normally only a foot (30cm) or so high, and the spaces behind are filled with the soil mixture described above. It is essential to fill in as you build each wall so that the latter do not dry out. To help with stability, build the walls so that they slope back towards the soil. The number of levels that you build depends on the contours of the land and your own preference. Keep it simple, as too many vertical walls begin to look overpowering; also, as the bed gets higher so the chances of the walls sinking into the increasing depth of compost become greater. On sloping ground a greater number of terraces will not look out of place.

Logs laid on their sides perform the same function as peat walls. If narrow ones are used, they must have stakes rammed into the ground to support two or more stacked on top of one another. Logs will eventually rot through and the peat blocks will disintegrate, allowing the filling to fall out; but normally, by the time this happens, the roots of the plants have bound together the soils and the peat so that the bank is maintained. The gaps between the logs and blocks can be planted with shade-loving plants such as *Ramonda*, that like to grow in vertical crevices. *Primula* also do very well in this type of moist situation. When planting in between the blocks, make certain that the roots of the plants are in contact with the soil behind and not hanging in space in an air pocket.

It is a good idea to incorporate a path or stepping-stones across the bed, as the soil should not be compacted by being walked on. Stepping-stones can either be of slabs of stone or, more appropriately, circles of wood cut from a large log. Paths can be marked by small logs or branches and filled with shredded bark, or just left as bare earth. A top-dressing of leafmould or chipped bark is helpful in retaining moisture and cutting down on the necessity to weed the beds.

Like any garden the peat bed suffers from weeds, which should be removed as soon as they appear. If they are allowed to get too large their root balls tend to take away a lot of the peat when they are removed. The bed must be kept moist and – more important than any other aspect of woodland gardening – watering should be carefully carried out, by sprinklers if necessary. The walls must be able to keep damp by drawing on reserves of moisture from within the beds. If they do dry out, they shrink and leave plants with their roots stranded in the air.

Another aspect of regular maintenance is to keep an eye on the levels of the beds. The peat or leafmould breaks down and the beds slump. This can be remedied by topping up every year, preferably in late winter or early spring before growth starts. Leafmould should provide sufficient nutrients, but if peat is used there will be the need to top-dress with a general fertiliser, at half the dosage recommended on the packet. This should be carried out at the same time as the peat is renewed.

The range of plants that can be grown in a peat bed is surprisingly large, especially the smaller plants grown by the alpine gardener. Anyone who is passionately interested in plants should create a shady peat bed, as it will considerably extend the range that he or she is able to grow. Twenty years ago that great gardener Alf Evans of the Edinburgh Botanic Garden wrote the definitive book on this subject, which you should consult if you want to go into it in greater detail.*

WILDLIFE

Although some of the gardener's hardest battles are against wildlife in one form or another, there can be few who do not appreciate the company of nature all around them. Creating a woodland garden is enough in itself to encourage a wide range of animals into the garden, but if you so wish more can be done to make the wood inviting.

Insects are the largest group of fauna that will be present. These may not appeal, but a wood that is rich in insect life will attract the birds and mammals that feed on them. Leave a few fallen trees around to rot if you have space and, if they are not dangerous, leave a few rotten tree trunks standing. Birch (*Betula*) is a good candidate, as it quickly rots, thereby inviting a wide range of insects and birds that prey on it. It will also attract fungi. Many butterflies will make use of the sunny spots in rides and glades if there are nectar-bearing wild flowers present. It is not only butterflies, of course, that are attracted to wild flowers: a great number of flies, bees, wasps, beetles and many other insects find sustenance in them.

The number of birds will increase as the wood matures and is able to give them more cover and potentially a larger number of nesting sites. These can be increased artificially by attaching nest boxes and platforms to trees. Some birds – nightingales, for example – prefer a dense undergrowth, and if your wood is large enough it is a good idea to keep part of it wild. Another way of encouraging

* Evans, Alfred. *The Peat Garden and its Plants*. J.M. Dent, 1974.

birds is to plant some fruiting bushes. For example, a crab apple tree will drop its fruit, which will lie on the ground well into winter and thus supply food to a number of birds and mammals. Rowan (*Sorbus*) berries are a great relish for birds, and usually disappear soon after they are ripe. Birds will also eat the seed from wild flowers. Some, such as chaffinches, will forage on the ground for the seed scattered from plants such as chickweed (*Stellaria media*), while others – goldfinches are a good example – like to take the seed direct from the heads of thistles (*Cirsium* and *Carduus*) and teasels (*Dipsacus fullonum*). It is more difficult in a small garden than in a large one to provide a wide range of food plants, and obviously some (such as the thistles) should be avoided if there is not much room or if they are likely to overrun everything else. Even so, there is still a large number of acceptable plants.

Mammals are a lot more problematic, as they can cause damage. Rabbits, sweet as they may look, are nothing but a nuisance in a garden, as anyone who has experienced them will know. Again, in a large wood this is not so much of a problem as long as the area they inhabit can be isolated from the main garden with a netting fence. Badgers are, likewise, a mixed blessing. Lucky are those who have this delightful creature in their gardens, but they can dig up some of the choicer plants in their search for food. Foxes are no trouble, unless you keep chickens and forget to lock them up. Smaller mammals such as mice and voles are really not a problem, particularly if there is a ready supply of berries and fruit to keep them happy. When they have to resort to eating bulbs, the gardener's generosity begins to wear a bit thin. Cats and foxes tend to keep the populations down to acceptable levels. One of my favourite mice is the dormouse. When our wood was wild we had some, but once my gardeners's sense of tidiness and design began to prevail they disappeared (there is a moral somewhere there). All these animals are shy creatures and will appreciate the cover that a woodland garden affords them. A wild patch, as already described, will be even more to their liking.

Aquatic life, as I implied earlier, will appear as soon as you create a pond or stream. Once the vegetation has grown up around and in it, it will be positively teeming. Most will come unbidden, but fish will have to be introduced. Whether you have a preference for native species or whether you want something more exotic is really up to you. Dragonflies, the most beautiful of creatures, will soon arrive in a myriad of colours to give a great deal of pleasure.

All these creatures are likely to start arriving in any woodland garden, but with forethought and the provision of shelter and food you will encourage a lot more.

When talking about wildlife, people seem to have a natural tendency to forget about the wild flora – the flowers, grasses, mosses, ferns, fungi and so on. Many of these will be at home in a woodland garden, and along its paths and rides.

Unless they become a nuisance, leave them where they are. Wildflower gardening is a very difficult art – much more so than many romantics realise – but in a natural situation wild flowers can be given their head and allowed to be untidy if they wish. They will need some control, and cutting a few times a year will keep the ranker weeds at bay – this is essential if you wish to keep the more delicate and less pushy plants.

One last word. As well as making a habitat that is suitable for wildlife, the gardener ought to make time to sit and watch. Sitting quietly while animals go about their business is one of the great delights in life. Find a comfortable position in the woodland garden about half an hour before dusk, and sit there until well after dark, watching and listening to the day shift pack up and the night shift begin; it is an experience you will never forget.

4 Maintenance

There is no such thing as maintenance-free gardening, but woodland gardening requires less attention than most other forms. Autumn and winter are good times for tidying up and doing any necessary pruning or removal. This ties in quite neatly with the rest of the garden, as it is often impossible to get on to the more cultivated soils at this time of year.

As with all gardening, one of the continual maintenance problems is to keep the area weed-free. Fortunately, once the canopy has developed there is less of a tendency for weeds to grow – grasses, in particular, are plants of open spaces. If a good loose top layer of leafsoil has been created, then what weeds do appear can be very easily removed by hand. The worst areas are going to be at the edges of the wood where there is more light. Some of the hedgerow weeds, such as goosegrass (*Galium aparine*), can form dense colonies here and can become a nuisance by smothering other, less rampant, plants. However, they can usually be removed by hand without too much difficulty. I would be loath to use chemical herbicides in the wood, as an accident might well rob it of much of its character. Imagine killing off a tree that you have patiently waited twenty years to reach maturity! Not that most herbicides are this powerful, but damage can be caused and it is not usually necessary to use chemicals, especially if the ground has been thoroughly prepared in the first place.

In a large wood, there is not the same need to keep the ground completely weed-free. Indeed, the only weeding necessary is to make certain that there is no competition in the areas where you have underplanted. In this type of wood it is quite normal to have wide paths and rides; these can be wonderful places, with wild flowers enjoying the sunnier spots. But they can also quickly be overrun by brambles, then bushes and finally trees, so they should be mown at least two or three times a year. The first cut should not be before late summer, so that any flowers that have already bloomed can first seed themselves. The centre of the path can perhaps be cut more frequently, to make it easy to walk on (wading through long wet grass, which flaps around the legs, is not a pleasant experience).

One potential problem to keep an eye on is the appearance of brambles

(*Rubus fruticosus*). Seeds from the blackberries are dropped by birds sitting in the trees and shrubs. Brambles are most easily removed as seedlings but, should they get a hold, be certain to remove the whole plant and not just the portion above ground – otherwise they will regenerate, seemingly with more vigour. There are several other pests dropped by birds, including ivy (*Hedera helix*) and elder (*Sambucus nigra*). These, similarly, crop up everywhere, and must be removed before a vigorous colony is formed. In a large natural wood this is not as important, since there is room for these 'weeds', particularly as the blackberries are good for pies and jam and the elderberries for wine. Both will only flower at the edge of the wood or in clearings, where they have sunlight.

Trees and shrubs use up a great deal of water. The annual rainfall in most areas is usually enough to sustain them, particularly if native plants have been used. However, some of the underplanting can suffer in dry weather, and it may be necessary to water these occasionally. Be certain to give them a good soaking and not just a quick sprinkle from a watering-can, which will be useless. Try not to water too frequently, or the trees will realise that there is water to be had and will soon send in an abundance of surface roots to mop it up, the situation soon becoming worse than if you did not water at all. If you build a peat bed, then this should be kept moist but not wringing wet.

Mulching helps to conserve water and, of course, to keep down the weeds. A good 10cm (4in) layer of shredded or chipped bark is one of the best kinds in a woodland garden. It is effective, and it looks right. Leafmould, if you can get sufficient, is another excellent material and looks even more natural than bark. Do not use sheets of black polythene covered with a layer of bark or leaves. In theory this is a good idea, but inevitably the polythene shows through and soon looks a terrible mess. It is the kind of thing that always looks neat and effective in a television gardening programme, but becomes extremely tatty as soon as the camera's brief visit is over. Grass cuttings make a cheap and effective mulch, and help to improve the soil. Do not spread them too deeply – 5cm (2in) is about the maximum depth. As mentioned earlier, the decaying grass heats up and the thicker the layer the hotter it will be, killing off any plants that pass through it. This does not matter if they are weeds – indeed, it is one of the reasons why grass has been used in the first place – but it does matter if they are ornamental plants. If you feel that rotting grass clippings look unsightly, put them at the back of borders or behind bushes where they cannot be seen.

There is generally no need to feed a wood with fertiliser. The falling leaves (as already described on page 13) provide a natural recycling of nutrients. Any supplement can be given by way of top-dressing with leafmould, or even grass cuttings (as described above). In a small area that does not get natural leaf-fall and where there is insufficient home-made leafmould, other organic materials such as farmyard manure can be used. This should be well rotted. If all else fails then a sprinkling of a general fertiliser in early spring will not go amiss. Apply it at about half the dosage recommended on the packet.

Unlike the more formal approach to gardening in herbaceous borders, there is no need to dead-head or cut down plants after they are over. They can be allowed to fall and decay where they are. However, in a small garden with only a small area of shade, it might be felt better to keep things tidy – otherwise, the border will stand out like a sore thumb. Most of the material can be composted and then returned to the border to feed it.

In a woodland situation there is rarely any need to prune trees or shrubs, except when they are damaged. Branches of trees should be cut off a little way from the trunk. First, make one cut beneath the branch to prevent it breaking off before the sawing is complete and tearing down the trunk (Figure 8). Then cut the remaining stub off cleanly, close to the trunk. In the past it was always advised to paint over the cut stem with a proprietary sealant, but this is now considered bad practice and the wound is left exposed.

Another reason for pruning trees is to reduce their canopy in order to allow more light to reach the plants below. This can be achieved by cutting off the lower branches (Figure 9) so that the effective canopy becomes higher, or by thinning out the canopy itself (Figure 10). This latter method is a popular way of growing apple trees (which make very good trees for a shade garden). These often have their centres almost bare of foliage and fruit-bearing branches, which not only makes it easier to pick the fruit but also allows light to get in to ripen it.

Shrubs are in greater need of attention, especially if you require them to flower well. As shade-providers they will need no more attention than the cutting out of any dead wood, but many of those used for ornamental purposes should be pruned annually. In many cases up to a third of the old wood should be removed every year, so that new young growth is encouraged. Those that flower on old wood should be pruned immediately after flowering, to enable the new growth to mature in time for the following year's flowers. Those that flower on new wood can be pruned over the winter or in early spring. The old-growth flowerers tend to be those that flower in the spring and the new-growth ones are those that flower later in the year, once the new growth has had a chance to mature. A few shrubs, such as the butterfly bush (*Buddleja*) and the elders (*Sambucus*), are best cut back to the ground every year during the winter. This all sounds very complicated to the inexperienced, but full pruning details are given when individual trees and shrubs are discussed.

The final reason for pruning is cosmetic, in that it is undertaken to help the tree or shrub to keep its shape. In a large wood this would not be a problem, but in a situation where trees and shrubs are seen as individuals they should be

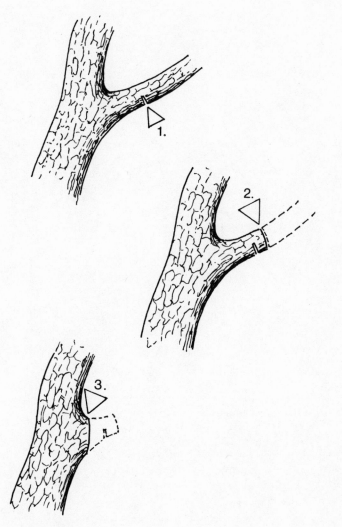

Figure 8.

kept in good shape by removing any branches that offend the gardener. Without going too much into techniques, one practical point about pruning should be mentioned: it is important to make the cut correctly. Using a pair of sharp secateurs, cut through the stem or branch at about 30 degrees just below a bud (Figure 11). Thicker stems should be sawn through.

Halfway between weeding and pruning, there is the problem of suckers. Some shrubs (and even trees) throw up a number of suckers, sometimes at quite a distance from the parent plant. In a large wood this does not really matter too

Figure 9.

Figure 10.

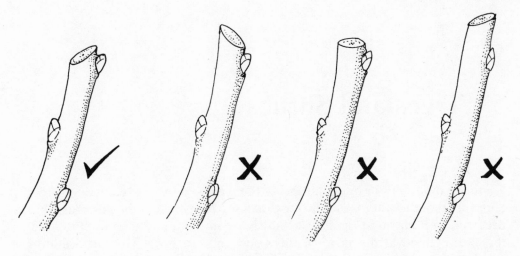

Figure 11.

much, but in a small garden it can become a nuisance. The best solution is to avoid this kind of plant in the first place, particularly as they are not very good as shade producers. Once the offending shrub has been planted, however, short of digging it out, the problem must be addressed some other way. The best method is to break off the suckers where they leave the parent plant. If you just cut them off at the surface, where they appear, they will throw up several more suckers from the same place, compounding the problem. Do not try to improve the situation by applying chemicals, as this will probably kill the parent plant as well.

This is not the place to go into a detailed description of the propagation of new material to increase the stock, but it should perhaps be mentioned that although woodland plants set seed, the majority of them depend mainly on vegetative means of increase. This generally means that the plants are spreaders and can easily be divided, either by lifting the whole clump and breaking it up, or by digging off a part without disturbing the rest of the plant. In order to build up a good-sized drift, especially of ground cover, from just one or two plants, this should be done quite frequently – once a year, possibly. It is surprising how quickly a large area of a plant can be worked up in this way. Most division should be carried out in autumn or in very early spring, just as growth is beginning. Methods of increase will be mentioned under individual plants in later chapters.

5   Trees and Shrubs

There are thousands of trees and shrubs that can be grown in temperate gardens. Some are more useful for our purpose than others. Many of the flowering shrubs need sun to perform at their best, but they can quite easily be used as long as they are planted at the front of the wood and not in it. The justification for some of them appearing in this book is that they, in turn, provide shade for other plants. However, it is mainly those shrubs that will tolerate shade that are listed, so do not be disappointed if some of your favourites are excluded. This does not mean that you should not grow them; the garden is yours and should reflect your tastes, not mine. So, bearing in mind the reasons why they are likely to have been excluded, plant them in an appropriate position.

Acer (maple)

The maples are a large and varied genus of which several hundred forms are available from nurseries. As this vast number indicates, they are very popular – especially those with decorative leaves. These are not a great deal of use in creating a woodland garden, and are best regarded as specimen trees.

Acers are generally thirsty trees that do not like the ground to be too dry. So avoid growing them on drier soil, or they are likely to be a disappointment. The biggest acers are the greediest of all, and trees such as the sycamore (*A. pseudoplatanus*) should be shunned at all costs. Its shade is too dense and the tree too thirsty and hungry to be of any use in our context. The only place where it might be used is in exposed areas, where it will protect the edge of a wood. Similarly, the popular *A. platanoides*, the Norway maple, should be avoided. Its shade can also be dense, but worse still is its ability to produce a mat of surface roots that will take up any goodness going, which makes it virtually impossible to grow anything underneath. I know, as I inherited a beautiful one with really black leaves, but its voracious appetite got the better of it and it fell to the axe.

The medium-sized acers are better, and produce a lighter shade that is more suitable for underplanting. They are ideal for planting along paths, because they do not create sufficient shade to prevent grass growing under them. Another advantage of planting them beside paths or at the edge of a wood is that the glorious autumn colours that many of them exhibit can be seen and appreciated. Warming to the subject, one can also recommend those that have decorative barks. *A. griseum*, the paper-bark maple, has a rich brown bark that peels off in an attractive manner, while others in the snake-barked series (including *AA. davidii, hersii* and *pensylvanicum*) have a decorative veining on the trunks.

The smaller ones, particularly the dwarfer forms of the *A. palmatum dissectum* group, can be lost in a woodland setting, but in a small garden they provide a good home for a few early-flowering bulbs such as snowdrops (*Galanthus*). Their own prettiness, though, often detracts from what is grown underneath. They also look particularly graceful beside a pond. No pruning is required, except if they need shaping.

Aesculus (horse chestnut, buck-eye)
A useless tree as far as we are concerned. Most species make very handsome specimen trees, but their shade is far too dense and their roots far too hungry to grow anything underneath, with the possible exception of cyclamen. This is a tree to enjoy in other people's gardens, if they are foolish enough to plant them.

Alnus (alder)
An odd choice, perhaps, but I find these trees quite attractive, both in the late winter when they have red catkins and later when their dark-green leaves have opened. However, the main reason for their appearance in this book is because they will happily grow in wet areas, even with their toes in the water. This makes them ideal for planting in boggy ground or alongside streams and ponds.

Many bog-loving plants will grow under alders – reeds and rushes, for example, as well as more colourful plants such as the kingcup (*Caltha palustris*). Outside boggy ground I would not bother about them. No pruning is required, but if the trees get too big they can be coppiced and started off again.

Arbutus (strawberry tree)
This is a wonderful genus of trees and ideal for our purpose as long as you do not live on chalk, because it is ericaceous (the commonest, *A. unedo*, is an exception and will grow on any soil as long as it is not *too* alkaline). It grows in either full sun or in light shade. I think it is best grown alongside a path, or better still in a thinning in the trees where one will suddenly come upon it. The first one I saw was in such a situation, and the unexpected confrontation was a great pleasure. The bark is a wonderful warm brown, revealed as the older, darker bark peels off. The most extraordinary thing for most people is the fact

that the strawberry tree bears its flowers and its fruit at the same time, during spring or autumn, depending on species. The white bells are reminiscent of those of heather, while the fruit is round and red, looking just like a strawberry.

Patience is required with this tree, as it is no more than a shrub for many years, taking up to twenty years to reach 5m (16ft). It dislikes having its roots disturbed, so do not try to beat the system by buying the biggest you can; a smaller one will transplant much more reliably. The foliage is evergreen and fairly dense, but the branches are usually quite open when mature, allowing light to reach the ground below.

The most widespread is *A. unedo*, which flowers and fruits in the autumn – a time of year when any flowering plant is welcome. Most of the other species flower in spring. The fastest-growing and probably the most attractive species is *A. menziesii* (madrona), although it might well be tender in colder districts.

Underplanting with ericaceous plants such as *Erica*, *Vaccinium* or *Gaultheria* seems to be in keeping with this tree. No pruning is required, unless you wish to have a tree with a single trunk, in which case it must be trained during its formative years.

Aucuba (spotted laurel)
A. japonica is a large, heavy-looking shrub that prefers shade, even quite deep shade, and can be planted under most shade-bearing trees. The heaviness comes from the large spear-shaped leaves which are a glossy green in the species. There are several varieties which have much lighter, variegated leaves, spotted or splashed with gold. These are invaluable for lightening up darker areas. They are not plants to set the world afire but they are useful in the larger woodland garden.

Not only are these plants accommodating in the amount of shade they will take, but they will also grow on most soils, including chalky ones. To add to their virtues, they need no pruning.

Berberis
These plants have their place in a garden, but not in a shade garden. They produce too dense a shade for underplanting. Another disadvantage is that those that have thorns make life hell if you are weeding anywhere near them. Little twigs with spikes seem to be lurking in every weed, ready to journey up under your nail. Use them by all means in a shrubbery or as specimens, but avoid using them for underplanting.

Betula (birch)
In spite of several drawbacks, birch should be found in any woodland garden. In a large wood they can be planted as individual trees or, better still, in groves.

Azaleas and bluebells in a woodland garden—easily grown but very effective.

A pond and sitting area in a small garden.
A colourful streamside border in light shade.

If your wood is big enough, a waterfall can create a fascinating focal point.

Silver and grey are not easy colours in a woodland setting, but here they make a welcome contrast to the usual green foliage.

Interesting leaf shapes and textures enhance the flowers in a shady area.

Acer palmatum can be spectacular in the autumn.

When walking through a wood you can always tell when a group of birch is coming up, because it begins to get lighter and there is more woodland-floor vegetation. Although found in woods, birch rarely grow under taller trees. Because the majority do not grow to a great height they make ideal trees for the small garden, possibly in association with shrubs to create a small shade area.

The drawbacks are that they have a tendency to scatter their seed far and wide, giving both you and your neighbours plenty of seedlings to pull up (not too onerous a task, though), and that they tend to be surface rooters. However, their demands on the soil are not too great, and it is perfectly possible to grow a range of plants underneath them. Their advantages are that they provide a fine dappled light which is ideal for planting under; they often have decorative trunks, many glistening white (*B. utilis jacquemontii* and *B. ermanii* have two of the best) or orangey brown (*B. albosinensis*); they have a graceful habit; and, although not spectacular, they have a reasonable autumn colouring. Their far-reaching root system makes them ideal for lighter, impoverished soils. They grow quite rapidly and soon reach maturity, often not lasting much longer than thirty years.

The leaves are small and are held on airy branches, which allows for a wide range of plants to be planted beneath them. Although they should normally be spaced at sufficient intervals to allow each to mature, they can be positioned together in tight groups (even as close as 1m (40in)) to show off their white trunks. Three planted in a flat triangle at this distance from each other will make an ideal grouping in a small garden. It will both act as a focal point and provide a good shade for underplanting.

The common silver birch (*B. pendula*) is ideal for woodland planting, but in smaller areas one of the more decorative cultivars or species may be used. Avoid the new, supposedly golden-leafed, form of the silver birch: it looks as though it is suffering from a virus attack and does little to enhance the appearance of any garden.

The widest range of underplanting can be achieved on richer soils; on more impoverished ones plants that prefer or that will tolerate a drier position should be used, as the birch will compete quite strongly for whatever water is going. No pruning is required, unless reversion (one or more branches returning to plain, undecorative form – for instance, the return to plain leaves in a cut-leafed form) occurs. Cut out any reverted branches.

Buddleja (butterfly bush)
Not a plant to put in the middle of a wood as it likes sun, but it can be planted on the edge of a shady area and can be underplanted with early-flowering bulbs or other early flowerers, such as *Anemone nemorosa*, that soon die back.

Buddleja should be cut to the ground every winter so that only a light shade is provided during the spring while the stems are regrowing. Later in the season the stems are likely to smother the ground, making it impossible for anything to grow under it.

Buxus (box)

Box will grow in conditions varying from full sun down to quite deep shade, but there does not seem to be a great deal of advantage in growing it in the latter. Its great virtue is that it is slow-growing and can therefore be used as hedging, or carved into topiary. Occasionally hedging, or rather edging, may be needed in a woodland setting – along a path, perhaps – and box makes the ideal material. Topiary would look out of place in a natural woodland setting, but it could be used as a surprise, or as a focal point in a clearing or at the end of a ride. It should not be used in dense shade for these purposes, as the plant will become very lax and open. I have never used box for either, I must confess, but I can see that it might have its uses and I rather like the idea of a topiary animal in a woodland setting. Certainly, box has no use as a shrub to be underplanted, because the shade is very dense and little will grow there.

B. sempervirens is the form that is usually grown. It has several cultivars, most with variegations in their leaves. *B.s.* 'Suffruticosa' is a dwarf, compact form that is much used in edging paths.

Box will grow on any soil, and it requires no pruning except for shaping.

Camellia

One of the all-time favourite flowering shrubs, this does well in any wood where it can get a reasonable amount of light. What it does not like is the early morning sun. The reason for this is that it flowers during the early spring when frosts are still around and, although the buds will tolerate frosts, they cannot stand the rapid thawing that an early morning sun induces. So plant in an open woodland or on the west side of a path or group of trees or shrubs. Camellias can be used as effective focal points where two or more paths join, but remember that although they may have quite attractive shiny foliage they only really have one season; so such places might be better reserved for plants that offer repeat flowering, autumn colour or some additional attribute to their normal flowering.

Camellias are lime-haters and must be planted on an acid soil. No pruning is required.

Carpinus (hornbeam)

This is a marvellous tree, related to the hazel but in appearance more akin to the beech. Although on first sight it appears to create dense shade, in fact it produces quite a nice dappled shade, and examination of hornbeam woods in the wild shows a complete ground cover of herbage. I particularly like to walk along rides or paths with hornbeam meeting over the top to form a delightful dappled tunnel. So, with a good leafsoil, it might be worth planting one or two trees, or even a grove if you have the space. Trees are cheaply available, as they are often used as hedging material.

Hornbeam will grow on any soil and there is no need to prune, which makes them trouble-free.

Castanea (sweet chestnut)

A commonly planted tree in woodlands in many parts of the country. However, except when very young their large leaves tend to exclude most light from the woodland floor, making it not a very good plant from our point of view. In a large wood, though, the odd tree is essential, even if it is only for providing the edible nuts in autumn. The twisted bark of ancient trees can be spectacular. The leaves take a lot of breaking down and therefore are not the best for making leafmould.

Cercis (Judas tree)

One of the most beautiful of trees, especially when in flower, as its rosy-purple blossom appears in clusters along all the branches, and even the trunk, before the leaves cover them. It is sun-loving, but will tolerate light shade. It is best used as a specimen tree to create shade in a small garden, rather than as part of a wood. Very slow-growing (only about 30cm (1ft) a year), it should be considered a shrub rather than a tree for the first part of its life.

The Judas tree should be planted while still young, as its fleshy roots resent disturbance. This does not make it the best of trees for underplanting, because disturbing the ground can wound roots and introduce disease. However, there are some plants, such as ferns and bergenia, that can be introduced when the tree is young and not disturbed again. Top-dress annually with organic material, and let the worms mix it into the top layer of soil.

The commonest and most readily available species is *C. siliquastrum*. It has a white form, but the rosy-purple one takes a lot of beating. There are six other species, if you have a collector's instinct.

Cercis like a rich soil, preferably on the acid side, although they will tolerate alkaline soils. No pruning is required.

Chaenomeles (flowering quince, japonica)

This is a wonderful plant that flowers in the late winter and early spring. For some reason it is treated as a wall shrub in most gardens, although it is perfectly hardy and has no need of this kind of protection. In fact, it makes a good free-standing shrub that will tolerate a surprising amount of shade. Many fine specimens could be seen in Cherry Ingram's old garden, The Grange, in Kent, dotted amongst the trees. These are good shrubs to plant alongside paths or rides. They make an untidy bush and love to throw airy stems through other trees or shrubs. They produce a curiously shaped fragrant fruit which is edible when cooked (but not when raw).

There are three species of *Chaenomeles*, of which *C. speciosa* is the commonest, both as the species and in its many cultivars.

Chaenomeles will tolerate a wide range of soils, but it is not too happy on chalk. In a wild situation it needs no pruning, but the plant will become very straggly. In a more formal position it should be pruned after flowering, back to the previous season's growth.

Clematis

This is a large subject to cover in a small space, but most of the genus can be dismissed as being too decorative for a woodland setting. Clematis like to have their roots in the cool and their heads in the sun, so they make ideal climbers to plant beneath a shrub or tree, where their roots get the shade, and their stems can ramble over the top of their host so that they are flowering in the light. Obviously, these are not plants for the centre of a wood, for they would never be seen there; they are much better planted on the margins, or round the edge of a clearing.

As already mentioned, the large cultivars are probably too ornamental for our purposes, but there are quite a number of species and smaller-flowered varieties which will blend in sympathetically with our wood. The native *C. vitalba* (traveller's joy, or old man's beard) is a plant that fits in well with its surroundings and does very well, especially on chalky soils. The small off-white flowers appear in late summer, and are followed by fluffy seedheads (the 'beard' of the common name). Another vigorous climber is *C. rehderiana*, which has small pale-yellow, bell-shaped flowers that smell of cowslips. This plant will rapidly grow away into the tops of the tallest trees. For a bit more colour I would choose one of the *C. viticella* varieties, which have delicate small flowers poised on long, thin stalks. These delightful plants have all the charm that their larger relatives lack, while retaining their floriferousness and range of colour. For spring-flowering clematis, *C. alpina* takes a lot of beating. This is not such a vigorous shrub and is more suitable for planting near a peat garden. The commonly seen *C. montana* can be an incredible sight in spring, and is certainly worth growing over a tree or a tree stump somewhere on the edge of the woodland garden. But do make certain that its host is not something important, as once the clematis gets going you will probably never be able to see it again. There are many more species to explore, if you have the space.

Clematis will grow on most soils but do particularly well on alkaline ones.

Most of these vigorous climbing varieties can be left unpruned, but there may come a time when they will become top-heavy with old growth and will then have to be cut back drastically, or replaced.

Clerodendron
There are two distinct species that are popular in gardens. *C. bungei* is perhaps not everybody's choice of shrub as it tends to sucker rather rapidly, but it is a wonderful plant for light shade, its flowers appearing in the autumn at a time when blossoms are in short supply. The flower heads are wide buns of rosy-purple flowers set off against large green leaves. Try to avoid crushing the leaves – the smell is rather unpleasant. *C. bungei* varies in height from 90 to 120cm (3–4ft). This is a shrub for planting in shade, rather than one to create shade.

C. *bungei* has no particular requirements with regard to soil. Because it suckers it should be planted in a position where this habit can either be accepted, or restricted. Pruning consists of cutting back to ground level in the winter or early spring.

The other common species is *C. trichotomum* and its variety *C.t. fargesii*. These are much taller shrubs or small trees, growing up to 3.6m (12ft) or even 6m (20ft) in favourable conditions. This species is useful not only as a shrub that will tolerate shade, but also as one that can be used for underplanting. The flowers are quite different from its relation, *C. bungei*, but are none the less very attractive, again appearing in the autumn. A good situation is near a path or at the edge of a large shrubbery or wood.

It will tolerate most soils and requires no pruning.

Cornus (dogwood)
A large genus of trees and shrubs with quite a number in cultivation, many of which would suit our purposes admirably. As a plant to underplant other shrubs, *C. canadensis* is to be strongly recommended. It only grows to about 20cm (8in) or so, but spreads quite rapidly when conditions suit it. It is really a subshrub (halfway between a hardy perennial and a shrub). The flower forms a boss in the centre of four conspicuous white bracts, which are set off, in turn, by a ruff of green leaves.

C. *controversa* has an interesting horizontal shape. It is best known in its variegated form, which looks stunning against the dark background of a wood. *C. kousa* is a small tree that enjoys light shade. It can be quite spectacular in the late spring when it is covered with petal-less flowers that are surrounded by large white bracts. It also has good autumn colour. Another member of the genus with the same liking for shade, and having the same kind of flowers with large bracts of white turning to pink, is *C. nuttallii*. A final species is *C. mas*, which has tufts of yellow flowers on the bare stems in late winter. It too likes light shade.

All the above are readily available. They will tolerate a wide range of soils and require no pruning. (See also page 91.)

Corylopsis (witch hazel)

A small genus of deciduous shrubs that prefer a light shade. They come into their own during the late winter, when they produce large open catkins. The yellow flowers are eye-catching and fragrant. Corylopsis are slow-growing, but will eventually reach about 3.5m (12ft). There is quite a number of forms available with not a great deal to choose between them. Go and look at several in flower, and make your choice. It is well worth acquiring at least one of them.

Corylopsis like either an acid or a neutral soil, and require no pruning.

Corylus (hazel)

This genus is not dissimilar from the last one, and yet it is not closely related. Hazels produce a good dappled shade and are widely used for underplanting, most famously in the nut walk, at Sissinghurst Castle, Kent, where a very large range of herbaceous plants is grown. For many years the nut walk was planted exclusively with a spectacular display of polyanthus, but the soil became polyan-thus-sick and they were replaced by a more varied planting. The shrubs themselves are not particularly distinguished, although they are quite pleasant to look at. They produce catkins on the bare branches in the late winter, and edible nuts in the autumn. *C. avellana* or one of its forms is the plant usually grown; the most spectacular is *C.a.* 'Contorta', which has corkscrew branches that are very eye-catching in the winter. Some give a good autumn colour.

Corylus will grow on any soil and can be planted in sun to give shade, or in a wood in light to medium shade (the purple-leafed forms prefer the sun). Unless grown as a tree, it should be coppiced every few years; but this can be done on a rotational basis, cutting out a few of the older stems every year.

Crataegus (hawthorn)

Hawthorn is mainly seen as a hedgerow shrub, although it will grow into quite a sizeable tree, given time. It is cultivated for its frothing flowers in late spring and its fruit (haws) in autumn. Some forms have a good autumn colour. It is a hungry tree, which makes it a difficult species to grow things underneath, although I have succeeded by keeping the ground fed with organic material. *Cyclamen*, *Anemone nemorosa* and *Ranunculus ficaria* all flower there in the spring, and *Liriope muscari* in the autumn.

Hawthorns will tolerate any soil, and need no pruning if grown as a tree.

They will grow quite happily in the light shade of other trees, making them especially good plants for the edge of a wood.

Daphne

Most daphnes prefer a light shade, although some are sun-lovers. *Daphne laureola* dislikes sun and will grow well under trees, even down to quite dense shade. The curious *D. blagayana* will grow in similar positions, although this must have a good leafy soil for it to be at its best. It runs underground, occasionally throwing up a shoot, often quite remote from its last appearance. Its scented flowers appear in spring and are creamy white. However, the more light, the denser the bush. Most of the other daphnes have scented pink flowers and prefer a lighter position, although they will tolerate a modicum of shade.

Most will grow on any soil, although a rich loamy one is to be preferred. No pruning is required.

Erica (heather)

These are not plants of deep shade, but they will tolerate a little light shade. However, they cannot be expected to stay as compact or to flower as well as when planted in the sun. They are useful as fillers between trees and shrubs in new plantings. There is a vast number of cultivars available with a range of different-coloured flowers and foliage.

Heathers prefer to grow on acid soils, although one, *E. carnea*, will tolerate chalk. This is also a winter-flowering plant, which is useful for providing colour at that time of year. Shear over after flowering. (See also page 91.)

Eucalyptus (gum tree)

I have a love–hate relationship with these trees. I cannot help feeling that they look alien in an English landscape, however well they may fit into an Australian, or even American, one. On the other hand, they are handsome, they have a delightful silver or blue foliage and an interesting bark, and the shade they cast is not dense. Another advantage is that if they get too big (and they generally do) they can be cut down and will regenerate.

They are not trees for dense woodland, but a group could well be planted together as a feature, and would provide a good light shade for growing a wide range of plants.

E. gunnii is probably the hardiest – it has taken temperatures down to 15°C (5°F) or lower in my garden, although it has lost a lot of leaves – and one of the most commonly seen, but there is a large selection of species available with variation in leaf shape and bark, although most are not so hardy.

Eucalyptus will grow on a wide range of soils, but they prefer light ones. They do not need pruning, although they can be cut down to the base annually if a more shrubby plant is required. If you have a group of these trees, do not cut them all at once, or the shade will be lost. The foliage is extremely good for cutting for floral decorations.

Eucryphia

A genus of trees and shrubs that is quite widely available, and yet is not seen in gardens as frequently as it should be. Eucryphias have large, saucer-shaped white flowers filled with stamens that appear in the late summer or autumn, often covering the whole tree. It can be an amazing sight. They prefer a light shade, and do well in clearings in woods or beside a path or ride. In fact although they prefer shade they will tolerate full sun as long as the base of the tree or shrub is in shade; so they can be grown in a small garden with a skirt of smaller vegetation – shrubs, for example – around them. The leathery leaves produce quite a dense shade, so they are not very good for underplanting.

There is quite a number of species and forms available, but there is not a great deal of difference between them. I grow *E.×intermedia* 'Rostrevor', which has long sweeping branches and fragrant flowers, much loved by bees. Although eucryphias are slow-growing, they do produce flowers right from the start, so it is possible to buy container-grown plants while in flower (which might help your selection).

Eucryphias grow best on rich acid and neutral soils, but will take a certain amount of alkalinity. No pruning is required.

Euonymus (spindle)

Most gardeners are familiar with variegated evergreen forms of *E. fortunei*, which are very popular with local authorities as ground cover (see page 92). But *Euonymus* is a large genus of deciduous and evergreen shrubs, most of which can be grown in light shade. The deciduous species are much larger and more open shrubs, grown mainly for their colourful fruit and fiery autumn tints (*E. alatus* being one of the best, with bright scarlet autumn colour as well as an interesting bark). *EE. alatus*, *europaeus* and *sachalinensis* can be under-planted. The evergreen species can tolerate quite deep shade, and are useful for forming dense ground cover.

They will all tolerate a very large range of soils, the evergreens, in particular, being able to grow in quite dry and exposed ones. No pruning is required.

Fagus (beech)

A wonderful tree, but not much use in a garden or wood for underplanting, because the shade is too dense and too dry. However, if your wood is big enough not to require every inch to be available for planting, add at least one.

But leave room – one tree could eventually cover a circle of 16m (50ft) or more in diameter.

Forsythia
It may surprise some people to see this shrub in this book, as it is so common that it is all too often sniffed at. Indeed, I do sniff at it myself occasionally, but for all its vulgarity it is still spectacular. It will grow in light shade, but it becomes drawn and does not flower very well. I have never seen it grown in association with a wood, but I suspect it would be too bright and out of character there. However, it is not dense, and since it is popular it might well make an interesting shrub to underplant in a small garden. Three bushes planted together at the bottom of a garden would certainly draw the eye in spring, and would make an interesting shady area for the rest of the year. *F.* 'Lynwood' is one of the largest and best forms, but *F. suspensa* is a softer yellow that might have more appeal for those who prefer to garden without sunglasses.

Forsythia will grow on any soil. For the best results, they do need to be pruned regularly. Take out about a third of the old wood every year, cutting it right to the base.

Fothergilla
In spite of its being not too difficult to find, this is far too rarely seen. The shrub is an open one with not too dense a canopy, so it is eminently suitable for planting beneath. It produces curious flowers in spring, just as the leaves are opening. They have no petals, but consist of bunches of fragrant white stamens looking like white pincushions or dumpy bottlebrushes. In autumn the leaves produce a show of their own, with a wonderful range of fiery tints. It is a shrub that is slow to establish, but it is well worth persevering with it.

The three main species grown are *FF. gardenii*, *major* and *monticola*. They prefer to grow in light shade under trees, or screened by them. The first is quite low-growing and is worth planting as an undershrub. The other two are much bigger, although very slow-growing. When they eventually reach a reasonable size they can be underplanted with a variety of bulbs or herbaceous plants.

Fothergillas need acid soil, and will not grow on chalk. Pruning is not necessary.

Fraxinus (ash)
The common ash, *F. excelsior*, is a hungry-rooted tree but one which produces a good dappled shade that is worth growing plants under. It is not attractive enough to warrant a place in the smaller garden, but should be included in any woodland scheme. Ash can become very tall and are useful for forming the high points of a wood. Another reason for growing them is that they can be

coppiced to produce straight poles or one of the best of firewoods – ash is one of the few that can be burnt green as well as dried. The weeping forms are more commonly seen in gardens, but do not particularly lend themselves to being underplanted. Be warned: ash seed themselves everywhere.

Ash will grow in a wide range of soil, including chalk. They require no pruning.

Fuchsia

Fuchsias are normally considered as sun-loving, but some will take a degree of light shade and will do well planted on the southern side of a woody border. *F. magellanica* and its various forms would be the best to use as they are relatively hardy, although likely to get cut to the ground by frosts. There are not a great many red-flowering plants for woodland conditions, and so the fuchsia might well earn its keep. The prostrate *F. procumbens* is a good plant to grow on the peat bed in shade, but it is not hardy and would need overwintering under cover. It has curious little flowers and bright-pink berries.

Fuchsias will grow on a variety of soils. They need hard pruning every year (cut them to the ground if frosts do not do it for you).

Garrya (tassel bush)

Garrya elliptica has its moment in the winter when the spectacular long silver catkins are set off against its dark evergreen foliage. After that it is, I am afraid, rather boring, to put it mildly. If it did not 'do its thing' in the winter when there is not much else happening, one suspects it would be a rare plant in our gardens. Apart from its flowers, its other virtue is that it is a classic plant for a north-facing wall. Although grown in this position it is by nature a free-standing shrub, and as such can be grown in light shade or on the north of other trees and tall shrubs as part of the woodland garden. Here it is likely to come more into its own, since its dark-green leaves can be used as a foil for something more interesting. *G.e.* 'James Roof' has the longest catkins.

Garrya is not at all fussy about soil, and it requires no pruning.

Gaultheria

This is a low shrub that makes excellent ground cover on acid soils (see page 92). Some forms are low enough to be used on a peat bed to give it permanent form and structure, particularly as their spreading roots are useful in binding together the peat blocks.

There is a surprising number of varieties currently in cultivation; over eighty are offered commercially. They are a specialist's plant and not usually seen in the general garden, and yet anyone who attempts to create a woodland garden of whatever size should include at least one. The flowering shoots carry many pendant, urn-shaped flowers, held in a red calyx and backed by evergreen leaves. The flowers are usually white – often pure white but sometimes tinged with pink.

There are so many that it is difficult to pick out any to recommend; they are all worth growing – and perhaps that is the answer, if you have enough space! The dainty Japanese *G. adenothrix*, about 30cm (12in) high, is one of the most beautiful. A much more prostrate form is *G. nummularioides*, which reaches only 10–15cm (4–6in). A taller one to give structure to a peat bed would be *G. hookeri*, that will grow to 60cm (2ft) or more (in the wild it can reach up to 1.8m (6ft) high). *G. shallon* is another of the same proportions and is more commonly available, possibly because it is rather rampant.

Gaultherias are plants of acid soils and are unable to tolerate alkaline positions. There is no pruning involved, except to keep them in check if they become too rampant.

Hamamelis (witch hazel)

A plant that any woodland garden ought to have for its winter flowers – bunches of strap-like petals, in yellow, orange or red, that are carried on the bare stems. Some forms have a sweet or even an astringent fragrance. The shrubs are a bit boring for the rest of the year, although they do contribute to the autumn colour scene.

H. mollis, the Chinese witch hazel, is the commonest and is none the worse for that. This and its various forms have mainly yellow flowers. *H.m.* 'Pallida' is undoubtedly my favourite, with its pale-yellow flowers, fine scent and good autumn colour: a real connoisseur's plant that I recommend anyone to buy. For something a little more exotic, try some of the *H.* ×*intermedia* forms which have red and orange flowers.

This is another chalk-hater; people are always bemoaning that they cannot grow rhododendrons on chalk, but it is shrubs of this type that I would lament. It needs little pruning, other than cutting bunches to take indoors.

Hedera (ivy)

Many see ivy as the scourge of woodlands, clinging to trees and often malforming them. What they miss is the decorative element that this wonderful plant contributes to the scene. I must admit that I do not go a great deal for some of the variegated and other special forms that are collected by ivy-freaks, but I have a great admiration for the common-or-garden ivy, *Hedera helix*. (I use several hundredweight to decorate my cottage at Christmas.) One of its most useful habits, in many woods, is to carpet the floor, creeping over anything in its path even in quite dense shade (see also page 93). I once saw a large low-maintenance garden in Belgium which was full of trees and entirely underplanted with ivy;

there was ivy everywhere you looked, climbing over objects to give the garden a three-dimensional look. It was not entirely maintenance-free, since the ivy was sheared over once a year, but it was the nearest I have ever seen to such a concept. Fascinating as it was, it was not the garden for me. And ivy is certainly not a plant to be encouraged if you wish to grow others.

There are many forms to choose from, and because it is evergreen you will be able to see what you are buying. Some of the variegated forms will lighten up a dark corner. Ivy will grow on any soil, and needs pruning only if it gets too rampant; or, if you want to keep it neat and even, give it an annual shear.

Hydrangea
Another plant that needs no introduction, as there can be few gardens that do not include at least one. Most prefer to grow in light shade, and therefore make admirable subjects for our woodland garden. The mop-head or hortensia forms (*H. macrophylla*) are the ones most frequently seen, usually in either blue or pink, but also white and red. The soil has a determining effect on the colour, the flowers being blue on acid soils and pink on alkaline. Many gardeners prefer what they see as the more refined shapes of the lacecaps (also *H. macrophylla*), which have flat heads with a few sterile florets floating around the outside of the much smaller fertile flowers; again, blue, pink or white are the usual colours. I must admit that these do have a luminous quality, if set in light shade against a darker background: their clean-cut quality can be magical.

There are many other hydrangeas to explore. *H. sargentiana* has similar flowers to the lacecap, though not so graceful, and it makes a more interesting shrub, the leaves being covered in stiff white hairs. *H. aspera* (*H. villosa*) is possibly a better plant, very much in the same mould, with pinkish-blue lacecap-type flowers and soft hairy leaves. *H. arborescens* has large round heads of creamy-white florets. In the form *H.a.* 'Annabelle' the flower heads are up to 25cm (10in) across. *H. paniculata* also has spectacular white flower heads (more conical in shape). *H. petiolaris* is usually grown up walls but it is equally at home in a tree, where it causes confusion to many visitors as to its identity.

Hydrangeas like a rich, moist soil, although they will grow in drier conditions in shade. They are one of the first plants to notify the gardener that there is a shortage of water: the leaves hang limp as soon as this condition is reached. Most do not require pruning, although many will be better for the removal of some of the older wood in the spring to help keep them rejuvenated. *H. paniculata* needs pruning hard each spring, to remove most of the previous year's growth. The general practice is not to remove old flower heads until the spring, because they afford a certain amount of protection from frosts during the winter.

Hypericum (St John's wort)

Most hypericums seem to flower best in sun, but many of them will take a modicum of light shade. However, the rose of Sharon (*H. calycinum*) will grow well even in quite deep shade – indeed, so well that it is a problem stopping it (see also page 94). It is a ground-cover plant *par excellence*, growing to about 30cm (1ft) high and producing bright golden flowers. I don't think I really like it very much, possibly because I don't like a sea of yellow. Tutsan (*H. androsaemum*) is another that will tolerate shade, but is nowhere as invasive. This is a taller plant, reaching 90cm (3ft) in height, and it has the added advantage of red berries. It often appears spontaneously, presumably carried by birds. I know of no plants near me, and yet I occasionally find seedlings in the garden. All the other, more bushy, types such as *H.* 'Hidcote' will tolerate light shade and so can be planted on the north side of other shrubs, but they are not keen on dense shade as they will not then flower very well – and a hypericum out of flower is a dull object.

Hypericums will grow on a wide range of soils. The shrubby ones should have a third of the old wood cut out each year in late winter. Shear *H. calycinum* to the ground at about the same time.

Ilex (holly)

Many gardeners like to include a holly somewhere in the garden. From the outset it must be said that this is for its decorative quality rather than the shade it casts, because this is so dense that nothing will grow under it unless the holly is pruned so high that it loses its shape. Another problem with creating a bed near holly is that the prickly leaves are not much fun when it comes to weeding. However, holly trees do well in a woodland setting, and should form part of it. They are grown mainly for their glossy leaves and autumnal berries which are usually carried into, and sometimes through, the winter. Holly is dioecious – that is, it has separate male and female trees. Since it is the female trees that carry the berries, these are the ones to have, but there must be a male in the area to offer the pollen. There are variegated forms, some of which are good for lightening a dark spot, and there are those with yellow berries, but I must confess that I prefer the ordinary wild *Ilex aquifolium*, especially in a woodland setting.

Holly will grow on any soil and will take quite a degree of shade. It does not need pruning. (See also page 94.)

Kerria (Jew's mallow)

Kerria japonica is the only species in this genus. It is mainly known in the double-flowering variety, but the single has been gaining popularity especially in its variegated form, *K.j.* 'Picta'. However, I still think the straight single is by far the best. This has a graceful simplicity about it that the brassy double lacks. For those who do not know it, perhaps I should mention that the flowers are yellow, about 3.8cm (1.5in) across, and appear in the spring on deciduous bushes that reach up to about 3.7m (12ft) (but usually much less). Whichever variety you choose, they can all be grown in positions ranging from full sun right down to a medium shade, a light shade producing the best results from our point of view. It is not a particularly attractive species out of flower, but the variegated form might add extra interest.

Kerria is not at all fussy about soil and will grow in quite dry ones, which makes it admirable for woodland gardens. It does need some pruning to keep it in good heart, and about a third of the older wood should be removed each year after flowering.

Leycesteria (Himalayan honeysuckle)

Leycesteria formosa is a strange plant that can be grown in light shade, although it produces too dense a shade itself to be of any use for underplanting. The main reason for growing it is because of the curious flowers that consist of white tube-shapes peeking out from a tassel of purple bracts. These are produced in late summer into autumn, and are followed by purple fruit which are relished by birds, particularly pheasants – stands of *L. formosa* are often planted in or near woods to satisfy their appetite. It is deciduous, but the dark-green stems have a certain attraction in winter.

Leycesteria is not particularly fussy as to soil, but it prefers it to be moist. Growing by a water feature would be to its liking. Pruning can be quite aggressive: cut it to the ground each spring.

Ligustrum (privet)

By many people this genus is considered a weed, to the extent that at least two of my past editors have wanted to have it excised from the books on which I was working. What they were thinking of, of course, is the maltreated shrub (*L. ovalifolium*) that makes a rather poor hedge. When left to grow free, it can make quite a decent shrub. However, it is some of the other species that one would prefer to grow, most of which are tolerant of a little light shade, some even taking quite a bit.

When I first came to my cottage there was a golden form of *L. ovalifolium*, called 'Aureum', growing in the small wood under the dense shade of an oak. As to be expected, it did not flower and it was a bit straggly, but it did brighten up that corner; growing in more light, it would have made a better bush. *L. quihoui* is a species that is worth looking at. It is a tall shrub, reaching 4m (13ft) or more. The flowers appear late in the summer, which is a bonus, but it is the size of the heads that makes it attractive, each one being up to 30cm (12in) long. One disadvantage ligustrum has is that most people find that its flowers all tend to be a bit unpleasant-smelling (but then there are others who enjoy it).

Privet will grow on virtually any soil. Unless you grow it as a hedge (not to be recommended), it needs no pruning at all.

Lonicera (honeysuckle)

No woodland garden should be without this wonderful genus of plants. Most people know the climbers, which we will come to in a moment, but what often comes as a surprise is that there is also a large number of shrubby forms. Some of these (*LL. fragrantissima*,×*purpusii* and *standishii*) produce fragrant flowers on bare stems in the depth of winter. They are not difficult to find in nurseries and at least one of this group should be considered for providing flowers at this time of year. They never grow bigger than 3m (10ft), and can easily be kept smaller than this by cutting branches to take into the house. It is very difficult to choose between the many other shrubby forms that flower later in the year. Certainly *L. syringantha* should be on the list of candidates, with its lilac-like (hence '*syringantha*') bunches of fragrant flowers, and *L. tatarica* with its mass of pink flowers. *L. involucrata* has very small yellow flowers surrounded by wonderfully rich crimson bracts. There are many others to look at, and to grow if you have the room.

Best-known of the honeysuckles are, of course, the climbers. Again, there are many more than the average gardener realises, to choose from. Many like a bit of light shade around their bases but will grow away up into the light. This means that they must be grown up shrubs or trees on the edge of the wood, or along paths or clearings; otherwise, they will disappear into the canopy way above your head. Not all are fragrant – indeed, many of the choice forms are not. There are so many that it is difficult to know which to recommend; whichever you get will be pleasing, even if it is the wild *L. periclymenum*.

Honeysuckles will grow in virtually any soil but they do not like to be too dry at the roots, so a rich, humusy soil is to their best liking. The winter-flowering shrubs need little pruning. The others need to have their old stems reduced by about a third each year. The same treatment should be meted out to the climbers, although if they go towering up into trees it becomes a terrible chore and they can be left to get on with it.

Magnolia

There are few gardeners who would not wish to grow at least one of these magnificent trees or shrubs in their garden. Fortunately, although there are some trees that almost defy the measuring rod, there are others that are small enough to fit into the smallest garden. One of these is the ubiquitous *M. stellata*, which is a wonderful plant. (Do not ever turn up your nose at a plant just because it is common – some of the most common are also some of the most beautiful.) It will grow well in light shade (indeed, I once successfully grew one under an 18m (60ft) lime tree!), and will in fact appreciate the protection from frost that the shading plant affords. Frost is a problem with all magnolias, and you should abandon the idea of growing them if you live in a frost hollow.

Some of the larger magnolias – *M. campbellii*, for example – make woodland trees that will tower above their surroundings, causing the viewer to crick his neck. Many have smaller proportions and will in any case take a long time, probably beyond the life of the gardener, to reach their full size. Many of the larger trees will take a number of years to start flowering, but smaller ones, like *M. stellata*, will flower from a very small size. It is difficult to know what to suggest when there are so many fine forms. Certainly, *M.×loebneri* 'Leonard Messel' is one that can be recommended, as can the chalice-shaped flowers of *M.×soulangiana* and many of its forms. A gardener should always be encouraged to walk round other gardens, searching for ideas as well as simply enjoying them. In the case of magnolias, a walk in spring round one of the many Cornish gardens, such as Trelissick, will show you the range of plants and how they grow (look at the camellias as well, while you are there).

×Mahoberberis

I am including ×*Mahoberberis aquisargentii* as it is fun, and gardeners, being hard-working people, should occasionally be allowed a bit of fun. It is a bigeneric hybrid between *Mahonia* and *Berberis*. The fun comes in the leaves, because on a single stem there will be several individuals that have a smooth outline with small, even spines (somewhat like those of the berberis), followed by several that are more reminiscent of holly leaves, with large flowing spikes on an undulating margin (similar to the mahonia). This is then followed by some of the smoother ones, and so on. The plant just cannot make up its mind which way to go. It can be a real teaser for friends who have never seen it before. Beyond its curiosity, it has little value. The evergreen glossy leaves are quite attractive, but the yellow flowers are insignificant. The bush is a very lax, sprawling one, and if space is short this is not a plant to grow as it will not earn its keep.

As to soil, ×*Mahoberberis* does not seem to be too fussy, as long as it is not too dry. It is quite happy in a light shade. Pruning can be restricted to shaping, if you want to, and occasionally taking out some of the older wood.

Mahonia (Oregon grape)

A group of very valuable early-winter- to early-spring-flowering shrubs. Fortunately, they are quite happy to grow in a light shade and can be placed under or next to deciduous trees, as long as these do not provide too much shade. They all have leathery evergreen leaves, usually with spiked margins, although these are not vicious. Some forms, such as *M. aquifolium*, take on purplish and bronze tints during the winter. The small flowers are produced in bunches or spikes in varying shades of yellow, and have the advantage of being fragrant. Later in the year they produce a bloom-covered, bluish berry.

There is quite a number of species and cultivars to choose from. One of the best is *M.×media* 'Lionel Fortescue', which bristles with large, upright flower spikes. Another good and popular form is 'Charity', along with its two seedling offspring 'Faith' and 'Hope'. *M. aquifolium* is not such an attractive bush; indeed, the leaves can be quite dull for most of the year, although it is used a lot for municipal mass and ground-cover planting. *MM. bealii* and *japonica* are also worth looking at.

Mahonias will live happily on most soils, as long as they are not too dry. They are hardy, but late frosts can cut back some of the early new growth. Pruning is restricted to cutting out the flowering stems after fruiting.

Malus (apple, crab apple)
Apple trees make good shade-producing plants, and a large range of herbaceous and other perennials can be grown under them. In old cottage gardens, even vegetables were grown beneath their boughs. The best are those that have been pruned properly so that the centre of the tree is relatively open, allowing the light to get in and ripen the fruit. Ornamental crab apple trees are usually more formal in shape but still are useful trees. Most apple trees prefer to grow in the open, but many can be found in old woods where they have been sown by passing birds. These are not particularly good for apples, although they often produce a good display of pink blossom in late spring. Many crab apple trees are very decorative in fruit and can be grown on the edge of a woodland garden for that alone. Most crabs fruit while still young, so buy in the autumn when you can see the colours and shape of the fruit and make a better choice. Purple-leafed forms need to be planted in a sunny position. Weeping varieties are decorative but can create too much shade close to the ground to be useful for underplanting.

Most apples will grow on a range of soils, but will do best on moisture-retentive ones. They need some protection from cold winds. Pruning for fruiting varieties is beyond the scope of this book, as there are different methods depending on the type of tree. Crabs and those not required for their fruit need no pruning, unless you wish to keep the canopy open.

Nothofagus (southern beech)

Unlike its northern cousin, the southern beech is one of the best trees for a woodland garden. The leaves are generally small and well spread, giving a wonderful dappled shade over a wide area, often, in the case of spreading species, some distance from the trunk, or trunks. Unfortunately, there are two problems. First, most of the species will eventually grow far too large for the average garden; and second, some are a bit on the tender side. Another caveat is that they should be planted on a sheltered site, as they are prone to wind damage; the one I knew best in Kent was completely destroyed in the 1987 hurricane. I think if I had to select one tree under which to grow plants, the choice would be between an oak and a nothofagus, although I would probably never live to see either of them mature. What I like so much about the nothofagus is the quality of its dappled shade: it is very gentle and restful, just made for sitting under. They are not widely planted in the northern hemisphere, although I notice that there are more than a dozen commercially available in Britain.

I have, of course, been talking mainly about the deciduous forms, as the evergreens produce a denser canopy – though in the mature trees this can be a long way from the ground. The one that I know best is *N. antarctica*, which can have a single or a multi-stem trunk, the latter spreading wide. This is perfectly hardy, and one of the best species to grow for our purpose.

The genus generally prefers an acid or neutral soil. They require no pruning.

Nyssa

These, like the southern beeches, form very large trees – up to 18m (60ft) or more. They are spreading, and provide shade that is not too dense for underplanting some plants. Their moment of glory comes in the autumn, when their leaves colour up beautifully. The one that is most commonly grown is *N. sylvatica*, although *N. sinensis* and a few others are commercially available.

These are lime-haters and must therefore be grown on acid soils. There is no need for pruning.

Pernettya

This is an interesting group of evergreen shrubs, grown mainly for their berries. These are round and shiny, and contrast well with the small, glossy, dark-green leaves. The colour varies from white to red, with pinks and purples as intermediates. They appear in autumn, following the flowers which are white and bloom in early summer. These evergreens are too dense for underplanting with other plants, but they can be grown in shade to add interest to the ground flora. They will do best in light shade, but I have seen them right up tight against large oak trees and yet still carrying large amounts of colourful berries.

There is a number of species and forms that are worth seeking out. More are now being stocked by garden centres, and since they carry their berries for some time it is easy to choose one that you like. In a darker situation one of the white-berried forms, such as *P. mucronata* 'Alba', will show up best.

They are ericaceous plants and therefore do not like alkaline soils. No pruning is necessary.

Philadelphus (mock orange)
This is a very popular genus of shrubs that are ideal for the edge of a woodland garden, or possibly hanging over a path or ride within the wood. The flowers are pure white, occasionally with a crimson central band round the boss of yellow stamens, as in *P*. 'Belle Etoile'. Apart from the virginal quality of their flowers and their wonderful individual fragrance, philadelphus have little to offer for the rest of the year, except for a couple of forms of *P. coronarius*, 'Aureus' and 'Variegata', which have golden and variegated foliage, respectively. These are particularly useful for brightening up a dark or dull corner. In the smaller garden one of the dwarfer forms, such as *P*. 'Manteau d'Hermine', which reaches only about 120cm (4ft) and has double flowers, can be used to advantage.

Philadelphus are not at all fussy about the type of soil they have. A bit of pruning is required to keep them in good heart: about a third of the older wood should be removed each year.

Populus (poplar)
Don't. It's hungry, extremely thirsty, the leaves are smelly and rattle like old bones, and it is likely to undermine your foundations if you live on clay.

Potentilla
I used to think potentillas dull and rather uninteresting, but in recent years I have begun to appreciate their simple beauty and the fact that they quietly, without shouting at you, go on flowering over most of the summer and autumn. Their many (usually) soft tints allow you to use them in a wide range of colour schemes, their flowering longevity making them a valuable colour link over the seasons.

They are really sun-lovers but will grow in a light shade, although the deeper the shade the fewer flowers they will produce. There is a wide range of cultivars to choose from, most derived from *P. fruticosa*. Most larger nurseries and garden centres stock quite a good selection, and since they are nearly always in flower, a visit will give you the opportunity to choose the colour you like best.

Potentillas will grow on a wide range of soils, but will show stress if the soil is too dry. I must confess that I never prune them, and they go on serving me year after year, but many authorities recommend reduction of the previous year's growth by half during the winter. Some older stems can be removed every year or so to encourage the new growth.

Prunus (ornamental cherry)

Most of the flowering cherries prefer to be in full sun, although most will also take a small amount of light shade. Only the gean (*Prunus avium*) is suitable for including inside a wood. Not much will be seen from the woodland floor, but these tall trees will soon out-top the others and in spring present clouds of white blossom above the canopy. This and any of the others can be planted on the edge of a wood, where their flowers will be well set off against the other trees, especially evergreens.

The evergreen *P. laurocerasus* and *P. lusitanica* are not the most exciting of plants, but they will grow and flower well in quite deep shade. The blowsy Japanese doubles look a bit out of place in a woodland setting, where trees and shrubs with simple flowers are more in keeping. There are two short shrubs that are good for a light shade: *P. glandulosa* forms a single shrub of about 150cm (5ft) or so with white flowers, and *P. tenella* grows to about the same height but has a suckering habit, forming quite a thicket when suited. The flowers on this are a lively rose-pink.

Cherries can also be used for creating shade. They are a bit hungry and thirsty, with widely spreading roots, but it is surprising what can be grown under them. At Savill Garden near Windsor in Berkshire there is a large cherry on the corner of an herbaceous border. Planted under it, and right up to the trunk, are varieties of annual nicotiana, which flower very well, as well as a number of perennials. *P. subhirtella* 'Autumnalis', which flowers throughout the winter, is a very good plant for this purpose. It can be bought as a tree or as a multi-stemmed shrub, the former being preferable for creating shade.

Cherries will grow on most soils but do better on richer ones. On the whole no pruning is required.

Quercus (oak)

This must be the doyen of woodland trees and absolutely ideal for our purpose; the only problem is that if you do not already possess one, it takes a long time to grow. An oak tree produces the ideal shade for growing plants, and most successful woodland gardens have employed them. They are generally deep-rooted and allow beds to be developed beneath them, right up to the trunk, without impoverishing the soil totally. Oak leaves produce one of the best leafmoulds, as can be seen by the amount of life it supports in its native habitat.

Quite a large number of plants can be grown even under a spreading oak, but for the best results it is best to take off some of the lower branches so that light can penetrate right to the trunk. In Britain the two native species of *Q. robur* (pedunculate oak) and *Q. petraea* (sessile oak) are probably the best to grow, although there are many other species and varieties now available. Some of these have large leaves and create a dense shade. The evergreens, such as *Q. ilex* (holm oak), are far too dense to grow anything under them satisfactorily.

Oaks will grow on any soil, but a rich mixture will help them get established. They need no pruning.

Rhododendron

Oh dear, where does one start with rhododendrons? There are so many, and in any woodland garden they are bound to be the one plant that everyone wants to grow.

Looking at them first from the point of view of creating shade, I must admit that most rhododendrons are not much use; their thick, leathery leaves create far too deep a shade for anything to grow underneath. Walk round any of the large gardens that grow them, and you will soon realise that even weeds give up. Some of the azaleas, however, cast a more moderate shade, especially, of course, the deciduous varieties, which are perfect for growing a wide variety of late winter and early spring bulbs and other plants. At the Royal Botanic Gardens at Kew there is a marvellous planting of bluebells (*Hyacinthoides non-scripta*) under a group of yellow-flowering azaleas (*Rhododendron luteum*) that is quite breathtaking when at its peak.

The number of rhododendrons that can be grown in shade is legion. Most, if not all, like shady conditions of one type or another. They will grow in quite dense shade, but then their flowering is somewhat impaired. Light shade will suit them all. In a large woodland garden they can be planted virtually anywhere. They make ideal plants for lining paths or glades, and are wonderful when glimpsed in the distance, their sudden bright flash of white, pink or yellow showing between other trees or shrubs and inevitably drawing one to investigate.

The rest of this book could be filled with suggestions as to which species or variety to plant. They vary in size from large trees to dwarf, procumbent plants that hardly lift themselves above the ground. In a large woodland garden any size will be suitable, except the very small, which might get lost. In the smaller gardens, the large bushes tend to be a waste of space as, although they have their moment of glory, they are quite dull for the rest of the year and their dense shade means that they are no use for underplanting. However, there are many intermediate and small shrubs that are admirably suited to the smaller garden.

Many delightful dwarf species and varieties are ideal for the peat garden. Indeed, no peat garden is really complete without some. *R. yakushimanum* is certainly one of the best of these, but there are many more, and all I can suggest is that you go to one of the specialist rhododendron nurseries in spring, look at the wide range on offer, and make your selection from whatever appeals.

The big problem with rhododendrons, as I am sure everybody knows, is that they will not grow on alkaline soils. It is possible to line a hole with polythene and fill it with a peaty soil, but it will not be long before the chalk or lime finds its way through and the rhododendron keels over. It is a bit better to construct a raised bed above ground, but even here the alkaline soil will eventually find its way in. If you really want to grow them on such soils the only way is to plant them in containers above ground level. You then have the problem of remembering to water them. No, if you live on chalk forget about rhododendrons – pretty as they are, there are plenty of other equally attractive plants that you can grow.

There is no need to prune rhododendrons.

Rosa (rose)
Roses may seem an odd choice for a book of this type, but they certainly have their place in a woodland garden, and in the small garden even the dreaded hybrid tea roses can be used to create shade for other plants if you do not mind gardening amongst the thorns.

There can be very few natural woodlands that do not have roses climbing up through the trees. Unless these are on the margins, the flowers appear way up, above the tree canopy and out of sight. On the margins they form cascades of white or pink flowers. These are the wild dog roses, and they make admirable climbers for any woodland garden, as long as it is big enough. Normally they do not even have to be planted; the birds will bring in hips and drop them at both appropriate and inappropriate points. They are, unfortunately, too rampant for the small garden, although they would look good growing through an apple tree as long as you did not intend to pick the apples (the dog rose has vicious thorns).

Many rose enthusiasts like to keep the ground beneath their roses bare of other plants, but I think beds of roses look sterile and the only way to enliven them is to underplant. On the whole the smaller shrub roses, such as the hybrid teas, produce only a light shade and can be underplanted with a very wide range of herbaceous plants. They root quite close to the surface, which makes it difficult to till the earth beneath, but with a top-dressing of compost and farm-yard manure this becomes unnecessary. The strange way in which hybrid tea roses and similar kinds are pruned gives them clumsy shapes, and any under-planting is likely to look a bit out of place, even artificial. In no way will it resemble a natural woodland planting (but, on the other hand, it will undoubtedly improve the rose bed).

Winter- and spring-flowering bulbs and other plants are ideal, because these flower before the eye is distracted by the often rather artificial colours of the roses. Later in the season you can use many herbaceous plants, particularly those that would look out of place in a more conventional woodland setting but do fine with well chosen roses.

Roses do well on most soils, but better on richer ones. The pruning regimes vary depending on the type of plant. If you want to go in for roses, I suggest you consult a good book, to help you not only to choose the right ones but also to grow them successfully.

Rubus (blackberry, bramble)

Again, this may seem a surprising choice of woodland shrub, but there are reasons for my apparent madness. In any natural woodland setting brambles play an important part, not only visually but for the support they give to wildlife.

Blackberries will not, in fact, grow very well in shade. They flower and fruit best on the edge of woods or hedgerows, where they can get some sun. Within the wood, rides and glades make ideal spots. Avoid planting on narrow paths: a bramble round the legs, especially on a cold, wet day, is not something to relish. The fruit is, though, and it's one of the few edible berries that can be grown in a woodland setting.

Another reason for considering this genus is that it is not restricted to black-berries. There are several other species which are grown for their flowers. In spite of being easy and attractive plants, these are surprisingly little grown. One of the finest is *Rubus tridel*, especially in its form 'Benenden'. This is a thornless shrub with glistening white flowers 5cm (2in) or more across, each with a central boss of golden stamens. Two other important plants of this type are *R. odoratus* and *R. spectabilis*. Both have deep-pink, fragrant flowers of nearly the same size as *R. tridel*. The first is without prickles, but the second has fine ones on its stems. All three will take a surprising degree of shade, although they do best in light shade.

There is another set of species that recommend this genus to us – those that have decorative winter stems. Both *R. cockburnianus* and *R. thibetanus* have wonderful white stems that glisten in the barren months. These are grown entirely for this quality and will in consequence take deep shade, since their ability to flower is unimportant. When positioning them make certain that they can be reached by the winter sun, which will illuminate their stems. A final group are those that are carpeters and make ideal ground cover. These often have red or orange stems and the leaves are usually silver beneath. They are not outstanding plants, but as ground cover for quite deep shade they are very useful. There are several to choose from, but one to be recommended is *R. tricolor*. Be warned, though: it can travel fast.

So what might appear to be a boring genus has some interesting and useful plants in it for the woodland gardener. Many are suckering or tip-rooting and so some form of control may be required, but in a large woodland garden they can be given their head. Pruning for the flowering forms should be undertaken after flowering, when you can remove a third of the old wood. With all the others, reduce them to the ground every year – the white-stemmed ones in spring and the rest in winter. In a wild situation they can be left to their own devices. They will grow on any soil. (See also page 96.)

Ruscus (butcher's broom)
Ruscus is another of those intriguing genera that are rarely grown. They are plants that will take deeper shade than most other shrubs; indeed, they dislike the sun. They are small, growing no more than 90cm (3ft) tall. The small leaves are very hard and end in a sharp spine. In the past they have been used for scouring butchers' cutting-blocks.

What appear to be leaves are, in fact, not leaves; they are cladodes – flattened portions of stem that look like and perform the same function as leaves. (Look at them closely and you can see that they are just a continuation of the stem.) The flowers are totally insignificant and appear in the centre of each 'leaf'. What is certainly significant is the resulting fruit. This is a bright red berry, somewhat larger than a holly berry. It used to be used extensively for Christmas decoration, but there are now fewer plants in the wild.

The species that is most commonly grown, by those who do grow it, is *R. aculeatus*. It is well worth obtaining for use in medium to dense shade. Butcher's broom needs no pruning (except for cutting for the house) and will grow on any soil, including chalk.

Salix (willow)
In a large woodland garden with plenty of space you can afford to have one or two willows. Indeed, you should have them; but in a smaller garden they have to be considered more carefully. Certainly, avoid the type described as weeping willows (*S. babylonica*), as nothing will grow satisfactorily under them. The others suffer from the same problem, but if you are using them as decorative planting rather than for creating shade then they can be used with discretion. Their problem is that they are very thirsty and hungry surface feeders, with masses of roots just below (and often on top of) the ground.

Having said that, I must admit that there are some attractive willows that can be grown in shady positions, especially near water. With some (*S. moupinensis*, for example) it is the spring catkins that are their main attraction, in others (for example, *S. melanostachys*) it is the winter stems, and in yet more (for example, *S. exigua*) the foliage.

Willows will grow on any soil, but prefer a moister one (including boggy ground in which few other shrubs will grow). Pruning is a bit more complicated. The shorter, slow-growing ones require no pruning. The faster ones that are mainly grown for their bark or leaves can be cut to the ground every four years or so, so that the shrub is rejuvenated.

Sambucus (elder)

Elders are good plants to grow on the edge of a wood or for lining clearings. They will take a little shade, but there is no point in growing them in too thick a part of the wood because any attraction they may have will be lost up in the canopy. Elders are grown either for their flowers or for their leaves – mainly the latter. There is now a surprising number of different leaf forms, some depending on their colour and others on their shape. Some, such as the vari-egated forms, especially the golden ones, need to have some shade or they suffer from sun-scorch. The purple-leafed forms, on the other hand, do need more sun to allow them to keep their colour.

Elders are odd plants: you either like them or dislike them. In a way their leaves are a bit coarse (and smelly if crushed), but I do not think this matters at all in a woodland setting. They are all easy to grow and quite cheap to purchase. Unfortunately, birds will provide you with seedlings, and these should be rogued out, or inferior forms will creep in (on the other hand, of course, they might just turn out to be a new and interesting form). Most of those in cultivation are varieties of *S. nigra*, although there are a few other species around, *S. racemosa* producing some interesting plants. *S.r.* 'Plumosa Aurea' is a great favourite, particularly for the woodland garden (it is liable to be scorched in full sun). The leaves really brighten up a dark corner.

Elders will grow on any soil, including chalk. In a wild situation they can be left to themselves without pruning, but for better results some attention is needed. With those that are grown for their flowers and berries, remove about a third of the old wood every year in spring. With those grown for their foliage, cut the whole shrub to the ground in winter or early spring. This will encourage much better leaves than if it is left unpruned.

Sarcococca (Christmas box)

These are very good plants for the woodland garden, although they may not look very exciting. They make dense clumps of suckering shoots covered in glossy, evergreen leaves in quite dense shade. Their main attraction is the flowers. Though these are somewhat insignificant in appearance, in the depths of winter their perfume fills the air for some distance around. Cut stems are wonderful, if somewhat overpowering, for the house.

There are several forms to choose from, but unless you are making a collection they are much of a muchness. *SS. confusa* and *hookeriana* var. *dignya* reach about 150cm (5ft) in rich soil conditions, while *S. humilis* is somewhat shorter but has the advantage of being able to tolerate more shade than the others.

Sarcococcas will grow on most soils unless they are impoverished. No pruning is required, other than cutting a few stems for the house.

Skimmia

This is a genus that has become more popular in recent times, partly for its flowers but more especially for its clusters of large red berries, which remain on the bushes unmolested by birds throughout the winter. The leaves are evergreen and glossy, making the bush attractive all the year. However, if the soil conditions are not to its liking the leaves will yellow and the bush become sickly. Skimmias will grow in quite dense shade, but will obviously not flower so well as they would in sun or light shade.

Until recently *S. japonica* was about the only species seen, but now more are widely available. Not that I think it is an improvement, but *S.j.* 'Fructu Albo' produces white berries rather than the usual scarlet. A more widely grown form is *S.j.* 'Rubellum', which has flowers that are red in bud but has no berries. The reason for the lack of fruit is that this particular form is masculine. Skimmia is dioecious, bearing male and female flowers on different plants. In order to produce berries you must have one bush of each, or at least there should be a male bush in your neighbour's garden if there is not one in yours. People who complain about never having berries on their plants have only either one or more males or one or more females. The ideal situation is to have a large-berried plant such as the female form *S.j.* 'Veitchii' along with an attractive-flowered male form such as mentioned above.

Skimmias are not at all happy on alkaline soils, and if planted in them will soon begin to look sick. Although they will take quite a degree of shade they do dislike being dripped on, so do not plant one where a shading tree or bush is likely to shed the rain directly on to it. (They will, of course, put up with rain!) Generally, there is no need to prune.

Sophora

Sophoras are rather fascinating shrubs with tiny leaflets arranged opposite each other along the shoots. They are generally considered to be sun-lovers, but a large bush of *S. tetraptera* grows in surprisingly dense shade under a big camellia at the Royal Horticultural Society's Gardens at Wisley. Certainly, production of the yellow flowers is likely to be impaired under these conditions, but the bush can hold its own as an attractive plant without them. The stems and shoots are light brown in colour and slightly twisted, which adds to the plant's character. Although not normally recommended for shade, for those who like something different it is worth a try.

Sophoras are not at all fussy about their soil, but they are tender and should, therefore, be given a protected site. (The Wisley plant is not only under the evergreen camellia but also in a south-facing angle between two walls.) No pruning is required.

Sorbus (mountain ash)

This is a very good genus for woodland gardeners, both those who have acres to play with and those who have only a small plot. The trees will grow in a light shade but are best used for creating shade (and, certainly, the silver-leafed forms are better in sun). Their shade is generally not too dense, and many plants will grow under them. The trees are attractive in their own right, especially those with white or silver leaves – mainly *S. aria* (whitebeam) and its various forms. These are best in the spring, but in the autumn the berries and the glowing colours of the turning leaves bring another season of interest. The large clusters of berries can be red, orange, yellow, white or pink.

There is a big selection of species to choose from, and most garden centres and stores stock several. Of the berried forms, good choices would include *S. hupehensis* for its white fruit, *S.* 'Joseph Rock' for its yellow, and *S. vilmorinii* for its pink. For autumn colour *S. matsumurana* is a wonderful sight. *SS. sargentiana* and 'Embley' are also plants not to be missed.

Sorbus are not fussy as to what type of soil they grow in. No pruning is required.

Stephanandra

These are small deciduous bushes with no merits other than that they are reasonably attractive and will grow in light shade. They produce racemes of white flowers in the early summer, which are pleasant rather than attractive. The most distinguished member of the genus is possibly *S. tanakae*, which has rich-brown stems in winter, making it a valuable plant for that time of year. It makes sense to plant this bush where the winter sun will strike it. Although stephanandras are not outstanding, they are useful shrubs as they will tolerate a reasonable amount of shade and they are completely hardy. But they are too dense and too low to be useful in creating shade in which to grow other plants.

Stephanandras prefer a rich soil, but will grow on most types. In order to rejuvenate the plant it is best to cut out about a third of the older flowering stems each year after flowering. This is particularly important on those with coloured stems, as their attraction lies in the new stems thrown up after pruning. (See also page 96.)

Symphoricarpos (snowberry)
This is a curious genus, related to the honeysuckles and grown mainly for its berries. Like the previous plant it is not intrinsically attractive, but it has merits from our point of view in that it can be grown in quite dense shade. The flowers, pink and bell-shaped, are generally quite small and relatively insignificant. The berries vary from white through shades of pink to almost red. The majority have a suckering habit which causes them to form dense thickets. They are really plants for the larger woodland garden, where they can be left to their own devices. In a smaller garden they might be difficult to control, and, besides, there are many more attractive plants that would be better given a home.

The most commonly grown is *S. alba* var. *laevigatus* (still often known as *S. rivularis*). This is a suckering form which carries white berries about the size of marbles from the autumn well into winter. These are useful for brightening up a dark corner and, for those who have a strong tactile sense, when squeezed they have a strange feel, almost like wet polystyrene. *S. orbicularis* has tiny leaves and pink berries. This species has a couple of variegated forms which make attractive foliage plants, but they tend to lose their variegation in the shade.

Snowberries will grow on a wide variety of soils. In a large woodland setting they can be given their head, but to ensure regular flowering and berry production it is perhaps better to remove about a third of the old wood every year.

Syringa (lilac)
Who could bear to be without this wonderful genus of plants? Some might argue that out of flower they are boring shrubs, but then so are thousands of others. In many ways I would rather put up with a shrub that does little for most of the year but puts on one glorious display, than live with one that supposedly has the same attractive foliage year in year out; that is the quickest route to boredom, and smacks of municipal roadside plantings.

Lilacs are known for their panicles (heads) of perfumed flowers that vary from white through the typical lilac to dark purple. For me and, I suspect, many others the scent of lilac is one of the glories of the late spring. It is also a wonderful shrub for cutting for the house. It will tolerate a little shade, but will not flower particularly well. For our purpose it is more valuable for creating shade, and in a small garden it is one of the shrubs that can be used for sheltering other shade-loving plants.

There are hundreds of different cultivars to choose from, and the best advice I can give is to urge you to go to a nursery or garden centre while they are in flower and choose one that appeals to you. Some of the species (as opposed to *S. vulgaris* and its host of cultivars) have a more open growth and smaller leaves that create just the right woodland-type conditions we are after. The flower heads are not quite so spectacular as in the cultivars, but their perfume is just as pervasive. Heights vary from the shorter (150cm (5ft) or thereabouts) *S. meyeri* 'Palibin' and *S. microphylla* to the taller (5m (16ft)) *S. josiflexa* and *S. vulgaris* and its cultivars.

Lilacs will tolerate a wide variety of soils. There is generally no need to prune, but from time to time some of the older wood can be removed to promote new growth.

Taxus (yew)

Yews are vast, ponderous trees that are best grown as specimens, although suddenly coming across one in a wood is a delight. From our point of view they are not of much use, as they produce a dense shade under which little will grow, apart from some cyclamen, perhaps. Certainly, they are not trees to plant if you wish to create a small shade garden, but if you are planting a whole wood then one or two would be well worth having, to add contrast and interest. Do not allow other trees to overtop them when first planted, as they are slow to grow and do not like too much shade. Once mature, they will hold their own. Incidentally, yews are not conifers: they produce pinkish-red berries in autumn after having small brownish flowers in early spring. The 'stones' in the berries are poisonous. There is little point in saying do not plant where there are young children, as they will be adults when the trees are mature enough to carry berries. On the other hand, do not plant where they can be browsed by cattle, as the foliage is poisonous to them.

Yews can be planted on any soil. No pruning is necessary unless you are using the trees as topiary or hedging.

Vaccinium

This is a large genus of ericaceous shrubs that includes bilberries, blueberries, cowberries, cranberries, deerberries, farkleberries, foxberries, grouseberries, huckleberries and whortleberries (and many other folksy names). As will be gathered from such a collection of names, it is the berries for which they are mainly known, although as garden plants the autumn colouring of the leaves is also important. Most prefer an open situation and they will often be seen on moorlands and other wild areas, but some can be grown under light shade.

They are generally evergreen carpeting plants that cover the ground in a low, tangled mass. The one most commonly seen in Britain is *V. myrtillus*, the bilberry. This has pinkish, globular flowers and black-blue berries. *V. vitis-idaea* is another that is seen both in the wild and in cultivation. It grows to about 30cm (12in) or so and has white or light-pink, bell-shaped flowers followed by red berries. There are several clones of each in cultivation that may be worth seeking out.

Since they are spreading, vacciniums should not be placed in choice positions. They are quite open in shady spots and, although creeping, are not dense enough to be considered ground cover in the sense of preventing weeds from growing through them. They do not like too much shade and do best where the autumn sun can catch and intensify the changing colours of their leaves.

Vacciniums must be planted on acid or neutral soils only. They need no pruning.

Viburnum

A genus of very garden-worthy plants that contain many members suitable for the small garden. They are attractive in flower, in berry and in autumn colour. On the whole they do not produce a very dense shade so are useful for under-planting, and are particularly suited to the edge of a woodland garden.

The winter-flowering species are those that first attract attention. *V. farreri* and *V. ×bodnantense* and their various forms are the ones to buy. These have clusters of sweet-smelling pink flowers on their bare stems throughout winter. In the spring they are followed by *VV. ×burkwoodii*, *carlesii* and *juddii*, which have larger heads of pale-pink flowers that, again, perfume the air. *V. opulus* has wonderful large white flower heads (which, unfortunately, are not scented), followed in autumn by great clusters of brilliant red or yellow berries. It also provides good autumn colour. There are several other autumn-colouring forms, including *V. lantanoides*. While no good as a shrub for underplanting, as its shade is too dense, *V. tinus* is a useful evergreen bush for planting in light shade. This produces slightly fragrant flowers (on a warm sunny day) which appear from late autumn right through to the spring. There are many others to explore in this remarkable genus.

Viburnums are not fussy as to what soils they are grown in and are good plants for a chalky position. Generally no pruning is required, although the winter-flowering species will benefit from the removal every few years of some of the old wood after flowering.

Vinca (periwinkle)

The two species *VV. major* and *minor* are very good ground-cover plants for growing in shade (see also page 98). They carpet the ground and, if there is sufficient light, produce star-like blue flowers. The former is more vigorous and is a good plant for growing through the lower branches of other shrubs or hedges to give them interest, particularly when the blue flowers unexpectedly peep out. They are best where they can have unrestricted growth, as the tips of the shoots readily root, forming new plants. This means that they can be invasive. There are several cultivars, including those that have white, purple or double flowers and those that have variegated leaves. *Vinca difformis* is probably my favourite species, as this flowers quite happily throughout the winter. The flowers appear to be white during this time of year but become bluer later. It is reputed to be tender, but it has survived winters with temperatures down to −15°C (5°F) and less in my garden.

Periwinkles will grow happily on most soils, but they seem to spread fastest when there is a good amount of leafmould in the top layer. There is no need to prune, although I often cut *V. major* and *V. difformis* back to the main plant to prevent them spreading too far.

Viscum (mistletoe)
Mistletoe is not a shrub in the conventional sense, as it is a semi-parasitic plant that grows upon others while at the same time having its own green leaves with which it can photosynthesise. I have never noticed it on trees and shrubs in the centre of woods, but I dare say that it occurs there. It is certainly more noticeable on the margins. Mistletoe does not add much to the appearance of the woodland garden, but it does have interest and is useful for adding to the Christmas decorations. It is characterised by twin pale-green leaves with one or two white berries between them. The host trees and shrubs are quite numerous and include apple (*Malus*), lime (*Tilia*), hawthorn (*Crataegus*), oak (*Quercus*), poplar (*Populus*) and maple (*Acer*).

The only method of propagation is by placing the seeds (which fully ripen in spring) on to the branches of the required hosts. Once you have got one to take, birds – thrushes in particular – will spread them to other trees but they do have a habit of placing the berries high up, in inaccessible positions.

6 Ground Cover Plants

The purpose of ground cover is to create a dense carpet of vegetation so that weed seed will not be able to germinate – or, if it does, will be starved of food and light and so will not develop.

As I have already intimated, I am not a great lover of ground cover. In most articles and books it is given as a soft option in gardening, a sort of panacea that will enable the gardener to have a wonderful garden with little effort. The truth, of course, is quite different. Ground cover takes a lot of effort to create in the first place, and then more to keep it looking good. Ground cover badly handled can also look extremely boring.

Perhaps all this is a little unfair, as the ideal for any border is to cover the ground with one's choice of plants to exclude those of nature's – that is, weeds – and ground cover is just taking it to its logical conclusion.

It is hopeless using ground cover anywhere that has not had thorough preparation. It is essential that all perennial weeds be totally removed. A small piece of couchgrass (*Agropyron repens*) will throw up a shoot, and before long will have set about recolonising the ground, taking scant notice of any ground cover. Indeed, the ground cover will make it difficult to see the weed until it is well away and then difficult to remove. So prepare the ground thoroughly.

Once planted, ground cover will take a while to establish itself and form a complete cover, so you must weed rigorously during this stage. Indeed, you must do so even after cover has been established; otherwise, there might be a battle of the fittest, with the ground cover coming off worst. Remember, ground cover reduces weeding – it does not eliminate it. Another thing to remember is that plants may become congested and need digging up and replanting before they lose their vigour and ability to keep weeds out.

Visually, this type of planting can become very boring. So try to avoid huge drifts unless they are likely to be impressive, such as bluebells. Add variety without making it look too bitty. Let one type of plant merge with another; do not have a rigorous demarcation line between them. Under trees that produce dense shade it might be better to have no ground cover, as it can look starved and scrappy in this situation; try leaving the earth bare, or covered with leaves.

Barks can create interest all year round but are particularly useful in winter. This is *Prunus serrula*.

Anemone blanda 'White Splendour' is one of the earliest flowers to appear, lighting up its surroundings. Here it is planted amongst hellebores.

The shining red berries of *Arum italicum* 'Pictum' make an attractive splash of colour in the autumn.

Cyclamen hederifolium grows and flowers well in quite dense shade and will tolerate dry conditions.

Cornus canadensis, a dwarf
perennial that makes a good
ground cover on neutral or acid
soils.

Clerodendron bungei is a
spreading shrub that has very
distinctive flowerheads in late
summer.

Dactylorhiza × *grandis* forms large clumps and is one of the easier hardy orchids to grow.

Crocus tommasinianus is one of the most accommodating of crocuses. It will flower in deciduous shade and it self-sows prodigiously.

Snowdrops are a favourite plant for the woodland garden. This is the large-flowered *Galanthus plicatus* 'Wareham'.

I always like the look of the bare earth under holly trees in woods. It should not be forgotten that moss makes an ideal carpeting agent. It will not keep the weeds out but it makes a nice cover, following the contours of the ground and tree roots. Do not allow your ground cover to encroach and destroy it.

Many of the plants that are listed below crop up elsewhere in the book, and are considered here only for their ground-cover ability. Of course, any plant grown in sufficient quantity has the potential to be used as ground cover, and many of the shrubs and herbaceous plants can serve in that capacity.

Acanthus (bear's breeches)
A tall plant that will suppress everything beneath its large lower leaves. Several plants together would create an imposing clump in a woodland setting, and would certainly give good ground cover throughout the summer. Perish the thought, though, of ever trying to remove them, because every piece of root left in the ground creates a new plant. Only suitable for light shade. (See also page 99.)

Ajuga (bugle)
This is a common sight in our damper woods wherever there is a gleam of sunshine. As a ground-carpeter it does well, sending out runners in the manner of a strawberry and soon making a mat of leaves; but these are not thuggish enough to prevent coarser plants pushing through, and will need constant attention. The forest of blue flower spikes produced by the common *A. reptans* is very attractive. There are several different-coloured leaf forms. (See also page 101.)

Alchemilla (lady's mantle)
Although common, *A. mollis* is a wonderful plant and should be found in most gardens. It will grow into dappled shade, where its pleated round leaves will produce sufficient cover to deter weeds. It spreads by seed, which can become a nuisance if not confined to the area in which you want it to grow. Once a sufficient cover has been established, remove the flowering heads before they set seed. Alchemillas will grow in a wide variety of soils, including quite dry ones, so they are valuable ground-cover plants. (See also page 102.)

Allium (onion)
Not ground-coverers in the conventional sense, as the leaves are above ground for too short a season to provide protection, but they are carpeters nonetheless. *A. ursinum* (ramsons) are a frequent sight in damp woods, their white flowers lighting up even quite dark shade. For lighter shade, *A. triquetrum* is a similar

plant. Both are extremely difficult to eradicate, once introduced, so be certain that you can stand their pungent and lasting smell before you plant them. (See also page 155.)

Anemone (wood anemone)
A. nemorosa, *A. blanda* and the other wood anemones are often given as an example of ground cover for woodlands. They do cover the ground, and very pretty they look too, but they serve no functional purpose as they have died back below ground before most weeds are even thinking of getting going. (See also page 103.)

Arisarum (mouse plant)
A curious plant with hastate (arrow-shaped) leaves that cover the ground rather efficiently until the late summer, when they die down. The curiosity is created by its flower, which is contained within a brown hood that tapers to a long point, giving the impression of the hind quarters of a mouse and its tail. This assemblage is often obscured by the leaves. *A. proboscideum* is the one to look out for. (See also page 106.)

Asarum (wild ginger)
The attraction of this plant is its dark-green, glossy, kidney-shaped leaves that can easily be mistaken for cyclamen at a casual glance. These prove to be quite an effective ground cover.

Bergenia
This is quite a different plant from the previous. For leaves it has big, glossy elephant ears that cover the ground completely, allowing no light through to promote the germination of other seeds. The leaves are up to 30cm (1ft) across and stay on the plant throughout the winter. The glossy green, often tinged with red, and the spikes of rosy-pink flowers make this an attractive plant with which to carpet the ground. Once planted, it rarely needs disturbing, which is an added bonus. This is one of the true ground-cover plants. (See also page 108.)

Claytonia
These will carpet the ground, but are not dense enough to constitute a weed-proof cover. *C. sibirica* is the one usually grown. This can be pretty with its rose-pink flowers, but once it finds its feet it can be invasive. Plant near bergenias which will act as a ground cover and keep it under control!

Convallaria (lily-of-the-valley)
Although lily-of-the-valley takes a time to settle down, once it is suited it romps away below soil covering the ground above with its upright ovate leaves that last throughout the summer months. The leaves are quite dull – there is a stunning variegated form, however, with fresh-looking gold stripes – but it is for the well known flowers that it is usually grown. As a ground-carpeter it is far from weed-proof, and would not be able to cope with much competition. On the other hand, it should not be introduced to a peat bed, for example, where it would probably oust other, choicer, plants. (See also page 113.)

Cornus (dogwood)
Most of the dogwoods are shrubs (see page 62) but *C. canadensis* is a subshrub with an herbaceous habit. Its underground stems (rhizomes) spread rapidly, sending up shoots with a whirl of green leaves surmounted by a white 'flower', made up mainly of bracts. It forms a dense shade 15–25cm (6–10in) above the ground, providing a reasonable ground cover.

Cotoneaster
These are not normally considered woodland plants, although several will grow happily against north-facing walls. One, however, makes a good dense ground cover and is suitable for planting in light shade and between denser bushes. This is *C. dammeri*, an evergreen, prostrate shrub with white flowers and red berries in autumn.

Epimedium
These are true woodland plants, and are dealt with as such in detail in chapter 7 (page 117). They form dense clumps that merge, forming an effective ground cover. They are not, strictly speaking, evergreen plants, but the new leaves appear before the old die back so that the ground is covered all the time, which prevents any weed seed from germinating. They are also good ground cover from the visual point of view, as they have both interesting foliage and attractive flowers. It is a ground cover that will grow in quite dense shade.

Erica (heather)
This must be considered along with *Calluna* and *Daboecia*, two other heathers that, to the gardener, are almost indistinguishable from *Erica*. These heathers are not really suitable ground cover under trees or bushes, as they become very straggly and open in shade, allowing all manner of weeds to grow through them. However, they do make ideal ground cover between bushes that have been newly planted. As the bushes grow so the heathers contract, keeping the inter-

vening spaces covered. They need shearing over after flowering, to keep them compact. (See also page 63.)

Euonymus (spindle)
It is only *E. fortunei* and its cultivars that can be used as ground cover. These evergreen ground-huggers will tolerate quite shady conditions. They are used extensively in municipal plantings, and the sight of them filled with litter and drink cans in shopping malls has put a lot of people off growing them; but they are one of the most efficient ground covers. (See also page 64.)

Euphorbia (spurge)
Quite a number of the spurges make large, spreading clumps and can therefore be considered as ground cover, but *E. robbiae* is the best one for shady areas. This can develop into dense clumps, and offers the benefit of being able to do so in quite heavy shade and in dry soils. Many of the other running forms, such as *E. griffithii* and *E. sikkimensis*, will also make large colonies, but they prefer a bit more light and are best planted between shrubs and trees. (See also page 118.)

Ferns
These have all been lumped together here, but are dealt with individually in chapter 10. Most ferns prefer to grow in shade, putting out large fronds to capture as much of the available light as possible. In doing so, of course, they starve the ground of light and thus become good ground cover. This is especially so of those that spread by underground runners, forming large colonies through which little else can grow. Bracken (*Pteridium aquilinum*) is the ultimate ground cover, but unless you have a very large wood do not introduce it, or you will be constantly battling to prevent it taking over everything, including the rest of the garden.

Galium (bedstraw, woodruff)
G. odoratum is a small plant which, once suited, will make large drifts through lightly shaded areas. Unfortunately, it is attractive rather than functional, as it is not in the slightest proof against weeds. The small leaves are grouped in whorls about the stems and are not large or vigorous enough to suppress any adversary. (See also page 119.)

Gaultheria
Gaultherias have already been dealt with under shrubs (page 66) but it is worth while mentioning them again because some of the more vigorous forms do make a good ground cover. The evergreen *G. procumbens* and *G. shallon* are two of

the best for this purpose. The former is low-growing, not reaching much above 15cm (6in), while the latter is much taller at about 180cm (6ft).

Geranium (crane's bill, hardy geranium)
Many of the geraniums make ideal ground cover for the open border, but there are far fewer that will do well in a woodland setting. *G. macrorrhizum*, one of the best, has large, fragrant leaves and will grow in light shade. One that smothers other plants as it goes and is often used to cover large areas is *G. procurrens*, but it prefers a lighter position and is a good plant for growing between developing shrubs, because it will pull back as the shrubs present it with deeper shade. *G. endressii* falls somewhere between the two, and will tolerate a light shade while making a dense ground cover. There are others that will grow in shade but are not particularly useful for our present purpose. (See also page 120.)

Gunnera
This is ground cover *par excellence*. The gigantic leaves will combine, on a mature plant, to create a weed-free zone covering 4.5m (15ft) across. A few plants of this dimension, and you will have a weed-free garden for life. They do prefer a moist position and therefore make ideal planting beside a stream or other water feature, which is often an area that is difficult to weed. They do not like dense shade but are ideal in glades, where they receive a little bit of sun.

Hedera (ivy)
Another perfect ground cover. It will grow in quite dense shade and will cover everything in its path, both upward and along the ground. As well as tolerating dense shade, it has the advantage of growing in dry conditions, which adds considerably to its value. The common ivy (*H. helix*) is a good cover but *H.h. hibernica* has larger leaves, which makes it more efficient. Although it means extra work, try and confine the ivy to the ground. (See also page 67.)

Hosta (plantain lily)
Hostas are yet another classic ground-cover plant. They will grow in shade as long as it is reasonably moist, and produce a dense cover of leaves. For our purpose those with the large broader leaves, such as *H. sieboldiana*, are best; those with the narrower leaves – *H. lancifolia*, for example – are not really dense enough to suppress weeds in the way that their bigger brethren can. While I like these planted in drifts, too large a planting of one species can look boring. (See also page 125.)

Houttuynia
H. cordata and its recent popular form *H.c.* 'Chameleon' are used extensively for ground cover in boggy areas, and will take a little light or dappled shade. However, in the invigorating conditions of moist ground I am not certain that they can really hold their own against weeds, in spite of their rampageous nature. There has been a lot of commercial hype about 'Chameleon', but I have my doubts as to its real worth. (See also page 126.)

Hypericum (St John's wort)
As we have already seen in chapter 5, there is quite a number of hypericums that will grow in shade. But there is only one that can really be considered as a ground-coverer, and that is *H. calycinum*, the rose of Sharon. This spreads rapidly by rhizomes (underground shoots), making a thicket about 30cm (12in) high. It will grow into quite dense shade, but it does not like it too dry. Do not put it near choice plants or near a peat bed, as it will take over. (See also page 69.)

Ilex (holly)
Although nothing grows under a holly tree, we are not really considering trees here as ground cover. What are a little more unusual are the low shrubs such as *I. crenata* that slowly grow to a maximum height of 60cm (2ft) or so. These have spreading branches with evergreen foliage that makes an excellent ground cover. They will grow in sun or light to medium shade, which means that they are useful to plant either between or under other shrubs. There are several variegated forms – the variegation adding considerably to their interest. (See also page 69.)

Lamium (dead-nettle)
L. maculatum and its mass of cultivars is a common ground-hugging plant in many gardens. It will also grow in shady conditions, although here it becomes more drawn and less of a ground cover. One that makes a much better plant for our purpose is *L. orvala*. This makes large dense clumps, even in quite deep shade, about 45cm (18in) high with typical dead-nettle-type leaves and dark-red flowers. It seems to be happy in quite dry conditions, although it does flag towards the end of summer. *L. galeobdolon*, yellow archangel (often still known as *Galeobdolon luteum*), is a native plant that carpets our woods. It is a vigorous spreader – much more so than the last-mentioned plant – and can become a nuisance in a small garden. It has yellow flowers and nettle-shaped leaves, usually flushed with silver. (See also page 128.)

Maianthemum
M. bifolium is a 15cm (6in) herbaceous plant that spreads by underground shoots. It forms a carpet of shiny green leaves overtopped with small spikes of white flowers. It likes a cool root-run in a leafy soil, and grows well in dappled shade. (See also page 131.)

Omphalodes
O. cappadocica is a spreading herbaceous plant that in theory should make good ground cover, but it is not dense enough and weeds will soon overcome it unless it is looked after. It likes dappled shade, and does best in the peat bed. (See also page 133.)

Ophiopogon (lilyturf)
O. japonicus makes a good low ground cover, producing tufts of shiny, green strap-like leaves that become quite dense as the plant increases by stolons (underground shoots). It produces short spikes of white flowers. Its relative *O. planiscapus* is very similar, but is better known in its black-leafed form, *O.p. nigrescens*. (See also page 133.)

Oxalis
It is a common mistake to consider plants that are invasive to be good ground cover. Well, I suppose they are in that they do cover ground, but not all of them have the strength to stand up against much competition. Wood sorrel (*O. acetosella*) is such a plant. It is wonderful in woodland, but do not expect it to suppress weeds. (See also page 134.)

Pachysandra
A classic ground-cover plant, *P. terminalis* grows only about 15cm (6in) or so tall and has shiny light-green leaves topped by insignificant clusters of white flowers. It quickly spreads by underground shoots, to form a dense colony that is tolerably weed-proof. It is mainly grown for this ability and for its leaves, which do much to lighten a shady spot. It likes a moist, leafy soil but, unfortunately, will not tolerate alkaline soils.

Petasites
This genus should be introduced only into a large garden, as the plants have a tendency to spread fast and furiously. They do, however, make a good ground cover. Although often seen on stony ground, they prefer a moist leafmould soil and will do well in light shade. Their flowers appear before the leaves and consist of very fragrant, rounded spikes. They tend not to flower well in shady positions. (See also page 135.)

Polygonum

This genus has been split up far and wide, but for the moment we will stick with the old names, since it is by these that they are still generally known. Many are rampant spreaders (*PP. cuspidatum* and *sachalinense*, for example) and should not be grown even in a large garden, but many spread at a more moderate rate and make good ground-cover plants. *P. affine* makes a low, tight mat that will grow in light shade. *P. campanulatum* is a much taller plant, reaching 90cm (3ft) or so; it can be a bit more rampageous, but is easily controlled. In between the two is *P. amplexicaule*, which will tolerate a reasonable amount of shade. It has large dock-like leaves that make it difficult for anything to grow through. (See also page 136.)

Pulmonaria (lungwort)

More will be said about this plant in chapter 7 (page 138) as it is one of my favourite spring flowers. It makes a dense carpet of large floppy leaves that are often spotted or flushed with silver. The flowers vary from red to blue, with the occasional white form. It is a spreading genus, although it does so at no great speed. Pulmonarias prefer a moist, leafy soil and do well in dappled shade. They make an excellent, attractive ground cover.

Rodgersia

A group of tall (90–120cm (3–4ft)) herbaceous plants with large leaves that soon block out the light on the ground. They form dense clumps, preferably in a moist soil, and make ideal ground cover for areas near a water feature such as a pond or stream. (See also page 139.)

Rubus (blackberry, bramble)

We have already seen in chapter 5 (page 79) the surprisingly large range of rubus that there are. The pink-flowered *RR. odoratus* and *spectabilis* make good thickets, but it is the low-growing *R. tricolor* that provides the best ground-covering plant. It does spread fast, so it is not really for the small garden.

Stephanandra

This is another plant that has already been considered in chapter 5 (page 83), but here we are concerned only with the low-growing form of *S. incisa*, namely 'Crispa', whose arching branches flow over the ground preventing anything from growing under it.

Symphytum (comfrey)

The large floppy leaves of comfrey make it very difficult for anything to grow beneath them and so it is an excellent ground cover – but only if you have space. Comfrey can become very rampant when suited, and once you have got it in the garden it is very difficult to eradicate. There is quite a number of different species and varieties to choose from, most of which will tolerate a little shade. Those with variegated leaves brighten up a shady spot, but a vast spread of them I find a little too 'busy' for my eyes. (See also page 143.)

Tellima
This and the next two plants in this list, all very similar to each other, are very much more delicate than the thug just mentioned. This one has bright green leaves and is about 25cm (10in) tall, with much taller stems of creamy-green bells. The leaves persist through the winter. It is a good ground cover for dappled shade with a lot of leafmould in the soil, although it will grow on a wide variety of soils. (See also page 143.)

Tiarella (foam-flower)
A shorter plant than the last one, growing up to 30cm (12in) tall, with spikes of very delicate fluffy flowers. The leaves will persist through a mild winter. It prefers a soil with plenty of leafmould or other humus in it. When suited, it can make a good ground cover even under quite dense shade. There is quite a number of species in the wild, but *TT. cordifolia* and *wherryi* are the two most commonly grown – the latter, though, is possibly too delicate to stand the rough and tumble of being a ground-cover plant. (See also page 144.)

Tolmiea (pick-a-back plant)
T. menziesii is a rhizomatous plant that is in between the previous two in height. It spreads at a similar rate, and in many respects it has similar leaves, but in one aspect these are quite different: young plants develop as buds on the older leaves. It makes a good ground cover on a variety of soils although, as with most woodland plants, it does best in a humus-rich one. (See also page 144.)

Trachystemon
This is a member of the borage family, and in common with many of them it is a coarse, hairy plant with large leaves that are good at suppressing other plants. It is a bit rampant and really only worthy of a larger garden, where it will grow into quite deep shade. Fortunately, it will grow on a wide range of soils, thus making it particularly useful as a ground-cover plant.

Vancouveria
This genus is very similar to *Epimedium* (page 117). When suited, it will make a very dense colony of plants that extinguishes anything that tries to grow through it. Its leaves stay on over the winter, so although not strictly evergreen

it creates a permanent cover. The leaves are attractive as well as functional, and the plant is further graced by delicate, arching stems of yellow or white flowers. (See also page 145.)

Vinca (periwinkle)

Periwinkles quickly spread, even into quite dense shade, to form vast mats under trees and shrubs. The leaves are generally quite small, but what they lack in size they make up for in quantity, and an area densely clothed in periwinkle is reasonably weed-proof. They will grow on most soils, but will grow fastest in a humus-rich mixture. They are evergreen, and so provide some interest throughout the year. They do not flower too well in dense shade, but in lighter conditions they produce bright-blue, purple or white flowers in profusion in the spring. (See also page 86.)

7 Perennial Plants

If woodland gardens were confined to trees and shrubs, they could become very boring. To me such a wood is a provider of congenial conditions for plants that prefer shade and a leafy soil. Not all will agree with this; many see beauty in the shape and texture of the foliage and in the trees and shrubs themselves – and, to an extent, so do I. But what changes a wood into a woodland garden is the degree of interference that the gardener allows himself, and underplanting with perennials is certainly something that tips the balance.

As we have already seen, most perennials will grow in shady conditions, but the majority will lose their shape and will not flower, and to all intents and purposes are useless. That leaves, none the less, a great number that either will do well in shady conditions or positively need them. The following list is a mixture of both.

To do well, plants growing under trees and shrubs need nearly as much attention as those in the open border. However, just as there are garden plants that do not like shade, so there are many weeds that find the position intolerable. This means that, at least in the denser shade, there is not quite the problem of weeding that one finds in the open garden. The other factor is that the conditions in the wood often become inhospitable after early spring, and while the early-flowering plants have retired below ground by then, the weeds, which are only just getting under way, are thus usually killed off by the lack of light and moisture.

The best time for working in the woodland garden is on days when it is just too hot to be out in the open. Then, being able to work in the cool interior of the wood is a joy.

Acanthus (bear's breeches)
These are statuesque plants that are generally seen growing in the open, but they will adapt well to growing in light shade, especially between bushes and trees. I have, in fact, known a clump for the past twenty years that is growing

on chalk under conifers. This is not by any means their ideal situation, but they will grow on most soils.

The most commonly grown species are large plants with big floppy leaves which are usually deeply indented, sometimes with spines on the ends of the lobes. The hooded, mauve-purple flowers grow in huge spikes up to 180cm (6ft) or more. These too can be prickly. As well as being planted between shrubs they can make a very effective focal point, particularly at the end of, or on a bend in, a path. The flower spikes can also be cut and dried for the house.

The most popular are *A. spinosus* and *A. mollis*. The former, and its variety *A.s. spinosissimus*, have prickly spines on the leaves and these are a good shiny, dark green, whereas the latter's are spineless and a duller green. *A. balcanicus* is a smaller plant – again, without the spines on the leaves. This plant is better where there is less room, while the others will spread, taking up quite a lot of horizontal as well as vertical space. Be certain to plant them in the right place, as moving them can be difficult. They are almost certain to leave behind fragments of broken root, which will all turn into new plants. In heavy soils, you may have to resort to weedkiller to get rid of them.

Although acanthus will grow in a wide variety of soils, they prefer one with plenty of rich humus in it. They can be increased from seed, by taking root cuttings or by division – if you are strong enough. (See also page 89.)

Aconitum (monkshood, wolf's bane)

Another plant whose flowers are carried in spikes. In this case they are usually a bright blue, although there are also yellow and white. They are best planted between rounded shrubs, where they create sudden vertical columns of blue. There is one, *A. volubile*, which is a climber and will make its way up through a shrub, speckling it with blue flowers. This blooms in late summer and is therefore useful for decorating a spring-flowering shrub.

However, the upright herbaceous species are the ones usually seen, and there are quite a number to choose from. *A. carmichaelii* is one of the commonest – a stiffly erect plant, up to 120cm (4ft) high, which carries purplish-blue flowers above a glossy-green divided foliage. Like all the aconitums it flowers late in the summer and into autumn, a valuable asset in a woodland garden, where the majority of flowers appear early in the year. *A. napellus* is a native of Britain, and has been grown in gardens for centuries; it is slightly taller than the previous species and has flowers of a violet blue. *A. vulparia* breaks the mould in that it has creamy-coloured flowers. This is a more sprawling plant that needs support in the open garden, but in a woodland position it can be planted under a low shrub, such as an azalea, through which it can grow.

Aconitums will grow on most soils, but do best in rich ones. They should not be allowed to dry out. Propagation can be from seed or by division of the tubers, which are highly poisonous – as, indeed, is the whole plant, including seed.

Actaea (baneberry)
These are the first of our truly woodland plants. They come mainly from the extensive woods of North America, and like nothing better than a cool, moist root-run.

They are curious plants in that they are mainly grown for their berries, which are either white, red or black, and are much more prominent than the minute white flowers that precede them. The flowers, however, appearing in late spring, should not be dismissed: they are attractive in their own right, forming spires of foam above the decorative dissected leaves. Actaeas grow up to 90cm (3ft) high. They can be planted in light to medium shade, the white berries, in particular, illuminating the darker shade.

There are basically two species in general cultivation: *A. alba* (previously known as *A. pachypoda*), with white berries, and *A. rubra*, with red. *A. spicata* has shining black berries and is a native of northern Britain.

Actaeas will grow on most soils, but do need a good layer of cool leafmould to give of their best. They should not dry out. Propagate them by seed or by division. As with the previous plant, the seed is poisonous.

Adonis
In this genus there are two or three yellow-flowering plants that are amongst the choicest for any peat bed. *A. vernalis*, in particular, is one of the most attractive plants ever introduced to gardens. The golden flowers offset against the very finely dissected leaves are a sight to behold in spring. *A. amurensis* is a similar plant, but is usually seen in its double form, 'Flore Pleno', which is equally stunning.

Adonis are normally grown in a rock garden or peat bed in sun, but are equally at home in a light shade. These plants appreciate a rich, moisture-retentive soil. While they are not often available from garden centres, many nurseries stock them and they are well worth searching out. Alternatively, they can be grown from seed – but sow it fresh to achieve best results.

Ajuga (bugle)
A medium-sized genus with a number of species in cultivation, several of which are annuals and not often grown. There is one perennial, *A. reptans*, which is a British native and is ideal for growing in a woodland situation. It is normally seen growing in shafts of sunlight at the edge of a wood, often along a path or on the edge of a clearing. Where the ground is moist the spikes of blue flowers can become quite large (up to 25cm (10in) or more), and very decorative. These

generally appear in late spring and early summer, but there are several attractive leaf forms, which extend the plant's appeal.

Ajugas form mats of plants joined to each other by runners in the same manner as a strawberry. The leaves are usually quite close to the ground, with the spikes of blue flowers rising from them. The different leaf forms come in different colours: there are deep-purple, and multicoloured variegated ones. The colours are not always stable in shady conditions; the purple, in particular, does need a bit of sunlight to sustain it.

Plant ajugas as suggested, alongside paths or between shrubs, where they can catch a bit of sunshine. Although they do form mats they are not the best of ground cover, and weeds will soon overpower them, especially in the sunnier spots, unless you attend to them from time to time.

They will grow on any soil, but really need a moisture-retentive one to give of their best. Propagation could not be simpler – just cut through a runner and remove one of the plants. (See also page 89.)

Alchemilla (lady's mantle)

Although many gardeners are a bit snooty about this plant because it is becoming very common, it is still well worth growing; indeed, I would go so far as to say that it is indispensable in most gardens. Its light-green pleated leaves always look good, but especially when they are young. The ebullient froth of green flowers is always a joy to see, but particularly if planted next to a path or by water. I find their fragrance very attractive, too, although most people seem unaware of this attribute. Next time you see one in bloom, sniff it. The flowers are very good when cut for the house, either by themselves or as a background.

The one that is mainly grown in gardens is *A. mollis*. This makes a plant about 45cm (18in) tall, but the flower stems do become floppy and so the height decreases as the season wears on. They also become a bit tired, and so it is worth shearing over the whole plant immediately flowering is over. This not only prevents it from seeding everywhere, but also produces fresh young leaves. There are lots of other, smaller species, most of which are virtually indistinguishable from each other and are not really of interest to us. The only other one I would mention is the delightful little *A. conjuncta*, which has shiny leaves with distinctive hairy silver margins. This is a plant for the peat bed, as it is only 10cm (4in) or so high. It does not have the habit of seeding about like its bigger relative.

A. mollis can be used in a variety of woodland positions. It will cope with light shade and will look good planted in drifts, especially towards the edge of a wood or along a path. It is a plant that is well suited to covering the ground between young shrubs as they develop. I once saw a planting of this and ivy together which made a surprisingly good effect.

Alchemillas will grow in most soils, even quite dry ones, but like most other plants will do best in a moisture-retentive soil. Propagation is from the self-sown seedlings that appear everywhere. *A. conjuncta* should be divided. (See also page 89.)

Anemone (windflower, wood anemone)

Anemone is a very big genus with lots of interesting plants in it. Here we are primarily concerned with the wood anemones (*AA. nemorosa, blanda* and so on), but we must also consider the autumn-flowering Japanese anemones, *A.×hybrida*.

The wood anemones are one of the glories of spring. I have loved them in the wild for as long as I can remember, and as soon as I had the right conditions I grew them in the garden. Until then, I had not realised the variety available. The simple wild *A. nemorosa* still takes a lot of beating. It comes up in early spring as it feels the sun's warmth on the earth above, and has flowered, seeded and disappeared below ground again by the time the trees above have got round to thinking about leaves. The drifts of the dainty white flowers are a joy to see. There is a whole host of purple and blue forms which seem to be increasing in number every year. The best blue one is still 'Royal Blue'. There are also different-coloured forms in a similar species, from Europe – *A. blanda*. This has a good white form called 'White Splendour', as well as blue and pink ones. *A. apennina* from further south also has the same range of colours.

All these grow in deciduous woods where they get the sun and moisture before the trees put on leaf. They can be grown in a similar position in a woodland garden, under trees or shrubs. They will tolerate most soils, but do best in a deep leafy mixture. Propagation can be by simple division of the running rootstock, and they can also be grown from fresh seed.

The Japanese anemones (*A.×hybrida*) flower at the other end of the season, in late summer and autumn. These are much taller plants, reaching 90cm (3ft) or so. They do best in a sunny position, but they will grow in between shrubs and, as long as the shade is light, under trees such as oak. I have grown them in denser shade but they flowered very unsatisfactorily and, being deep-rooted, found the competition with the roots of the tree above them too much. There are several hybrids, white or pink, to choose from. White looks best in shade. They do best in a deep, rich soil. Propagate by root cuttings.

Another anemone that enjoys a light shade is *A. narcissiflora*. This flowers in between the two types already mentioned, in early summer. It is an herbaceous plant that forms a clump and throws up flowering stems, each having several buttercup-like white flowers, stained with blue on the reverse. These grow to 30cm (2ft) when well suited. They prefer a moist soil and should be planted with plenty of leafmould in dappled shade, possibly in a peat garden, which would be very much to their liking. Propagate from fresh seed. A very similar plant to this is *A. rivularis*. (See also page 90.)

Anemonopsis
This is a genus of only one plant, *A. macrophylla*. It is quite tall, reaching up to 90cm (3ft). The flowers, held on upright stems, appear in summer and consist of four outer petals and a ball of inner ones – a bit like a cup and saucer, except that the flowers are nodding. The petals are white, tinged with a purplish blue. The leaves are fern-like. In its native habitat, Japan, it frequents woodland areas, so will do well in our own woodland gardens as long as the shade is not too dense.

This is another plant that likes a good, humusy woodland soil. Increase from seed or by division.

Angelica
A wild herb that is sometimes grown in a light woodland setting, especially in clearings. It is a tall, robust plant, related to the next one, *Anthriscus*. Its stout stems carry heads of greenish-white flowers that are almost spherical and appear in summer. It is well known, and is usually grown in a vegetable or herb garden, but does well in light shade as long as the ground is moist.

Angelica often grows up to 120–150cm (4–5ft), when suited. It has a statuesque quality that makes it worth planting – just one plant, perhaps, at some strategic position. It will grow in most soils and can be increased from seed.

Anthriscus (cow parsley, Queen Anne's lace)
This is a plant for the larger woodland garden. It grows wild in Britain in hedgerows and along the edges of woods, where its foaming white flowers are one of the joys of spring. Be warned, however: it is a weed with deep tap roots and, pretty as it is, will cause a nuisance in a small garden.

A. sylvestris is the native form that flowers so prolifically in May. It looks well with other native plants, and I particularly like it under or next to hawthorn trees or bushes which continue the frothy white theme up into the sky. It would do well on the edge of rides or in a clearing in your wood. It is up to 120cm (4ft) tall or more, and can become floppy in wet weather, so do not plant it near narrow paths. There is a variety called 'Ravenswing' which has purple foliage and stems, but this does not really improve on the delicacy of the white flowers against the green leaves and stem of the type plant.

Anthriscus will grow in most soils and can easily be grown from seed.

Aquilegia (columbine, granny's bonnet)

A. vulgaris is another native species; it will do well in a light shade but will fade away if planted in too deep a position. An ideal place might well be between shrubs or under taller ones, or under trees that produce a light dappled shade. I grow it successfully under hazel, for example. The flowers are like delicate ballerinas with raised arms. There is a large number of species to choose from, but the wild columbine mentioned above is probably the best. Some of the modern cultivars such as the long-spurred strains are really a bit too brash for my taste, and look out of place in a woodland setting.

A. vulgaris has blue or purple flowers with a number of pink, white and even near-red forms. The white ones in particular look good in a woodland setting, as they really shine out, especially against a dark background. The white seedlings can be recognised before they flower by the pale yellowish-green of the foliage and stems. *AA. formosa* and *canadensis* both have delicate flowers that hover like brightly coloured moths in red and yellow. These look better in a cool woodland setting as they tend to get lost in an herbaceous border.

Aquilegias prefer a deep, rich position, but will grow on a surprising range of soils. They are best increased from seed, but are notably promiscuous and so the seedlings will not necessarily bear the same-coloured flowers as the parent plant.

Arisaema

This is a genus of curious plants that have recently gained tremendous popularity. Their curious property is the spathes (hoods) that surround the flower. They are similar in many ways to the common arum, lords and ladies, that grows in many British hedgerows and woods. It is the shape and colour of the hood that make these plants intriguing and sometimes very attractive. Some can grow to several feet, while others stay much closer to the ground.

A. candidissimum is one that has been grown for many years. It throws up a three-part leaf and large hooded flowers. The hood is white-striped and flushed with pink. This striping is found on most of the species but the colours vary dramatically from plant to plant, many being green-brown, purple, or even red with green or white stripes, or some other combination of colours. *A. triphyllum* is one of the oldest in cultivation, and still one of the most popular. This is a variable species, with a green or brownish ground striped with white. In fact, there are so many variations that it is impossible to list them all. More and more nurseries are stocking them, although they are difficult to find in garden centres.

Arisaemas are plants that are best enjoyed at close range; it is the individual that is interesting, not the effect of a whole drift, so plant near a path. Many are worth growing on a peat bed, where they can be not only easily seen but also cared for. One word of warning: they are late above ground, sometimes not appearing before June, so do not assume they are dead and dig them up or overplant them by mistake.

Arisaemas do best in a moist woodland soil of leafmould, in which they should not be allowed to dry out. They have tuberous roots which can be divided for increase, or you can grow them from seed, but they may take four or more years to reach flowering size.

Arisarum (mouse plant)

This is another curiosity for the garden, and one that has much appeal for children. At first glance it is just a ground-cover plant with glossy, arrow-shaped leaves, but on closer examination it can be seen that the flowers are protected by a brown hood that tapers off into a long point, very reminiscent of the hindquarters and tail of a mouse. The reason that these are not immediately apparent is because they have a tendency to hang down beneath the leaves. *A. proboscideum* is the species concerned and is the only one of the genus in general cultivation.

It will grow well in shade. There are no particular recommendations as to which plants it best associates with, as it is basically just a low, carpeting green plant. However, to exploit its mouse-like qualities some should be planted near a path or other point where they can be easily seen.

Arisarums will tolerate a wide range of soils, but a leafy one is best. Plant the small tubers just below the surface of the soil. Increase by division. (See also page 90.)

Arum (cuckoo pint, lords and ladies)

This and the previous two genera are all closely related. *Arum* is probably the most familiar, as it is a British native. Like the others, it has a hooded spathe enclosing a spike of a flower, and grows to about 25–30cm (10–12in) in height.

The native plant, *A. maculatum*, has shiny leaves and a stalk of orange-red berries in autumn. There are more attractive forms, in particular *A. italicum* 'Pictum', which has silver markings to the leaves. These leaves appear in autumn and overwinter in spite of frosts, whereas our own native tends to wait until spring before venturing forth. They are all useful plants, especially the overwintering forms, since they provide a green ground cover in quite dense shade. The silver variegated leaves are particularly good in this position.

Arums are not really fussy as to soil. Birds will distribute the seed, so that new colonies will crop up here and there. Pull out any seedlings you do not want; once the tubers have formed, they are awkward to get out of some places – such as in between choice plants, in which they invariably seem to seed.

Aruncus (goat's beard)
Here we are dealing with a much larger plant, one that will grow up to 180cm (6ft), when suited. Its lower part is a dense clump of rubus-type leaves through which stems bearing feathery creamy-white flowers grow. These are at their best in the middle of the summer, but, as with so many white flowers, they begin to look tatty as they turn brown. They will grow in shade but their height means that they need to be planted under a tall tree, such as oak, or in between shrubs. They are tremendously good plants for lightening up a dark corner, the froth of creamy flowers looking almost like a fountain.

The species that is normally seen in cultivation is *A. dioicus*. The male and female flowers are found on separate plants, and the male is usually considered to be the finer of the two. *A.d.* 'Kneiffii' is a very lovely form with delicately cut leaves, and is preferable to the species in a small garden as it takes up less space.

Aruncus will grow on a wide range of soils and are particularly useful for planting in drier areas. They can be increased by division or from seed. Since there are male and female forms, both will be required if seed is needed.

Asarina
A delightful plant that is, unfortunately, not well known. The species that I am particularly referring to is *A. procumbens*. If I tell you that it used to be known as *Antirrhinum asarina* you will guess that the flowers are of a snapdragon type. They appear throughout the summer and are a pale yellow, well set off by the grey-green stems and foliage. The plant is procumbent, as its name suggests, spreading to form a carpet. It is very useful, as it will grow in dry shade, which few plants find accommodating. The pale flowers show up in darker positions and often look best when growing on a bank.

Asarinas are very easy-going and will grow on most soils, although they are reputed to do best on alkaline ones. They self-sow, but they are also easy plants to transplant; so they have either to be left where they are or specially raised in pots and planted out. I have had best success by simply scattering the seed where I wanted it to grow.

Astilbe
Astilbes are some of the most colourful plants that can be grown in the woodland garden. On the whole I would recommend soft tones, as these seem more in keeping, but this genus gives a range of bright colours from white through luminous pinks to the very strong purples and reds of the modern cultivars that can be used to brighten up the woodland garden. Although I hate to describe them thus, their upright feathery flower heads make them look like the punks of the woodland garden.

The majority of species are quite tall, up to 120cm (4ft) in good conditions, but some such as *A. chinensis* and *A.* 'Sprite' are very short and are best grown in the peat garden. The large, tapering flower heads overtop an attractive, deeply cut foliage which is often shiny. Astilbes will grow in a light shade, but too much will impair their flowering ability.

There is a great number of varieties to choose from, most of them based on *A.×arendsii*. As there are too many to describe, the best thing is to go to a nursery or garden centre, see them in flower and choose the ones you like. I would be inclined not to have too many different colours, or the cool and tranquil quality of the garden may be upset.

It is essential to give astilbes a moist position, but having said that, they will take a drier spot if it is in shade. They are really best next to water; not only do they look at home there – even the bright ones – but they also grow well because of the moisture. Because the majority are cultivars, the best way of propagation is by division so that the plants come true.

Astrantia (masterwort)
Many gardeners bemoan the fact that there are few plants that will grow in shade. They must have very limited horizons; I think I would be happy filling such an area just with plants beginning with the letter 'A'. This comment is prompted by yet another very worthy plant that I would not want to be without in any garden.

Astrantia has curious but attractive flowers. The main part is a series of pale-green bracts forming a ruff, and inside this, like pins in a cushion, are tiny pale-green florets. Sometimes, as in *A. major* 'Rosea', the flower is greenish pink. 'Shaggy' is a very large but attractive cultivar. Astrantias always have a fresh, clean look about them, and retain it even after the flowers are finished. They vary in height, normally growing to about 60cm (2ft) or so. The variegated forms really need sun to keep their colours, though most astrantias do well in either sun or light shade. They are plants to grow in drifts and are happy in a dappled shade, such as under hazel or in between denser shrubs, forming a river between them.

They grow on most soils but appreciate a cool, moist root-run. They can easily be divided in spring, or you can grow them from seed. They do self-sow, so a drift can be quickly built up.

Bergenia
I never liked these plants as a child. I found their big leathery leaves a bit frightening, but I now have them in several parts of the garden. They must be one of the most accommodating of plants, because they will grow in sun or shade and in dry or moist soils, and, if happy, never need any attention.

The leaves form a dense cover about 15–25cm (6–10in) above the ground (see page 90). They are thick and glossy, smothering everything beneath them. The flower heads rise above the leaves on stems of up to 30cm (12in). Their colour varies from a light pink to a deep rosy pink that verges on red. There are also white forms, but these are not always so floriferous. The flowers appear in early spring, but odd blooms can be met with at virtually any month. There is quite a number of species and cultivars to choose from, and not enough space to go into them here. Two of the best are *BB*. 'Abendglut' and 'Ballawley Hybrids'. 'Silberlicht' is a good white form.

Bergenias will grow into even quite deep shade, but the deeper the shade the more impaired is the flowering. They are always grown as a drift rather than as odd specimen plants. Their low stature means that they do best at the edge of a wood or next to a path. For some reason they always seem to look right on a corner, where they can outline the edge of the path.

They are not fussy as to soil and will take it quite dry, although they undoubtedly do better in a leafy soil. You can propagate them by division or by taking cuttings from the thick rhizomes.

Brunnera

This is a small genus of which *B. macrophylla* is the only one generally in cultivation. It is a coarse plant with green leaves that get bigger as the year proceeds. The coarseness does not extend to the flowers, which are of the dainty forget-me-not type that float airily above the foliage. This is particularly effective in shady areas, as the flower stems are not easy to see and the blue flowers do appear literally to float.

It is a good plant for the shade, quickly forming large clumps when it is well suited. Fortunately it will take quite a degree of shade, and can be planted under trees and shrubs in the second row.

Brunnera will do well on most soils, but is happiest in a deep rich one that is moisture-retentive. Propagation is by division or seed – it does seed itself around. If you remove the spent flower heads you can often induce a second crop of flowers.

Caltha (kingcup, marsh marigold)

Caltha is another genus that contains a native plant, *C. palustris*, that does extremely well in a shady place. It is a waterside plant and therefore does best by a stream or pond, but will grow equally well in boggy ground.

The flowers, of a rich golden yellow, gleam in the late winter before the trees above put on leaf. It shines out so well that it is a plant to put in a position where it is suddenly come across, causing unexpected pleasure. There is a double-flowered form, *C.p.* 'Plena', which is nearly as good as the single, but

I prefer the shine that the cup-shape of the latter produces. There are several other species such as *CC. leptosepala* and *polypetala*, but little matches the simple *C. palustris*.

Plant out in a moisture-retentive soil, preferably one that is boggy for most of the year. Propagation is easily achieved by division or by seed, which should be sown fresh.

Campanula (bellflower)

This is a very large genus, mainly consisting of sun-lovers, but fortunately from our point of view there are a number that will grow in shade – even quite dense shade. One such rather surprised me when it sowed itself in dense shade in my wood and then proceeded to flower year after year. This was *C. persicifolia*, not a plant you would normally associate with shade. The blue really shines out in the dim light. Since this first happened I have noticed in other gardens that it is occasionally grown in light shade, and there both the blue and white forms are very effective. The plant grows to about 90–120cm (3–4ft). Three of much the same height that are good for growing amongst shrubs, but not under them, are the similarly named *CC. lactiflora*, *latifolia* and *latiloba*. These have flowers of various shades of blue. At the other end of the scale are two that often get confused with each other; *CC. poscharskyana* and *portenschlagiana*. These are both rampant carpeters that will do well in sun or shade. The latter will also happily climb up into low shrubs and spangle them with its starry blue flowers.

There are some campanulas that are far too rampant to include in a small garden. *C. rapunculoides* is one of these, but it can be planted in a large woodland garden to do its worst – or, when you look at its flowers, its best. A final plant that I have grown successfully in light shade is *C. alliariifolia*. This grows only about 45cm (18in) high, but it has graceful arching stems covered in white bells and interesting heart-shaped leaves. There are hundreds more species of campanula, many of which will undoubtedly grow in light shade. It is worth experimenting.

Campanulas tend not to worry too much over their soil, as long as it is not too dry or too wet. Propagate either by division or from seed, which is usually abundantly set.

Cardamine (cuckoo flower, lady's smock)

The native *C. pratensis* is a delightful plant, and not one that should be sneered at because it is a wild flower. It generally grows in open, boggy places, but can also be found in shady ditches, indicating that it will grow in dappled shade as long as the soil is moisture-retentive.

The flowers are a delightfully fresh mauve colour, and they appear in small heads on 30cm (12in) stems. There is also a double form, 'Flore Pleno', which has been in cultivation for many years and will also grow in light shade. Another rare native that actually grows in light woods is *C. bulbifera*, coral root, which has pinkish flowers. This plant has little bulbils in the leaf axils (where the leaf stalk meets the main stem), which, if 'sown', produce new plants. *C. asarifolia*, from the Alps, is well worth considering if you can find it. It has dense heads of white flowers, and blooms well even in quite dense shade. The final one I want to mention is *C. trifolia*, which is more commonly available than the last mentioned. This has white flowers, borne on 15cm (6in) stems, and tufts of trifoliate (cut into three) leaves. This too will grow in shady conditions. *Cardamine* also includes a number of plants that were, until recently, members of the genus *Dentaria*, and since they are still generally known under that name I will leave them until we reach the letter D.

Cardamine must have a moist soil, or it will peter out. A good leafy one will generally suffice, unless there is intense competition from other plants. Planting beside a stream or pond is ideal. It can be increased by division or seed.

Caulophyllum

Although it belongs to the berberis family, which is mainly shrubby, this genus is an herbaceous one. It is represented by one of its two species, *C. thalictroides* – a true woodland species that likes nothing better than cool, dappled shade with plenty of leafmould around its toes. It throws up a single thalictrum-like leaf (see p. 143), followed in late spring by a shoot bearing small yellow flowers. These in turn are followed in autumn by round, deep-blue berries.

This is not a common plant in cultivation, but one worth acquiring for a woodland garden as long as you can provide it with a good leafy soil. It can be increased either by division or from seed.

Chelidonium (greater celandine)

C. majus is a native British plant that has been grown in gardens for many centuries as a medicinal herb (the sap is good for curing warts). It is still often seen growing in hedgerows outside country cottages. It has bright yellow flowers of about 2cm (0.75in) across that shine out in shady areas. The form most commonly seen in gardens today is the double-flowered *C.m.* 'Flore Pleno'.

It will gently seed itself around, making a small colony in either sun or shade. It is quite tall – about 60cm (2ft) or so – making it a plant for further back in the shade, as long as it is not too deep.

Chelidonium will tolerate a very wide range of soils, including dry ones. It is easy to propagate from seed.

Cimicifuga (bugbane)

These are dramatic plants that prefer to be out of the sun, although they do not like too much shade. Their beauty lies in the tall spires of white flowers (looking like rockets going off) that appear above their cut leaves. The flowers generally appear from mid-summer onwards, making them a valuable addition to the woodland flora. There are several species, all of which tend to have green foliage, but there is one form, *C. ramosa* 'Atropurpurea', which has a wonderful dark-purple foliage that offsets the creamy-white flower spike in a superb fashion. If you only have space for one, this is the one to go for. *C. racemosa* is another that is well worth considering. Both grow to 180cm (6ft) or more. There are several more species to look for.

Cimicifugas will all grow in a light shady spot, but their dramatic spire shape makes them ideal for growing between rounded bushes, particularly against a dark backdrop. They must have a soil that contains a lot of rich humus, and they must never dry out. Propagate them by division in spring.

Circaea (enchanter's nightshade)

This is not a particularly interesting plant from most gardeners' point of view – indeed, it can be a positive nuisance, because once you have got it it is difficult to get rid of. However, *C. lutetiana* is a native British plant and its natural haunt is woodland, often in very dense shade, so it is perhaps worth choosing it for a large woodland garden in which there is a certain element of wildness. Not that it is very big – it grows to only about 25cm (10in) or so – but it does romp around a bit, its thin rhizomes spreading rapidly underground. The leaves are a dull green, but it does have a spike of dainty white flowers which, when seen in their thousands, have a pretty, misty effect.

Circaea will grow on any soil, even a dry one, which is a plus. To propagate, divide it in the spring, or simply sow the brushings from your trousers when you have walked through a drift in autumn.

Clintonia

A small genus of plants, related to the lily-of-the-valley, that are well worth growing in a woodland setting if you can get hold of them. They are quite similar to their more popular relations, with the same sort of leaves and bell-like flowers. *C. andrewskiana* has reddish flowers and *C. borealis* has yellow ones; *C. umbellulata* has white bells. *C. andrewskiana* is the tallest, when happy, at about 60cm (2ft). As well as its red flowers it produces blue berries, making it one of the most interesting.

Clintonias all grow in shady conditions and have a tendency to form colonies, although nowhere near as rapidly as lily-of-the-valley. They prefer a lime-free soil with plenty of leafmould or other humus in it. They can easily be increased by division, or from seed if it is available.

Codonopsis
These are climbing plants that like nothing better than a shrub in a sunny position to climb through. They grow only to about 60cm (2ft), so the host shrubs should not be too large or too far back in the wood – on its edge or along a sunny path would be ideal.

The charm of the bell-shaped flowers usually lies within the petals, which means that you either have to crawl along the path or tip them up to get full pleasure from them. *C. clematidea* is one of the best. This has what appears to be pale-blue flowers, until you tip them up to reveal a surprising red and orange interior. I do not wish to dwell on these for too long as they are not true woodlanders, but there are plenty more species worth trying.

Codonopsis are not too fussy about soils, as long as they are neither too wet nor too dry. Seed is probably the best method of increase.

Convallaria (lily-of-the-valley)
C. majalis must be one of the best-loved of the woodland plants. In the spring the young leaves encircle the stem of bell-like flowers in a natural posy. Part of the charm is the flowers' beautiful, distinctive scent.

To most people the species is more than sufficient but, man being man, there have been selections of so-called improved forms. 'Fortin's Giant' has larger leaves and flowers and is slightly later flowering, which does have the advantage of allowing a succession of flowers. 'Prolificans' is a double form (if you like that kind of thing), and 'Rosea' has pinky-mauve flowers. If you like variegated plants, *C.m.* 'Albistriata' has fresh-looking yellow stripes along the green leaves. This will occasionally revert to plain green leaves, which should be rogued out before the whole colony changes back to green. The variegated form cannot take quite as much shade as the type, but I have it planted in a light shady spot under a quince tree and it is doing very well.

Lilies-of-the-valley sometimes take quite a while to settle down, but once happy they set off in all directions making a large colony. They do not grow very tall – up to 25cm (10in) – so they can be planted towards the foreground. But since they are not particularly interesting when out of flower and since the white flowers show up well, they can be placed some way from a path as long as no tall herbage intervenes when they are in flower.

They will grow on any soil, but are especially happy and easier to get started in a leafy soil. Propagation is usually by division, and I have found that digging up a clump and transplanting it whole is the best method of ensuring an easy start. (See also page 91.)

Cortusa (alpine bells)

Cortusa is not a very well known genus, but it does contain one or two fine garden plants. In many respects they are very similar to the primulas, to which they are closely related. The species that is most commonly grown is *C. matthioli*. This has hairy stems and leaves surmounted by a hanging head of purply-red bell-shaped flowers, held at about 30cm (12in) above the ground. The flowers appear in late spring and early summer.

Cortusas are natural woodland plants and so are ideal for our purpose. They need a bit of attention to make certain that they are not over-run by competition, and so the best position would probably be in a peat bed. If the soil is leafy enough, though, they will grow in any part of a woodland garden.

As intimated, they like a humus-rich soil that does not completely dry out. Propagate either by dividing the clumps in spring or by sowing seed when it is ripe.

Corydalis

This genus is one that has suddenly risen in popularity, and gardeners are ever seeking new species. And new species there are aplenty – over 250 in China alone that have not yet been introduced. Putting all this aside, there are already enough in cultivation for our and most others' purposes. Some species are bulbous and belong theoretically in chapter 9, but it is better to deal with them all here.

Many of the corydalis grow in shady conditions, either in woods, under shrubs or in the lee of rocks. The flowers are very delicate and hold several to a stem above a ferny foliage. There are some, such as *C. lutea*, which seed themselves around and seem indestructible, but the majority are rather fragile and break if roughly handled, so give them a position out of strong winds. A peat bed is ideal, as long as the shade is not too dense and preferably receiving a little dappled sun.

In Europe one of the commonest seen in woodlands is *C. solida*. This varies in colour from blue to red – the latter is particularly fine in the form *C.s.* 'George Baker'. For the peat bed, one of the most beautiful is the electric-blue *C. cashmeriana* from the Himalayas, which must be grown in a peaty soil that is not allowed to dry out. An even more beautiful blue has recently been introduced from China, *C. flexuosa*, which likes a similar position. This species has a long flowering season. One of the easy ones to grow is *C. caucasica alba*, which produces wide creamy-white flowers in spring.

I have talked at length about this genus, which, in spite of its popularity, I like very much. In any woodland garden it is worth creating a peat bed for a few of the more delicate plants that need extra attention, and these would be some of the most valued of its inmates.

Plant out in a peaty, gritty soil that is moisture-retentive and yet well drained. Propagate from fresh seed or by dividing the tubers. (See also page 150.)

Dentaria

Most of this genus has been moved to *Cardamine* (see page 110), but since they are still generally known by their former name by most gardeners I am going to stick to it. They are some of the most perfect of woodland plants as they naturally grow in the shade, and will soon make large colonies. They grow to about 45cm (18in) or so in height, and consist of deeply cut, fresh-looking green leaves surmounted by heads of very decorative white or lilac flowers in spring.

They like a dappled shade and will grow well under hazel, oak, or some similar shrub or tree. They can be in the front or the second rank of the ground vegetation, depending on how much room there is. They will also grow well in drifts between shrubs, possibly with some later-flowering plant, such as lilies, growing through them.

D. digitata (*Cardamine pentaphyllos*) is one of my favourites: it has fresh lilac flowers that look very cool in the shade. One that brightens up deeper shade is the white-flowered *D. pinnata* (*C. heptaphylla*). A third member, *D. enneaphyllos* (*C. enneaphyllos*), has pale-yellow flowers. All these look very good in drifts, which they quickly make when they are well suited.

Dentarias will grow on most soils, but they undoubtedly do best in a layer of good leafsoil. They are easy to increase, as they are readily divided in spring.

Dicentra (bleeding-heart)

These are essentially border plants, but since they do not like full sun they make ideal plants for lightly shaded areas. I particularly like the white ones in shade, and I grow two under hazel in dappled shade.

For my taste, the pink and white flowers of *D. spectabilis* look a bit out of place in a woodland context, but the white form, *D.s. alba*, is perfect. This is quite a tall plant, with the flowers – which appear in spring and can be susceptible to late frosts – dangling from long arching stems reaching 60cm (2ft) or more. The smaller varieties, like the pink *D. formosa*, the pearly-white *D.* 'Langtrees' and *D.* 'Pearl Drops', are excellent plants for the front of a woodland garden, as they have a dusky pink-mauve foliage which they retain through the summer.

Dicentras should not be planted too far from the edge of the wood or path, because not only do they require some light but they also need to be reasonably close to be appreciated. Plant in any good garden soil that does not dry out. Propagate by division in the spring.

Digitalis (foxglove)

The common foxglove (*D. purpurea*) is a biennial and is dealt with in chapter 8 (page 151), but there is a number of foxgloves that are perennial and well worth growing in a woodland garden. They generally do not like too much shade and do best on the edge of paths, or better still in clumps on the edge of clearings.

One of the easiest, but not the most spectacular, is *D. lutea*. This is a smaller plant than the wild foxglove, growing to only about 60cm (2ft). It has small yellow flowers which are most effective when planted in a group. Its bright green foliage is evergreen. Another yellow is *D. grandiflora*, which has much larger flowers and coarser leaves. Another coarse plant is *D.×mertonensis*, which has large floppy leaves and large flattish flowers of a soft crushed strawberry colour suffused with yellow (it is a cross between *D. purpurea* and *D. grandiflora*).

Foxgloves will grow in any soil (or even poor soil, but they will not grow so big). Propagation is generally no problem: they seed themselves around in a most generous manner.

Disporum

This is a little-known genus of plants that are true woodlanders, liking nothing better than a bit of leafmould and some shade. They are closely related to the Solomon's seals (*Polygonatum*, page 136); they have the same tubular flowers, hanging down from arching stems.

One of the commonest is *D. smithii*. This is a short plant, with whitish flowers in spring, but its main attraction for many gardeners is the orange berries that it carries in the autumn. A slightly larger plant is *D. sessile*, which in its variety 'Variegatum' is very attractive. This has arching stems of fresh-looking white-striped leaves, and is very good for lightening up a dull spot in shade. Like all the genus, it runs underground and soon builds up into a drift. A taller member of the genus is *D. pullum*, which has dark stems and flowers that are attractive when looked at close to but likely to be missed at a distance. They are tubular like the rest, but are of an intriguing smoky-green colour. One of the latest to have been introduced to cultivation is of a similar height (about 90cm (3ft)) but has yellow flowers. This is *D. flavum*.

Disporums grow well under shrubs or trees that do not obscure too much light. They will all be best planted in the second rank of the border. They must have a good loose leafmould soil that does not dry out, to give of their best. They can all readily be increased by division or from seed. *D. smithii* tends to self-sow.

Dodecatheon (shooting stars)

Although at first glance it does not seem like it, this is, in fact, a member of the primula family. When one remembers that cyclamen is also a member, the family resemblance becomes clearer. The vernacular name is a very descriptive one: the cyclamen-type flowers seem to be shooting off in all directions from the top of the tall flowering stem. Their basic colour is either purple-pink or white, but with a yellow ring round the deep-purple centre of the flower.

There are several different species, of which the best for our purposes is *D. meadia*. When suited, this can reach 60cm (2ft). There are others, but they need more specialist attention. They are probably best grown on a peat bed in light shade.

Most dodecatheons need a moisture-retentive soil. They can be increased, like most primulas, either by division in spring or from freshly ripened seed.

Epimedium

Epimedium is another genus that has become very popular in recent times. As a consequence there have appeared a number of new hybrids, and even several new species, from China. They are true woodland plants, and no woodland garden should be without at least one. They all form a dense mass of shield – or heart-shaped leaves, above which airy, arching flower stems carry starry flowers coloured either red, white or yellow. The shape of these small flowers is difficult to describe, but they always remind me of a jester's cap with horns sticking out.

E. grandiflorum and its different forms is one of the commonest species, with flowers in a variety of colours of which 'Rose Queen' is often considered one of the best: it has deep-pink flowers tipped with white, and the leaves are flushed with copper. *E.×rubrum* has flowers that have crimson horns and a yellow centre. This also has very fresh green leaves flushed with a coppery brown. *E. perralderianum*, with its bright yellow flowers and shiny green leaves, is another well worth considering. There are many more for the enthusiast to start collecting, if he or she so wishes.

Being natural woodlanders, epimediums can be planted in light to medium shade. As they creep underground, they gradually form large drifts. They are tall and bold enough to be given any position in a woodland garden, but can be particularly effective if planted on either side of a path so that you have to walk through them.

Epimediums will grow in any fertile soil, but seem to do best in one reasonably rich in humus or leafmould. Propagation is most easily achieved by division in the spring. They can also be grown from seed. (See also page 91.)

Euphorbia (spurge)

This is an enormous genus of up to five thousand species, but some are trees and many grow in tropical areas (for example the Christmas poinsettia (*E. pulcherrima*)). The number that we grow in our gardens is considerably smaller, and even fewer are grown in a woodland setting.

All the same, there are still a large number left to consider. They all have a freshness that makes them attractive plants, and although the flowers are insignificant, they are surrounded by bracts that are usually a bright greeny-yellow and occasionally a reddish orange, which glow magnificently in dappled shade.

Euphorbia robbiae is one of the best for woodland gardens, as it will grow in quite dense shade and on quite dry soils. It is not one of the most exciting, but it can look very good when there is a large colony of it. Related to it is the British native wood spurge, *E. amygdaloides*. This is not particularly exciting either, but there is a purple form, *E.a.* 'Rubra', which can be a stunning plant as long as it gets enough light for it to retain its colour. Plant it where the winter sun can catch it, and it can be breathtaking. *EE. sikkimensis*, *schillingii* and *wallichii* are somewhat similar, and all have that characteristic freshness. The first two reach about 120cm (4ft) or so, while the last is a bit shorter. These will not take so much shade, but are ideal for planting between shrubs. The first will spread quite rapidly on lighter soils. Also spreaders are *E. griffithii* and its varieties 'Fireglow' and 'Dixter'. These are tinged a rich orange-red, and are certainly worth growing if you have the space. Again, they look good growing between bushes, especially those with a darker foliage. This whole book could be filled with descriptions of euphorbias, but I have covered some of the most interesting ones that can be used in shade. One word of warning: do not introduce *E. pseudovirgata* (sometimes known as *E. uralensis*) to your garden, as it will run riot and give you a terrible job getting rid of it, especially if you live on a heavy soil. The same advice applies to *E. cyparissias*.

Euphorbias will grow on most soils, including quite dry ones. They can be increased by division or from seed. Some can also be propagated by taking cuttings. Many people find they are allergic to the white sap that euphorbias produce, so take care and at all costs avoid getting it into your eyes, as it creates one of the most excruciating pains possible. (See also page 92.)

Filipendula (meadowsweet)

The British native *F. ulmaria* can often be seen growing in ditches in the shade of overhanging hedgerows. It can also be planted in similar moist situations in a woodland garden, as long as the shade is not too deep. The attractive thing about filipendulas is their fluffy flower heads, and some also have pleasing foliage. For example, the form of the plant just mentioned, *F.u.* 'Aurea', is mainly grown for its golden foliage. This plant is quite short, reaching only about 90cm (3ft), but there are others such as *FF. palmata* and *purpurea* that will reach another 30cm (1ft). These both have flowers in differing shades of pink, and can make very handsome clumps.

Filipendulas should not be in too deep a shade, and are best used in association with a waterside planting: the use of grasses with them, for example, can be eye-catching. As already indicated, they prefer a moisture-retentive soil, which, if it is not near water, should have plenty of humus in it. They can easily be propagated by division.

Fragaria (strawberry)
The wild strawberry, *F. vesca*, will grow in shade and is a useful plant for those who have a woodland garden on chalk. It is like a miniature version of the plant we normally grow in the fruit garden: a smaller plant; smaller, white flowers; and ultimately smaller fruit. There is one that has double flowers – *F.v.* 'Multiplex'. In recent times, *F. daltoniana* has been introduced. This covers the ground at an incredible rate of knots, sending out new runners in all directions. The runners are red and the leaves are a shiny dark green. It will grow in quite deep shade, but seems to require a moister soil than our native wild strawberry.

Fragarias are useful ground-coverers, but as they are almost flush with the ground, put them near the edge of the wood or beside a path. They will grow in virtually any soil, but as already mentioned *F. daltoniana* does better on a moisture-retentive one. You can easily increase them by dividing the new plants from their runners.

Galium (bedstraw, woodruff)
This is included for the British native *G. odoratum* (once known as *Asperula odorata*), sweet woodruff. It makes a low, creeping carpet of small whorled leaves, with tiny star-like white flowers appearing in the spring. It is not a plant of great presence, and is really of use only in a larger woodland garden where there is space to accommodate plants that only marginally earn their keep. I grow it and sometimes look at it and wonder why, but it is in quite deep shade in which I do not want to grow anything else, so I just smile at its gentle presence and wander on.

It is not the easiest of plants to get established, but once it has found soil that it likes – this usually means a reasonably fertile leafmould – it thrives. Propagate it by division. (See also page 92.)

Gentiana
Gentians are wonderful plants to grow; their blue trumpets are unlike anything else grown in the garden. Many like a bit of sun to grow well and so should be

planted on the very edge of a wood, although one of the tall ones, *G. asclepiadea*, the willow gentian, will tolerate quite dense shade. This one grows to about 90cm (3ft), with long arching stems bearing willow-like leaves and the typical rich-blue flowers of the gentian family. There is a white variety, *G.a. alba*, but I do not think it is as beautiful as the typical blue form.

The low-growing ones such as *G. sino-ornata* and its many varieties do need that extra little bit of light if they are to flower well, but they can be grown under tall-growing trees such as oak where the sun can get in to them. What they also require is a good humusy soil that will hold plenty of moisture – they dislike it dry. This also applies to the willow gentian, which needs a deep, rich soil to give of its best. This species is best increased from seed, but *G. sino-ornata* can easily be divided in spring, when the crowns will fall apart in your fingers.

Geranium (crane's bill, hardy geranium)

As with the rhododendrons in chapter 5, it is difficult to know where to start with this genus. It has become extremely popular over the past few years, and new cultivars and hybrids are being introduced all the time. Many are but minor variants on what we have already, but others add to the richness of the genus. Unfortunately, my task is made worse by the fact that most will grow in a light shade. It is a very varied genus with plants of all sizes from ground level up to 120cm (4ft), and from tight little buns to large sprawlers that are continually spreading. Surprisingly, the colour range of the flowers is somewhat limited, although within the limits there is great variation: it goes from blues (reddish blues, usually) to reds and pinks, taking in deep purples on the way. As with most flowers of these colours, most species have a white form.

Starting with those that, given the chance, prefer shade, *G. phaeum*, the mourning widow, is a clump-forming plant with intriguing reflexed flowers of a very dark purple, almost black – hence its common name. It grows to about 60cm (2ft). *G. nodosum* is another such plant, but not one that I would choose to grow as its flowers are not particularly interesting – neither is the plant itself, for that matter. Its main virtue is that it will grow in quite dense shade where not much else will. The flowers are a mauvy pink.

Moving on to others that will tolerate some shade, *G. macrorrhizum* is one of the better ground-cover plants (see page 93). It is evergreen, with nicely scented leaves that take on a red tinge. The flowers vary from a very pale to quite a dark pink. It spreads quite quickly to form large colonies, but can easily be removed if it becomes a nuisance. *G. endressii* and *G. × oxonianum* are similar, forming large hummocks covered with pink flowers. These spread by seeding and can become a nuisance in a small garden, especially as they do not always come true, producing plants that are inferior to the parent. In spite of

The dainty flowers of *Epimedium perralderianum* arch above the solid mass of leaves borne on wiry stems. The plant makes good ground cover.

Drifts of *Erythronium* 'White Beauty' growing in a leafy soil in light shade.

In spring delicate pincushions of flowers appear on *Fothergilla major* before the leaves fully develop.

In contrast to the flowers, the autumn colour of the *Fothergilla* is quite startling.

Gunnera manicata is a very dramatic plant for wet spots in the larger woodland gardens.

The willow gentian, *Gentiana asclepiadea*, has vivid blue flowers and likes moist, leafy soil.

Hellebores are becoming increasingly popular and grow well in light shade. This is a yellow-coloured seedling.

The grace and beauty of the native bluebell, *Hyacinthoides non-scripta*, takes a lot of beating.

The beautiful snowflake, *Leucojum aestivum*, does well in a woodland situation so long as the soil is not too dry.

The scruffy golden heads of *Ligularia × hessei* are extremely useful for lighting up dark corners in autumn.

The white-berried form of *Pernettya mucronata* growing in the dense shade of a large oak tree.

this they are well worth growing on the edge of a woodland garden. *G. pratense* and *G. sylvaticum* and all their cultivars have a lot in common and are all worth considering. These are plants of the open meadow as well as hedgebanks and woodland edges. They have finely fingered leaves and large flowers varying from blue to purple. A geranium I have grown for years in light shade is *G. versicolor*. This is not a spectacular plant for the open border, but in shade the small flowers, pale pink, striped darker, stand out well. The low-growing *G.* × *cantabrigiense* is another that I have grown in the shade. It produces few flowers in this position, but it does spread, and the leaves make an interesting ground cover.

There are many more species that you can explore; many of them you can grow in the open garden, and then you can take a piece and try it in the shade. An average garden can accommodate at least twenty different geraniums without looking over-run by them.

Geraniums will grow on most soils but they do best on a richer diet. Most can be divided or grown from cuttings. The species can be grown from seed sown in the spring.

Gillenia

Gillenia trifoliata is a delightful plant that most gardeners seem oblivious to, although it has been in cultivation for over two hundred years. It grows into a small bush of wiry stems and is covered with airy white flowers that float above it, each encased in a red calyx (the spent bud sheath). Although it is herbaceous, dying back to the ground each autumn, its habit when in full flower makes it appear to be a shrub. I love this plant, and although I grow it in a sunny border it will also grow well in light shade.

It needs a moisture-retentive soil – otherwise, it does not appear to be fussy. It can easily be grown from seed, although it takes several years to obtain a mature plant this way. A speedier method is to divide an existing plant.

Glaucidium

This is another beautiful plant that is not grown as much as it ought to be. *Glaucidium palmatum* is a true woodlander, relishing dappled shade in rich, humusy soil. It grows to about 60cm (2ft), and has good-looking, fresh green leaves offsetting a large dish-shaped lilac flower, centred with golden stamens. It really is a choice plant and one well worth acquiring; indeed, I would go so far as to say that it is well worth creating a woodland garden just to be able to grow this one plant, even though its flowering season (late spring) is quite short. There is a white form, *G.p.* 'Album' – but, fine as it is, it is not really a patch on the type plant.

In spite of its being quite tall, it is a plant to put where it can be seen. It will grow well under an oak or hazel; or, even better, a whole colony would look tremendous in the light dappled shade created by a *Nothofagus antarctica*.

Glaucidiums must have a deep, rich soil that is moisture-retentive, to do well. Although it is a long-winded process – it takes several years to reach a decent flowering size – glaucidiums can be grown from seed. It is quicker to divide an existing plant, if you have one.

Glechoma (ground ivy)

From a plant that is not often seen to one that can be too often seen, for ground ivy is usually considered a pestilent weed. However, in a large woodland setting where there is plenty of room to entertain native plants it is a pleasant addition. It most commonly occurs in hedgerows, where it not only covers the ground but climbs up into the bottom of the hedge. In the woodland it can be given the same scope and allowed to climb through some of the low shrubs. It is low-growing, with furry leaves and purply-blue flowers that shine out in quite an attractive way. Be warned, however: it is a plant only for the largest of gardens, where there is space to tolerate rampant plants.

Ground ivy does well in most soils, and is often to be found on quite dry banks where its growth will be quite sparse, its leaves taking on a purplish tinge. On a richer diet it becomes more luxuriant. It roots at the nodes as the stems extend, so it is easy to take one of these rooted stems and transplant it.

Hacquetia

This is a single-species genus with *H. epipactis* as its sole representative. It is a woodlander by nature but a very small one, as it grows only a few inches tall. The first signs of activity are around the turn of the year, when little greenish-yellow flowers push through the soil followed by a ruff of bracts and finally the leaves. It will grow in any woodland conditions as long as there is not too fierce a competition from other plants, but it probably does best in a peat bed.

Hacquetia seems happy with a wide variety of soils. It can be divided, but this is not an easy process and the plant takes a while to settle down again; so propagate by seed.

Helleborus (hellebore)

Hellebores are yet another favourite genus, not only of myself but of many other gardeners. Perhaps if hellebores flowered in the summer when there is much more around, they would not be so popular, but since they flower in winter when there is little else to look at, it is not surprising that they are so appreciated.

In their natural habitats the majority are woodlanders, and so they will fit well into a woodland garden. They tend to form large clumps, which can be viewed in isolation or in drifts. I think I prefer them in isolated clumps; I find drifts a bit fussy, as there is usually variation in flower colour. I would choose one or two good colour forms and enjoy those, rather than building up large colonies of indifferent ones. Hellebores are best planted under deciduous trees, as they flower when the trees are out of leaf. They will take quite a bit of shade later in the year, as long as the soil is kept reasonably moist.

The most popular species is *H. orientalis* and its many cultivars. These grow to about 45cm (18in), and have saucer-shaped flowers in a range of colours from green through yellow to pink and purple to almost black. Some have spots on the petals and some are plain. Go for those with clear colours and an even spotting; so many on offer are very muddy in appearance, or have spots that look like an ugly rash. They flower from late winter into early spring. Slightly earlier are the Christmas roses (*H. niger*). These can be difficult to grow and disappointing, if the slugs find them or they get splashed by mud. A good form with beautifully even white flowers is 'White Magic'. A different-shaped hellebore that does very well in a woodland setting is *H. foetidus*. This has very attractive deeply cut leaves which sometimes appear to be almost black. It is a handsome plant, reaching up to nearly 60cm (2ft) tall and topped by a large truss of nodding green flowers, each tipped in red. These do look good growing in a drift. Of the several other species that are worth considering, *H. argutifolius* (previously *H. corsicus*) forms a large sprawling clump with large, prickly-edged, pale leaves. The flowers are pale green and persist for a long time.

All these will grow in light shade in a rich soil, preferably one that does not dry out, although I have some that linger on in very dry soil. They can be increased by dividing in autumn, or immediately after flowering, or by sowing the seed as soon as it is ripe.

Heloniopsis

H. orientalis is a small plant that is worth growing on the peat bed. It forms a perennial clump of strap-like leaves, and every spring it throws up a 30cm (12in) stem topped by nodding pink flowers. Not a startling plant, but a pleasant one. There is a very similar but much shorter species called *H. breviscapa*, that likes similar conditions. The leaves of both make good slug fodder and can become tatty.

Plant heloniopsis in a good leafy soil. They are rhizomatous, so can be easily divided if more plants are required.

Hemerocallis (day lily)

Day lilies are usually considered plants of the open border, but they will grow surprisingly well in light shade. There are literally thousands of hybrids and cultivars to choose from – too many, really, as a lot of them are very similar to each other. For those who do not know them, the plants form large clumps of arching strap-like leaves with straight flowering stems extending above them; each of these carries a bunch of buds, of which one opens every day, each flower lasting for only one day. One plant has so many buds that it seems to be in flower for several weeks. The flowers are lily-like in shape, and the colour is based on shades of yellow, extending to mahogany red.

Most of these modern cultivars look best in the open border, but some of the species, such as *H. lilio-asphodelus* (previously *H. flava*) and *H. fulva*, are much more refined plants with smaller leaves and flowers, and somehow I think these look better in a woodland setting.

Hemerocallis are not particularly fussy as to the soil in which they grow, although they do not like it too dry. You can increase them by division – which you should, in any case, do every three or four years to prevent the plants becoming too congested.

Hepatica

These are delightful little plants that are natural woodland inhabitants. They form hummocks of three-lobed leaves and tiny, jewel-like flowers of mainly blue, although there are also pink and white varieties. Sometimes there are double forms. They are related to anemones, a genus to which they used to belong, and flower at about the same time as the woodland species (early spring).

The commonest species is *H. nobilis* (formerly *H. triloba*). This is the smallest of the genus and is probably best grown in a peat bed, although it can be quite happy under trees or shrubs as long as it has not got too much competition. The flowers vary in colour from blue through to a deep pink. There are also white forms. *H. transsilvanica* and *H. × media* 'Ballardii' are not so common. These have larger, pale-blue flowers and are larger, more lax plants that can stand on their own in a woodland garden, although they will make good candidates for the peat garden.

Hepaticas do best in a gritty, peaty soil. You can increase them from seed, but sow it as soon as it is ripe (usually in late spring or early summer).

Heuchera (coral bells)

Heucheras are normally considered to be open-border plants but, in fact, they appreciate a modicum of shade and can therefore be grown to advantage in a woodland garden. They are best on the margins, where they can be easily seen.

The flowers are held on long arching stems and consist of dainty bells of mainly white, pink or red. In recent times one of the most popular has been *H. micrantha* 'Palace Purple', which has shiny purple foliage. Unfortunately this is likely to turn green unless the plant gets enough sun, so it should be planted on the very edge of the wood. I have one in such a position and it manages to retain its colour. There are several other species that are worth considering: *H. americana* has greenish flowers and *H. sanguinea*, the native coral bells of North America, has red or sometimes pink.

Heucheras will grow in any fertile soil in a light shade. Propagate by division in spring.

X Heucherella
This is a bigeneric cross between the last genus and *Tiarella*, producing plants with very dainty flowers, much lighter and starrier than *Heuchera*. It grows in similar conditions to the latter.

Hosta (plantain lily)
This is another of those large genera that do well in shady conditions. Not only is there a large number of species, but there are also thousands of varieties, with new ones seemingly appearing every day. To be honest, I find great difficulty in distinguishing between them, and I wonder, anyway, if this is necessary for the average gardener. It is a bit like choosing between the millions of different michaelmas daisies – you just choose the ones you like, and hang the name. Being a writer, I have to be rather more scientific than that and differentiate between the species, even if I find the varieties a bit of a trial.

Although hostas have flowers (usually pale blue) that look particularly attractive when they are in groups, it is the leaves for which they are mainly grown. They have a great diversity of colour, shininess, degrees of ribbing and so on. They are best in large clumps or drifts, but I find that if the drifts get too large they can be a trifle boring. Similarly, if too many forms are mixed up together they become bitty and uncomfortable to look at – so use hostas with discretion. They do look good along a path, possibly on both sides of it so that you are walking through them. They also look good flowing between shrubs or contrasting with plants of a more upright growth or with strap-like leaves.

Some, such as *H. sieboldiana* 'Elegans', have very large leaves and can make a dramatic impact. Others (*H. lancifolia*, for example) have smaller, strap-like leaves which depend on their shine to add interest to them. There is a large number of varieties that have variegations of one sort or another, either of a pale cream or of a rich gold. In recent times there has been a lot of interest in some varieties with golden leaves (such as the old favourite *H.* 'Semperaurea' or the newer *H.* 'Sum and Substance'). The variegated and golden forms are very good at lightening a dark spot. There are so many to choose from that the only way is to go and see your local supplier, and see what he has that appeals to you.

Hostas will grow in a wide variety of soils but do best in a rich, moisture-retentive one. To make certain the plants come true, the only satisfactory method of propagation is by division, often by using the crude method of splitting a clump in half with a spade. (See also page 93.)

Houttuynia
H. cordata, at least in its form 'Chameleon', is a very fashionable plant at the moment and yet, somehow, I have never got on with it. It is a rampant spreader that is best placed in damp ground. It can be grown in full sun or in a light shade beside a water feature. It would do very well in a peat bed, but under no circumstances introduce it to such a choice position, or it will swamp every-thing in it.

The plant is grown for its dark-green, heart-shaped leaves and its small white flowers. There are several forms, with different-coloured foliage. 'Chameleon', for example, has leaves that are variegated in green, cream and red.

A good ground-cover plant, perhaps, but one to miss unless you really like it. Grow in a moist soil, either in boggy ground or in soil that has had a lot of moisture-retentive humus added to it. Propagate by division. (See also page 94.)

Hydrastis
H. canadensis is a woodlander from North America that is worth considering, although it is rarely seen in gardens. It is a tuberous species with divided leaves and strange, but attractive, flowers consisting of small bunches of yellow stamens. The whole plant is about 30cm (12in) high. Although not outstanding, it does make an interesting drift when planted in the front of the border where it can be seen.

Being a woodlander, it likes a moist, leafy soil. Increase it either by division in early spring or by sowing freshly ripened seeds.

Hylomecon
This is a genus of one species: namely, *H. japonicum*. It is one of the poppy family, as can readily be seen from the bright yellow flowers, well set off against fresh green leaves, that it carries in spring. The whole plant is only about 30cm (12in) in height and is summer-dormant, so it disappears back below ground once the flowering cycle is complete.

It spreads, slowly, to make delightful little colonies. It is not a plant that is well known, but it deserves to be found more regularly in our gardens. It can be planted in isolated drifts or along with ferns that will take over the space vacated by its summer dormancy.

Hylomecon must have a cool, moist root-run, and so the usual leafy soil is the ideal medium. It can easily be increased by division.

Iris

Iris is a very big genus, but I do not wish to dwell on it other than to mention *I. foetidissima*, which is a true woodlander. It will, in fact, grow in any situation from full sun to deep shade. This iris grows up to 90cm (3ft) in favourable conditions, with typical sword-like iris leaves and flowers with the falls (the lower petals) a pale-bluish colour, netted with purple veins, and the standards (the erect upper petals) a brownish lilac, sometimes flushed with yellow. The flowers appear in summer, followed by bright red berries which stay in the seed capsules after they have split. These berries are persistent, and it is surprising how they show up at quite a distance, especially in the winter. The dried stems with berries still attached are much desired by flower arrangers. From our point of view, this is the only iris of interest. Being tall, it can be planted further back in the wood.

Iris foetidissima* is happy on most soils, including chalk, on which it is frequently seen growing in the wild. Increase by dividing the clumps in the autumn or spring, or by sowing the seed.

Jeffersonia

Jeffersonia – yet another of my favourites – is a small genus of only two species, but our woodland gardens would be much the poorer without them. *J. diphylla* comes from North America and has two leaves on each stem, each divided into two. The flowers are white with a central boss of yellow stamens. The whole plant is no more than 15–20cm (6–8in) high. The other, *J. dubia*, is even better. It has the most beautiful mauvy-purple flowers, cradled in the emerging leaves, which are blue-grey-green, on purple stems. There are few more lovely sights than this in spring when it first flowers. When all is over, the seed pods are worth picking and displaying indoors. Both species are a bit too precious to leave to the rigours of the large woodland garden, but they make perfect denizens of the peat bed.

Jeffersonias need a cool, gritty leafmould mixture that does not dry out but is reasonably well drained. Propagation is best carried out by sowing fresh seed. They can be divided in spring, but this is not the easiest of tasks.

Kirengeshoma

K. palmata is a very beautiful plant, and valuable in the woodland garden for its late autumn flowering. It is tall, growing up to 90cm (3ft), but even before it reaches that height it exhibits interest. The leaves, noteworthy at all stages, are shaped a bit like a sycamore's, and their pale green is well set off by the blackness of the plant's stems. The bell-shaped flowers are a pale creamy yellow, and hang from arching stems. There is an even more rarely seen species, *K.*

koreana, which is smaller and has upright and more open flowers. Both are well worth growing, even in a small garden, if the right conditions can be supplied.

Kirengeshomas look good planted in drifts, especially if they are associated with ferns. They like a dappled shade and will take quite an amount of it, but the beauty of the plant is lost if it is too deep. It does not like drying winds or frosts, so plant in a position protected from both.

They should have a deep, leafy, moisture-retentive soil to give them their best chance, but it must be lime-free. Increase by division.

Lamium (dead-nettle)

Common as they are I think lamiums are very good value as garden plants. Some have a very long flowering season, and their leaves too provide a great deal of interest. One of the commonest is *L. maculatum* and its host of cultivars. This grows to 30cm (12in) or so, with typical nettle-shaped leaves and heads of white, pink or red flowers. The leaves are usually flushed with silver. Lamiums flower from spring through until the autumn frosts; they often appreciate a shave half-way through, to rejuvenate them. They spread rapidly making a dense mat, but can easily be removed if they become invasive.

I have a particular fondness for *L. orvala*, which I grow in my wood. This makes rounded hummocks about 45cm (18in) high, with green leaves and a dark, maroon flower which for me appears in early spring, but I know that for some it comes later.

Another popular dead-nettle for the woodland garden is *L. galeobdolon*, yellow archangel (which has finally, we hope, settled under this name, having shuttled to and fro several times between this, *Galeobdolon luteum* and *Lamiastrum galeobdolon*). It is a vigorous spreader, and should be used only where there is space for it. It has bright yellow flowers in the spring, and dark-green leaves usually splashed with silver. A native woodland plant, it thrives under such conditions.

Lamiums will all do well in shade, and the spreading quality of the first and third mentioned makes them good ground cover that can be used anywhere in the wood. The yellow archangel, being a native, looks particularly good in a wilder part. They are not fussy about soil, but will travel faster in a light, leafy one. They can all be increased readily by division in spring. (See also page 94.)

Lathraea

This is a fascinating genus, of which *L. clandestina* is the form usually seen. It grows only 5–7.5cm (2–3in) high, and being a parasite it has no green foliage. It appears above the roots of host trees in the spring, as a group of mauvy-violet or purple hooded flowers. These always excite comment. Being parasitic, lathraeas are in no need of light, and their host provides all their needs. They can therefore be planted anywhere, even in deep shade, but of course they are restricted to where their host trees grow.

Lathraeas mainly grow on willow, poplar or alder, although I also know of some growing on sycamore. They will grow in any soil, but a bare soil is best, or they cannot be seen. Most of the hosts prefer to live on dampish soil. The only way to grow this plant is to obtain some seed and spread it round the potential host.

Lathyrus (peas)
Most peas are sun-lovers, but there are a couple which will put up with a little shade. The first is a natural woodlander and can be found growing in oak woods in parts of Europe. This is *L. vernus*, a short, non-climbing plant that reaches only 30cm (12in). Tufted and erect, it flowers in the early spring before the leaves are on the trees. The small, typical pea-like flowers are a reddish purple which changes to blue as they age. There are several varieties in cultivation that have pink flowers. The other pea is *L. grandiflorus*, a climber reaching up to 180cm (6ft) if given the chance. It loves to scramble through shrubs and can be planted on the outskirts of a wood where it will get some light. The rounded flowers are pink and maroon, appearing throughout the summer. This pea increases quite rapidly by underground stolons.

They will both grow in a variety of soils and are not too worried if they are quite dry. They can be increased by seed or division.

Ligularia
This is a very valuable genus for the large woodland garden, as it is one of the few daisy-type plants that can be grown in shade. There is quite a number of species that are suitable for our purposes, all with flowers of yellow through deep gold and some that are almost orange – colours that are not frequently met with in a woodland context. They can be planted under trees or shrubs, but they often look better cradled in between shrubs. What they all require is that the ground be moist, and they make ideal plants for growing in shady areas in boggy ground or beside ponds.

One of the commonest seen is *L. dentata*, especially in its form 'Desdemona'. This is about 120cm (4ft) tall, with quite large orange flowers and large rounded leaves that are purple beneath (the slugs love them – be warned). *L.d.* 'Orange Queen' is similar, but with larger flower heads. Equally popular but quite different is *L. przewalskii* 'The Rocket', which has tall (180cm (6ft)), straight black stems with a tapering spire of small yellow flowers. Different again is *L. macrophylla*, which has large upright-pointing leaves from which rise sturdy stems topped with enormous dumpy spikes of yellow flowers.

Many people find these plants too coarse or object to the rich colour, but I love them and would not wish to garden without them. They can be very dramatic in a woodland setting, as long as you have the moisture they require. Plant in a very moist, even wet, soil. Propagate by division in spring.

Liriope (lilyturf)
L. muscari is a valuable plant for the woodland border, because it flowers late in the autumn when little else is around. It forms dense clumps of narrow, strap-like leaves and throws up spikes densely packed with tiny violet-blue flowers. The whole plant, in shade, does not get much more than 30cm (12in) high, but the flowers shine out against the dark-green leaves. There are several other species, but this is one of the best and the easiest to obtain. It can either be planted in drifts (for some reason that I cannot work out, this never appeals to me) or in isolated clumps.

Liriope will grow in most soils but – although I have mine in a dry soil – does best in a moist, leafy soil. It can be easily divided.

Lunaria (honesty)
These are wonderful plants for a woodland garden. The commonest, *L. annua*, is dealt with in chapter 8 (page 152), but we must consider *L. rediviva* a perennial relative. This is a medium-height plant (60cm (2ft) tall), with lavender-white to purple flowers that appear in the spring. I find it delightful; it has a certain freshness about it and, certainly, an enjoyable fragrance. It is particularly useful for lightening up a darkish spot. I like lunarias to seed gently around so that they appear dotted about the wilder part of the wood.

They grow in any reasonable soil and can be increased from seed sown in the spring.

Macleaya (plume poppy)
Plume poppies are very stately plants, and although they are more associated with the herbaceous border, I have seen them planted in some odd but very effective positions. From our point of view they can look very impressive between green shrubs, or even in a sudden thicket in a small clearing in the wood. One of the joys of the plants is the sun shining through their leaves, and to glimpse them as one approaches a clearing is a breathtaking sight.

They are tall plants, reaching 2m (7ft) or more, with grey stems and lobed leaves. The flowers are fluffy plumes of bronzy buff and usually held well above the viewer's head. They have a tendency to run like mad, so they are not plants for the small garden. Plant only in very light shade where they can catch some sun – preferably evening sun, in which they look superb. The species to look for are *M. microcarpa* and *M. cordata*, the latter having whiter flowers.

Plant in any good, fertile soil. Increase by division or cuttings.

Maianthemum

This is not a plant that is seen very commonly in gardens, but it is a native British woodlander and has a certain appeal if you have enough space to spare for it – not that it takes up much, but there may well be other plants that you would rather grow. *M. bifolium* (see also page 95) is related to the lily-of-the-valley, but at a superficial glance it seems to have more in common with enchanter's nightshade (*Circaea lutetiana*).

As its name indicates, it has two leaves and a small spike of dainty white flowers, followed by red fruit. It is only about 15cm (6in) high. This is a plant for an odd corner, where it can spread around making a green carpet of leaves much in the manner of its commoner relative.

Plant in a moist, woodland soil in light shade; it may well run into deeper shade by itself. It can easily be increased by division.

Meconopsis (blue poppy)

Meconopsis may be the reason why many people want to take up woodland gardening. When seen for the first time in a woodland setting, these blue poppies are literally breathtaking. Get the conditions right, and you stand a good chance of having them as well; get them wrong, and a lot of money is wasted. Having a good woodland garden has part of the battle won.

Most meconopsis come from the Himalayas and China, but there is one that is much nearer to home – the Welsh poppy (*M. cambrica*). Now this is not one that is difficult to grow; in fact, once you have it, you have it for ever. The only snag is that it is yellow (or orange) and not blue. However, it is a delightful plant, and it will grow into quite dense shade, illuminating it with flashes of gold and orange. A drift of mixed colour under trees is a wonderful sight. Welsh poppies like any soil, and can easily be started by scattering a handful of seed around.

The more difficult ones are the blue ones. The commonest and easiest for our purposes is *M. betonicifolia*, which grows to 120cm (4ft) high. It likes a dappled shade, but must have moist conditions. It is hopeless trying to grow it on a dry, sandy soil. It must have plenty of rich humus, and preferably a moist, buoyant air about it, such as created by a stream or pond. Lacking these, it is more than possible to grow it on a moist peat bed or its equivalent. Plant *M. betonicifolia* in drifts, either along a path or, better still, between green shrubs so that they appear to be growing in a green valley. They produce masses of seed, and if sown fresh and kept moist a large number of plants can be established.

There is quite a number of other species and hybrids in cultivation, but I would be inclined to start with *M. betonicifolia* and then move on when the right conditions have been achieved. (See also page 153.)

Melittis (bastard balm)

M. melissophyllum is another native British plant, although it also grows throughout Europe. It is of medium height (about 45cm (18in)), and has white-hooded flowers with a purple lower lip that appear in the summer. It is a fresh-looking plant that will grow happily in shade and will tolerate quite dry conditions – which makes it useful to many gardeners. It looks particularly good if backed by dark-green or evergreen foliage.

Plant in any soil – even, as indicated, quite dry ones – although it will obviously do better in more typical woodland soils. Increase by division in spring, or from seed.

Mentha (mint)

Mints are usually sun-lovers, but some, such as the native *M. aquatica*, grow in ditches, often overshadowed by hedges; and I have often seen mint growing alongside streams that run through light woodland or in damp patches where there is dappled shade. I would introduce it only in the larger woodland garden, where plants can be left to run wild; it is far too rampant for a small or more formal garden.

Plant in any moist, boggy soil. Increase by division, at any time of the year.

Mercurialis (dog's mercury)

M. perennis is a British native that is not worth considering unless you are creating a natural woodland. In the wild it grows in great drifts under trees, often in very dense shade where nothing else will grow. From this point of view it can be considered valuable, but from the visual standpoint it is a bit boring. It produces dark leaves which last for most of the year, and in late winter little green, petalless flowers in which the yellow stamens contribute the only bit of colour. The plant is about 25cm (10in) tall and spreads quite rapidly by underground stolons.

Mertensia (Virginian cowslip)

Most mertensias are light-lovers for which woodland conditions would be too dark, but the North American *M. virginica* appreciates a dappled woodland position in a rich leafmould soil. A peat bed is the ideal spot.

This is a lovely plant. The stems and leaves are a glaucous blue-green and the flowers are nodding tubes of brilliant blue. It deserves a choice position on a peat bed. It dies down in summer and should be marked to prevent anything being accidentally planted on top of it. A backdrop of ferns makes a pleasant scene.

This particular mertensia really needs a good moist, leafy soil, so it is no use trying to grow it in dry conditions. Propagate either by division, or from seed.

Myosotis (forget-me-not)

The usual garden forget-me-not is dealt with in chapter 8 (page 153), but here it should be mentioned that there are several perennial forget-me-nots of which one, *M. palustris*, the water forget-me-not, is eminently suitable for planting in damp spots, especially at the sides of streams or ponds. It grows well in the same places as mentioned for the water mint (*Mentha aquatica*); indeed, they often grow together, the little forget-me-not uncoiling its stems of bright blue flowers so that they shine out amongst the other vegetation.

Plant forget-me-nots in a moist, even boggy, soil. They can readily be increased by division in spring.

Omphalodes

This genus is related to the forget-me-nots and has very similar flowers. For the woodland garden the only interesting species are *O. cappadocica* and *O. verna*. The former is the larger (up to 23cm (9in) high) and stronger of the two, the latter being 15cm (6in) tall. These are pleasant, spreading plants whose green leaves set off the blue flowers to advantage. They create large mats which are useful at the edges of woods or beside paths.

Both like a leafy soil and will do well in a peat bed. They can be easily increased by division. (See also page 95.)

Ophiopogon (lilyturf)

Ophiopogons, almost entirely due to the black-leafed variety *O. planiscapus nigrescens*, have become fashionable plants. There is no denying that this *is* a beautiful plant, in the right position, and one that can be useful in most gardens. Ophiopogons have narrow, strap-like leaves and spikes of small whitish-pink flowers. They are usually about 20cm (8in) high, but can reach 30cm (12in) in lush conditions.

The marvellous black form mentioned has been used in a lot of arty associations in show gardens because it mixes well with a surprising number of colours. White is an obvious one – try growing snowdrops through it – but there are many more subtle ways of using the plant. Needless to say, it goes well with green, and a backing of ferns makes a nice contrast. I – unadventurously, perhaps – have it growing with its relative *O. japonicus*, which has green leaves and white flowers.

Plant out in a gritty leafmould soil in light dappled shade. Ophiopogons can easily be increased by splitting, in spring. (See also page 95.)

Ourisia

This is a genus of plants from the southern hemisphere that ought to be better known, as it contains some very good ones. The reason they are infrequently met with in ordinary gardens is that they are best treated as subjects for the peat garden. They are not all small and delicate, by any means. *O. macrophylla* grows to 30cm (12in) or more in height, and has large heads of white, almost primula-like, flowers. There is a good hybrid of this known as 'Snowflake' that is worth hunting out. The other species that is particularly beautiful is *O. coccinea*, from Chile. This has heads of flowers that are more like a hanging form of penstemon, in a rich scarlet. Most unknown garden plants have only sufficient attraction for the specialist, but this genus is truly a beautiful one and should be explored.

Ourisias will grow in full sun if the soil is moist enough, but they will also grow in light shade in drier conditions. Although they will take a dryish soil they are much better off in a gritty leafmould where they can spread at will. Propagate by division in spring.

Oxalis (wood sorrel)
O. acetosella has the appearance of a delicate plant. The dainty white flowers, veined with violet, appear over the low mat of fresh green, clover-like leaves, but beneath the surface are spreading rhizomes which make it, in fact, rather invasive. Still, it is well worth growing in a woodland garden. It has to take quite a lot of summer shade, as it appears above ground only in the spring when deciduous trees have yet to apply their coat of leaves. In this way it is able to colonise bare patches of ground where nothing else can grow. I think it is a very pretty flower, and have liked it since childhood. I enjoy seeing it growing up through the fallen leaves under trees or shrubs, sometimes in association with moss.

Wood sorrel will grow on most soils but prefers to be in leafmould. It can easily be increased by division. (See also page 95.)

Peltiphyllum (umbrella plant)
P. peltatum is a curious plant, for those who have got space for it. (It has undergone a name change in recent times – *Darmera peltata* – but I have left it under the name by which it is still generally known.) The leaves are quite conventional; they look like round rhubarb leaves (about 30cm (12in) or more across), with the leaf stalk (90–120cm (3–4ft) tall) in the centre. These appear after the flowers, which are carried in a small flat cluster at the top of a long, waving stalk. The nakedness of the tall stem and the nakedness of the ground (the leaves suppress any weeds) give the impression of some strange alien landscape. The flowers are pink, and look like small bergenia flowers. Once flowering is over, the leaves come up and create an impenetrable ground cover.

These fascinating plants grow only in moist areas, and do particularly well in boggy places that are liable to flood in the winter. Full sun or light shade are equally tolerated. They will eventually spread to cover a wide area, so do not try and plant in a small garden. The soil can be of any type as long as it is moist. Peltiphyllums can be propagated by dividing the rhizomes in late autumn after the foliage has died down, or in early spring.

Pentaglottis

This is a single-species genus consisting of *P. sempervirens*, which looks a bit like comfrey (*Symphytum*) but with bright blue flowers more akin to *Anchusa*, of which this used to be considered a member. It is a bit of an untidy thug, and in spite of its beautiful flowers should be introduced only in the wild part of a very large woodland garden, as it seeds itself about and is extremely difficult to get rid of.

You have been warned – but if you want to grow it, it will thrive in any soil in light shade. There is no need to propagate it, as it will do it for you.

Petasites

Yet another plant not to grow in a small garden (the latter half of the alphabet seems full of them). These have the advantage of flowering during the winter when there is little else around, and the further advantage of being highly scented. The species *P. japonicus* is one of the best known, as it has become naturalised in many places in Britain. It produces a club-shaped flower head about 15–20cm (6–8in) tall covered in white flowers, followed by huge leaves 120cm (4ft) wide. *P. hybridus*, the butterbur, is similar, except that the flowers are mauve. On a smaller scale is the winter heliotrope (*P. fragrans*), with slimmer flower heads and much smaller leaves. All three have naturalised, probably where they have been thrown out of gardens.

These plants do well in light shade and are not too fussy about the soil, although they prefer it moist. They spread vigorously under ground, forming huge colonies when they are happy; and should you wish to propagate them, they can be divided. (See also page 95.)

Phuopsis

This is really a sun-lover, but I have successfully grown it in light shade and it is worth doing so, as it makes its own contribution to the woodland flora. It is a low-growing plant, although it will climb up through or over others. It produces whorls of small fresh green leaves, and globular heads (about the size of a golf ball) of very pretty rose-pink flowers. I am extremely fond of it, and it does a lot to brighten up a woodland border in summer. The foliage has a kind of foxy smell, particularly when it is wet, which some people object to, but it has never worried me. The only member of the genus that is usually grown – and the one just described – is *P. stylosa*.

Phuopsis seems to be quite happy in most soils, but undoubtedly does better in those with more humus in them. Its stems root as they spread, forming new plants which can easily be detached for propagation purposes.

Polygonatum (Solomon's seal)

Cool and extremely elegant, Solomon's seal must be the epitome of woodland gardening. Nearly all the members of the genus are quite tall, with long, arching stems that have outstretched leaves, and dangling beneath them are pairs or small clusters of bell-shaped flowers. These are usually 2.5cm (1in) or less long, and coloured white with green tips. You have only to look at these plants to feel at peace with the world. They spread by underground roots and soon build up a colony. The taller ones (up to 90cm (3ft) or more) look particularly good in drifts, as you can see through and underneath them. They can be some way back from the edge of the wood or path, as they will take quite a degree of shade.

There is a fair number to choose from, and unless you want to really take them seriously and collect several, which you choose does not matter too much. The commonest, *P.* × *hybridum*, is still one of the best and certainly worth getting. It has both a double and a variegated form but, for me, these interfere with the simplicity of the plant.

Solomon's seal will tolerate a wide range of soils. I have had it for many years (I keep meaning to move it) in deep shade and very dry soil. It lingers on, but has not made a very big group. It would certainly be happier in a rich leafmould soil. You can propagate by division in spring.

Polygonum (knotweed)

This genus has gone through several revisions in recent years, and the various species have been moved from one genus to another at blinding speed. In keeping with current trends, I am sticking with the old names. Most of the plants that we are concerned with produce spikes of tightly packed pink or purple flowers. *P. affine* (now *Persicaria affinis*) is a very low-growing plant that makes a dense, colourful carpet of leaves with 23cm (9in) flower spikes. This is eminently suitable for a small garden, and is good for lining a path or border. *P. amplexicaule* (*Persicaria amplexicaulis*) is a much bigger plant (120cm (4ft) high), with large, floppy green leaves and much taller flowering stems, although both the flower spikes and the flowers themselves, which are usually red or deep pink, are about the same size. It also spreads, making a large clump rather than a carpet. *P. bistorta* (*Persicaria bistorta*) has large green leaves and short spikes of pale pink on tall stems. This makes an ideal waterside plant, but it does spread and really has no place in a small garden unless it is kept under control. There are many more, but the last I will mention is another plant that is, again, too vigorous for the small garden: *P. campanulatum* (*Persicaria campanulata*). This is around 90cm (3ft) tall, with a constant display of pink flowers in little round heads.

Polygonums will all grow in light shade, and except for the first mentioned can be planted further back, in the second rank. The last two do particularly well near a water feature. *P. bistorta* looks good pouring between green shrubs. They will all grow on a wide variety of soils, but do best in a moisture-retentive one. (See also page 96.)

Primula (cowslip, polyanthus, primrose)
This is a huge genus, with many garden-worthy plants. Several books have been written on them, so you see the daunting task that besets me in writing about them in just a few words. Most primulas like a moist soil and most, but not all, prefer a light shade. All the ones that we commonly come across in gardens will grow in shade, so there is no need to worry unduly about the others.

I think I must start with our native primrose (*P. vulgaris*). This is a superb plant, one that can never be bettered. Its lovely yellow flowers, set off against the fresh-green leaves, is one of the high points of the spring. Primroses will do well in our woodland garden, planted in light shade. If left to their own devices they will seed around, but you can give a helping hand by dividing them in autumn. Both procedures will ensure a large colony or drift that can look magnificent under hazel bushes, for example. I always like to see them on a bank, so if there is one in your wood try planting them there. Always plant at the top – then the seed will fall and fill up the rest of the bank.

The cowslip (*P. veris*) is another much loved native. It is more a plant of the open field, but the first I ever remember seeing as a child was in a hazel wood, miles from anywhere. I can remember going back to pay homage to it every year. This, of course, has nodding heads, smaller than the primrose. A combination of the two produces the common garden polyanthus. This is a very wood-worthy plant. The famous nut walk at Sissinghurst Castle was once totally underplanted with them. Another variation is the oxlip (*P. elatior*), that grows in Britain and throughout Europe.

Looking towards some of the bigger species, the tall *P. florindae* and *P. japonica*, along with many of the other candelabra primulas, will grow in light shade as long as it is moist. These really prefer to grow beside water and, indeed, look best in that position.

All primulas like to grow in a moist, leafy soil; they will grow in drier ones, but in times of drought they will turn up their toes. You can easily increase them by division in the autumn, or by sowing freshly harvested seed. Most, once established, will self-sow.

Pulmonaria (lungwort)
Yet another favourite genus. I would not like to be without these in the garden, as long as I had conditions to suit them. They form a low-growing mat (up to 25cm (10in) high, sometimes more) of bristly, dark-green leaves, overtopped with pink or blue – often both on the same plant – funnel-shaped flowers in late winter and early spring. Once the flowers are over, the leaves continue to make a good display. Many are either spotted or flushed with silver, adding to their interest. There are also red- and white-flowered forms.

P. longifolia and *P. angustifolia* both have narrowish leaves and very intense blue flowers. *P. saccharata* has long leaves that are usually heavily spotted. 'Margery Fish' is one of the best cultivars of this species, with good leaves and lovely pink and blue flowers. *P. rubra* has red flowers, with the cultivar 'Bowles Red' being one of the best. *P. officinalis* is one of the oldest in cultivation, and has forms of various colours, including 'Sissinghurst White', which is as pure a white as you could get.

Pulmonarias will grow in light to medium shade. They must not have too dry a soil, or their leaves will flag later in the season. They are not fussy, apart from moisture, as to what soil they grow in, but the best will be a good leafmould one. They can easily be propagated by division in spring. (See also page 96.)

Pyrola (wintergreen)
Pyrola is a small genus of perennial plants that, as their common name suggests, retain their leaves during the winter. These are complemented in the spring by fresh new leaves and spires of nodding, cup-shaped flowers in white, yellow or pink. *P. rotundifolia* is a British native and will do well in a woodland situation. It grows to about 30cm (12in) and has white flowers, delicately flushed with pink. There are several other species that are worth looking at by the devotee, but plants are not easy to obtain. Seed is the best way of getting them, and this is sometimes available from seed exchanges.

Pyrolas do need to have a good humusy root-run, so a typical leafsoil is the one to go for. As well as being grown from seed, they can be increased by division in spring.

Ramonda
Ramondas are usually grown by alpine gardeners, but the woodland gardener should also attempt them as, given the right conditions, they are not difficult and they are such beautiful plants. They can be grown on the peat bed and do especially well if planted on their sides in the peat block or in gaps in the log walls.

They make rosettes of leaves close to the ground, from which extend stems with heads of lavender-pink flowers. The commonest, *R. myconi*, is the one that I would recommend any woodland gardener to try. It will grow in light shade, but must have a gritty leafmould soil. You can increase it from leaf cuttings.

Ranunculus (buttercup)
This is a large genus of which a few serve our purpose. *R. auricomus*, goldilocks, is a British native that grows in woodlands, often in quite deep shade. It is a rather lax plant with many narrow stem leaves as well as more typical buttercup foliage growing from the base. The flower is also typical of the buttercups: a shallow saucer of gold, not as large as those of the garden weeds, and liable to lose its petals, so it often looks ragged.

If you want to have a wild woodland garden, then introduce the ordinary creeping buttercup (*R. repens*) to the lighter areas, but on no account let it into a small or formal garden – otherwise, you will rue the day. There is also a double form, *R.r. pleniflorus*, but this is just as badly behaved. The common lesser celandine (*R. ficaria*), of course, belongs to this genus; it definitely has its place in a woodland garden, especially along the paths, where it can catch sunshine through the bare winter branches. The native one has a wonderful golden colour and takes a lot of beating, but there is also a number of cultivars that have orange or near-white petals, are double, or have coloured leaves. All are worth growing. They can be planted in very deep shade as long as this is deciduous, as they are above ground only during the winter and early spring.

Ranunculus are happy in any soil, and can easily be propagated by division.

Ranzania
A single-species genus from Japan that makes an ideal woodland plant. *R. japonica* grows to about 45cm (18in), and consists of nodding pale-mauve flowers (appearing in early summer) held above fresh-green leaves. It looks good against a background of dark ferns and does well in a rich humusy soil, as it likes moist woodland conditions. Propagate from divisions taken in spring.

Rodgersia
This is an important genus in any ornamental garden, but especially a woodland one. Rodgersias are worth growing both for their decorative leaves and for their flowers. They are 90–120cm (3–4ft) in height, and their large, bold leaves make them imposing plants. They do well in any position of light shade, but they are another of those plants that I like to see erupting from between green-leaved shrubs. Being tall, they can be used as a background for other perennials. The leaves are often tinged with bronze; the flowers are spikes of fluffy cream or pink that are extremely effective in a dull corner or against a dark background.

R. aesculifolia has very distinct leaves, much in the shape of horse-chestnut leaves, after which the plant is named. The flowers are creamy white, sometimes tinged with pink. *R. podophylla* is another good species. This has leaves that are more lobed and its flowers are also creamy white. *R. pinnata* has pinnate leaves and pinkish flowers.

They all must have a moist, leafy soil and a light shade, and can be increased by division in spring. (See also page 96.)

Sanguinaria (bloodroot)

S. canadensis is a wonderful plant, and most gardeners fall in love with it on sight. The form usually seen is not the species but the variety 'Plena', which has a double white flower made up of many narrow petals in a sphere a bit bigger than a golf ball. This is held in a natural posy by one of the grey leaves that circles around it. The species is a simpler affair, and although I love the double, I think the single has a pure elegance that rivals it. This is also white, but sometimes flushed with pink.

Sanguinarias spread around beneath ground with roots that, if cut, produce a red sap – hence their common name. They like a gritty, peaty soil and therefore do very well in a peat bed where care can be taken that they are not swamped by other plants, as they only grow a few inches tall. You can easily propagate them by division in spring.

Sanicula (sanicle)

Sanicle is not a particularly spectacular plant – in fact, it is quite dull – but it is a British native that can be introduced to a woodland garden, where it will do a pleasant turn. It is an umbellifer related to cow parsley; though much shorter, at about 23cm (9in), it has the same type of white flowers. Where the plant scores is that it will grow in quite dense shade where few others will.

Plant in a moist soil, because it will not tolerate a dry one. It does not mind chalk, as long as it has a good layer of moister soil on top of it. It can be increased from seed sown fresh.

Saxifraga (saxifrage)

This is a big genus that is mainly devoted to small cushion plants much beloved by alpine gardeners. Many of these appreciate shade, but a more refined shade than we are able to offer in a woodland garden. Having said that, I must add that I have grown *S.* 'Bob Hawkins' for many years in a shade bed under a quince tree. But then, this is one of the mossy saxifrages, and these generally prefer a bit of light shade. They form fresh green mats of leaves with a mass of white, pink or red flowers floating just above them, no more than 5–7.5cm (2–3in) high. They are quite tough, but generally too delicate to be let loose in a general woodland garden; they are much better off in the more refined atmosphere of the peat bed.

However, the saxifrages that are more commonly grown in a woodland garden are the larger ones such as *S. fortunei*. These have shiny round leaves and graceful, arching stems of dainty white flowers which appear in late autumn. A plant that used to be more popular than it is now is London pride (*S.* × *urbium*). It has evergreen rounded leaves and flights of airy pale-pink and white flowers that lighten up a dark patch in summer. One of its parents, *S. umbrosa*, has a similar habit.

All three are stoloniferous, putting out runners on which new plants grow, much in the manner of strawberries. You can easily take these off for propagation purposes. They will all grow in light shade, as long as they have a gritty, moisture-retentive soil. Being low-growing, saxifrages can be smothered in falling leaves, so be certain to remove them.

Shortia

These are choice plants for the peat bed. *S. uniflora* is probably the most beautiful of this small genus. The leaves are a shining evergreen, often with tinges of red at the margins. The flowers, which are quite large and a delicate shade of pink, appear above them in the spring, on long stems up to 15cm (6in) tall. The species *S. soldanelloides* carries many flowers per stem – nodding bells that have cut petals so that they appear deeply fringed. The leaves are toothed, and vary in their colouring.

This is not an easy genus to grow, but one worth persevering with. Shortias like a gritty, moisture-retentive soil such as would be found on a peat bed, and it must be remembered that they dislike lime. They need to have light shade. Propagation is by division, but it is not at all easy and many losses may result before success is scored.

Silene (campion)

S. dioica, red campion, is a common British inhabitant of woodland margins and hedgerows. It is a beautiful plant, growing up to 90cm (3ft), with flowers of varying pink that shine out of the shade. They look particularly good when growing with bluebells. They will not tolerate deep shade, but along a path or at the edge of a glade will suit them well.

Campions are not at all fussy as to soil. You can easily raise them from seed, either sowing them in pots or simply scattering where you want the plants to grow.

Smilacina (false spikenard)

This is a genus that is very closely related to the Solomon's seals (*Polygonatum*). Smilacinas have the same general appearance as their relatives, but the stems are more upright and the flowers appear in fluffy spikes at the ends of the stems instead of along their length. The flowers are a creamy white, eventually turning to a dirty brown, and have a lovely fragrance. They are at their best in late spring and early summer. *S. racemosa*, which grows up to 90cm (3ft), is the species normally seen. *S. stellata* is a similar plant but on a smaller scale; unfortunately, it has not quite got the beauty of its larger relative.

Smilacinas are natural woodlanders and so will tolerate quite a bit of shade. They are rhizomatous, and will therefore slowly spread underground to form colonies. The large fluffy heads make them superb plants for lightening a dark corner, especially against a dark evergreen. They need a moist soil, preferably lime-free. When suited, they will creep about, making it easy to propagate simply by dividing.

Solidago (golden rod)

This may seem an odd genus to include in this book, as solidago are usually associated with sunny borders, but if you take a stroll through many of our sandier woodlands in late summer or early autumn you will see short (up to 60cm (2ft)) but pretty golden rods scattered throughout them. This is the British native, *S. virgaurea*. It is an attractive little plant in a woodland setting, but take it into the ornamental borders and its big brothers will outshine it. The tall plants normally associated with gardens can also occasionally be seen in woods, where they have been dumped by gardeners after tidying up their gardens. These will grow in similar conditions, but for me it is the small one that seems most at home in our context.

The plant is very upright, with light-green leaves and spires of small golden-yellow daisies. As far as I can recall, I have never seen it in drifts but as individual plants scattered around the lighter spots, especially on banks and other dry areas. Follow the same principle when planting.

Golden rods will accept any soil, but are valuable in that they will grow in dry soils that few plants will tolerate. Most solidago can be easily divided in spring, but as it is a species and not a cultivar, *S. virgaurea* can also be grown from seed.

Stylophorum (celandine poppy)

S. diphyllum is a plant that flowers in the early summer. It has a yellow poppy-like flower and greyish-green foliage. The whole plant, which grows to about 45cm (18in), is a bit like the British native *Chelidonium majus*, the greater celandine. By no means could you call *S. diphyllum* spectacular, but it is useful for light shade. The other species that is occasionally seen is *S. lasiocarpum*, which is similar in appearance. They can both get a bit scruffy by the end of the summer, and should be cut down if they are in any sort of formal position. They look good when planted with ferns, which offer the advantage of covering them when they are cut back.

Plant in a moisture-retentive soil, in a light or dappled shade.

Symphytum (comfrey)

One can have a love–hate relationship with this genus. The plants are coarse-leafed, with unwinding spirals of blue, red or cream tubular flowers. They are attractive enough when they are in flower in spring or early summer and the leaves make good ground cover throughout the season (see page 97), but they do spread, and should you decide to move them, every little bit of root left in the ground produces new plants, so they can become a pest. My favourites are *S. caucasicum*, which has pure-blue flowers, and *S.* 'Rubrum', which has rich red flowers offset by fresh-looking green leaves. There are several variegated forms that brighten up dark spots and have their uses, especially when mixed in with green plants.

This is certainly a candidate for the larger garden, but think carefully before introducing it to the smaller one. Control can be helped by shearing over after flowering, which will prevent it from seeding. The leaves will soon regenerate and will be fresher-looking. Any soil will suit comfrey, but the richer the better. You can propagate it easily, by simple division.

Tellima

A genus of but a single species, *T. grandiflora*. It is very similar in appearance to heuchera. It has pale-green, rounded but lobed leaves, above which rise arching stems carrying tiny green bell-shaped flowers, which appear in late spring. The whole plant is about 30cm (12in) high. Tellimas have a coolness about them that makes them ideal for planting in a woodland setting. They will do well in light or dappled shade, contrasting in colour with the darker greens, or in shape with variegated hostas.

Tellimas will grow in any good garden soil and can be propagated by division in early spring. (See also page 97.)

Thalictrum (meadow-rue)

This is a genus that is normally associated with the open border, but most species can be grown to advantage in a light shade, often between bushes, where their frothy heads can appear like a cloud of coloured steam. The heavier ones, such as *T. flavum* and its variety *T.f. glaucum* or *T. aquilegifolium*, look good planted in solid drifts in between shrubs, but the more delicate, airy ones such as *T. delavayi* (formerly *T. dipterocarpum*) look best peering over the top of other perennial plants or shrubs. The flowers are either cream or light purple, and it is the stamens, which add to their light frothy nature, that are their most prominent feature. *T. minus* has insignificant flowers, but a delicate foliage which makes a good contrast to bold hostas. This plant will run, quickly making a large colony.

Meadow-rue will tolerate only a little light or partial shade. The soil must be moist, or it will soon show signs of stress. It can be grown from seed or from divisions.

Tiarella (foam-flower)
Tiarella is a woodland genus from North America. The plants have a delicate quality about them but some, when suited, are rampant spreaders. Not that this matters, as they are delightful. *T. cordifolia* is the one generally seen. It has lobed, heart-shaped leaves that are soft in texture, overtopped by spires of airy white flowers on stems reaching up to about 30cm (12in) high. A drift looks wonderful, especially when it either tails off into the distance or is edged with something more solid. Tiarellas spread rapidly by runners, to form large colonies. In recent times *T. wherryi* has become more widespread in gardens. I like this plant, as it is even more refined, with graceful pinkish-white flowers. It is a clump-former, and has to be helped to form colonies by being split up.

These plants must be grown in a cool leafmould soil. You can easily increase them by division. (See also page 97.)

Tolmiea (pick-a-back plant)
T. menziesii is the only species in this genus. In many respects it resembles *Tellima* (page 143). It forms carpets of hairy, ivy-shaped leaves and carries spires of green, bell-shaped flowers. The species is not particularly attractive, but it makes good ground cover (see page 97). It has been somewhat superseded by a form that has leaves splashed with gold (*T.m.* 'Taff's Gold'). This is very good for brightening a gloomy area, or for contrasting with darker-leaved plants. The common name comes from its habit of forming young plants in the axils of the leaves.

Plant out tolmieas in a moist, humus-rich soil; they dwindle in drier soils. You can propagate them by detaching the young plantlets.

Tricyrtis (toad lilies)
To many woodland gardeners these are the glory of the autumn scene. They do not make an impact from a distance; it is only when you look at the strange shape and distinct colouring of the flowers that they become attractive.

The general shape of the plant is a vertical stem rising to about 90cm (3ft), clustered on top of which, in autumn, are flowers that are very difficult to describe. They consist of six narrow petals, heavily spotted all over, splayed outwards with the stigmas exploding from the centre. One of the most frequently seen in gardens is *T. formosana*, which is pinkish-purple with dark purple spots. As do many of the others in the genus, this spreads under ground by stolons and is sometimes referred to as *T. stolonifera*. *T. latifolia* is a bright yellow with brown spots. There are many others to explore, all of which like the same dappled woodland conditions. They look good in swaying drifts, but do put them near the edge of your wood or along a path so that they can be seen.

Plant toad lilies in a humus-rich soil, as they dislike drying out. Propagation is easily achieved by division in spring.

Uvularia (bellwort)

Uvularias are not plants to set the world on fire, but they have a certain cool quality that appeals to me. They are closely related to the Solomon's seals and have captured some of their elegance.

The tallest (*U. grandiflora*) grows only to about 60cm (2ft), and consists of a slender, arching stem with pale-green leaves and loose, hanging yellow flowers that always remind me of strips of yellow rag. There is not a great deal of difference between the various species, and the one already mentioned is probably the best to start with. It does have a form called *U.g.* 'Pallida', which has paler yellow flowers. Uvularias are woodlanders, and seem completely at home in such a situation. They run underground and will soon make a small colony. I like to see a clump quite close to a path, so that they can be easily seen and enjoyed.

This genus is another that must be planted in a good humusy soil, and would do well in the second rank of a peat garden where the plants would give a bit of height. They can easily be increased by division in the spring.

Vancouveria

This is a genus that is very similar to the epimediums, already described (pages 91, 117). They are running plants that soon form a dense colony, making them ideal as ground cover (see page 97). Besides this utilitarian quality, they have their own intrinsic attraction. The leaves are small and often of irregular shape, and basically green but often flushed with bronze. They are quite leathery and tough, lasting throughout the year until they are replaced by new ones in spring. Above the leaves wave airy stems of small white or yellow flowers that appear very dainty and graceful. The whole plant is no more than 30cm (12in) or so in height.

These marvellous ground-cover plants can be used as such anywhere in the wood. I would be inclined not to plant them in a peat bed, as they can take over. Although the flowers are pretty, it is for their long-lasting leaves that they are generally grown. The commonest species is *V. hexandra*, which is one of the tallest and has white flowers and small, roundish leaves. A more recent introduction is *V. chrysantha*, which has more oval-shaped leaves and sprays of yellow flowers.

Vancouverias will all grow in any soil, being most vigorous in a leafy mixture but still doing quite well in dry conditions. They can all be easily increased by division.

Veratrum

Veratrums are superb plants, both when only in leaf and when in flower. The leaves are large and heavily pleated, forming a clump a bit like a turban. They have a nice freshness about them which is spoilt only by the voracious appetite of slugs, which seem to adore them. It is a good thing that the foliage is so attractive, as it can take seven or more years between germination and flowering. But the flowers are worth waiting for. They throw up statuesque spires, with outstretched branches each covered in small flowers.

V. nigrum is my favourite, with its very deep, almost black, flowers that appear in summer on the 180cm (6ft) stems. *V. album*, on the other hand, has greenish-white flowers and blooms a bit later. *V. viride* is shorter, and has a denser spike with green flowers. They are all worth growing, either as specimen plants or, better still, in drifts if you can propagate enough. They will be quite happy in a light shade, but they must have a humusy soil that does not completely dry out. Being such a dark colour, *V. nigrum* should be planted in a lighter spot, or the flowers will not be seen. It looks best if the evening sun can shine through it, when it will glow. Since the other two are much lighter in colour, they allow you more freedom in their positioning.

Plant in a rich, moisture-retentive soil. Propagation is usually by division, but they can also be grown from seed if you have the patience.

Viola (viola, violet, pansy)

I love all of this genus and have quite a number of species dotted around the garden. While a few are sun-lovers, the majority do best in moist woodland conditions. Some, such as *V. pensylvanica* and *V. glabella*, have tiny yellow flowers that sparkle out of the woodland floor. Others, such as the sweet violet (*V. odorata*), are valuable not only for the rich blues of the flowers, but for the scent that goes with them. There are some that make ideal companions for low shrubs, as they enjoy clambering through them. *V. elatior* will do this, as will the larger *V. cornuta*. The latter comes in a range of violet-blues, mauves and white, the last mentioned being especially impressive when climbing through shrubs or other vegetation that has dark leaves. *Viola* is an extremely large genus, and anyone with a woodland garden can easily build up an interesting collection without using up too much space.

Although they do not like direct sun, most do not like too much shade, either, so plant them on the very edge of the wood; but take care that they do not have too much competition from more vigorous neighbours. The ideal position may well be in a peat bed, where they can be more easily cared for.

Most do not like being dried out, and will die if they do not have a moistish soil. The usual leafmould mix will be ideal. For species, division is in the main from seed, but those with fleshy stems can be easily rooted from cuttings taken from non-flowering shoots. (See also page 154.)

8 Annual and Biennial Plants

As we have already seen, woodland conditions are not entirely conducive to seed production, and so most plants that grow in this kind of environment have developed other, vegetative, methods of reproduction. Thus we find that many of them creep or run around, with underground or above-ground stems forming new plants as they go. Even those that do produce seed may have difficulty, through lack of light and moisture, in their germination. Plants such as foxgloves (*D. purpurea*) rely to a great extent on seed lying dormant until the right conditions are met with, usually when trees accidentally fall or are felled, thereby providing the necessary light.

Since depending solely on seed, as do annuals, for reproduction in woodland conditions is not a good method for securing future generations, most woodland plants have developed as perennials, with alternative means of reproduction. This means that, for our purposes, the number of annuals we can grow is somewhat limited.

There are two types of annuals: those that happily self-sow about and, once sown, become almost honorary perennials in that they appear year after year without any attention being paid to them; and those that are used as bedding plants. These are generally much brasher in colour and general appearance, and need not only to be raised but also to be coddled a bit. While the former fit well into a woodland garden, the latter usually look decidedly out of place, and will probably involve you in more work than you are prepared to spend on them. A few of the self-sowing kind can be included in the woodland garden. On the whole, they will grow only in very light shade, preferably where the sun occasionally bursts through. I list a few below, and it is quite likely that you will be able to add more.

In some cases the plants may produce different colour forms: for example, *Digitalis purpurea* may be purple or white. If you decide that you want one particular colour – say, white – to dominate, then rogue out all the purple ones before they seed. In this way, after a few years nearly all the seedlings will be white.

Do not be over-anxious to clear up plants that have finished flowering, as some may take some time for the seed to ripen and fall to the ground. It is all too easy to forget and tidy up, only to wonder why there are no plants the following year.

Adlumia (climbing fumitory)
This is a genus of only one species: namely, *A. fungosa*. It is a hardy biennial from North America that will climb up through other plants to a height of about 3m (10ft). The flowers are small white or purplish tubes a bit in the manner of fumitory or corydalis. They are carried in clusters throughout the summer. The delicate leaves are pale green and deeply divided, adding to the attraction of this plant.

Adlumias can be grown up through any shrub, but it is pointless growing them where they will be above the viewer's head, so shrubs on the margins of the wood or in a clearing would be the best site.

They will grow in most soils. They are hardy and will withstand the first winter, flowering in the second year. The seed should be sown fresh or in spring, where you want the plants to grow. It is not easy to come by, but seed exchanges occasionally supply it. Once you have acquired the plant, save your own seed.

Antirrhinum (snapdragon)
Having put down bedding plants, I immediately include one. Antirrhinums have been part of the garden for so long, especially in the informality of the cottage garden, that they rate consideration beyond their role of bedding plants. In fact, in many gardens they are never used as such. I cannot remember the last time I actually planted an antirrhinum, and yet I have them dotted around the garden every year, where they have self-sown. They are usually treated as annuals, in spite of being short-lived perennials that can be left to grow another year – although they generally do not do as well the second time around. Normally plants of the sunny border, they will nevertheless tolerate a little light shade. There is a classic planting at Sissinghurst Castle, of white antirrhinums growing under a magnolia tree, the white lifting the shade.

There is a large number of varieties in seed-merchants' catalogues to choose from, but I would go for the simple colours on full-sized plants. Leave the fancy ones for the bedding borders. When they start self-sowing they will come up with all kinds of colours, often biased to red, but white is not unusual. Rogue out any colours you do not want, and the strain is likely to come true.

Antirrhinums will grow in any good soil. Sowing can be directly where you want them to grow, or they can be raised in pots and planted out. Sow seed in autumn or in spring.

Asperula (woodruff)

We have already met some closely related plants, the *Galium*, which are perennials. There is quite a number of plants in the *Asperula* genus, but they are nearly all sun-lovers. However, there is one annual, *A. setosa azurea*, that will grow in the shade. It is similar to galium, except that the flowers are a pale blue. Fortunately, it is not too formal, and can be used in our context along paths at the front of the wood, possibly sprawling in a carpet under a tree or shrub.

It is not fussy as to soil, as long as it is reasonably moist. The seed can be scattered where you wish it to grow.

Calceolaria (slipper flower)

This is a large genus of plants that are mainly tender and need a lot of care. However, *C. mexicana* is one that will not only tolerate shade but can be sown directly into the ground. It has pale-yellow, typical calceolaria flowers which appear throughout the summer and autumn. The plant reaches up to 30cm (12in) high and has divided leaves.

Calceolarias are a bit alien-looking for a woodland garden, but with careful siting they can add to its attraction at the latter end of the year. Be careful not to line them out like bedding plants! They are probably best grown in a gritty but humus-rich soil. Sow seed under glass in spring, or in the open in late spring. (Seed is not too difficult to acquire.)

Collinsia (blue lips, innocence)

This is a genus of hardy annuals from North America. Fortunately, they fall into our category of self-sowers, so once you have grown your first batch, with luck they will always be with you. They are pretty flowers with white or pink upper petals and tube, and a lower lip of a darker colour. The main species that is available at the moment is *C. bicolor* (sometimes called *C. heterophylla*). This has upper petals that are white and a pinkish-purple lower one.

Collinsias are mainly sun-lovers, but will tolerate light shade. They are best used in between decorative shrubs rather than placed in isolation under trees. They will grow in any gritty but moist soil. Initially, sow seed in pots, or broadcast it where the plants are to grow. Once established, they should self-sow.

Corydalis

Detailed consideration has already been given to this genus, as the majority are perennials (see page 114), but there is one annual, *C. sempervirens*, that I would like to mention. This is a delightfully airy plant that grows up to 30cm (12in) tall, with small flowers of an unusual combination of pink and yellow. It will tolerate light shade, and should be planted on the woodland's margins where it can be seen. Like many others in this chapter, it will seed itself around happily and not make a nuisance of itself. Scatter some seed on a peat bed and just let it get on with it.

Digitalis (foxglove)
The common foxglove (*D. purpurea*) is the main biennial that one finds naturally under trees. In the countryside, foxgloves will be seen on the margins of woods, or in clearings where trees have been felled by woodmen or have fallen through natural causes. The sudden appearance of light is enough to trigger germination, with the result that a whole forest of waving foxgloves suddenly appears. In woodland gardens the same positions should be used. Once the foxgloves have become established, they will sow themselves around the spots that they prefer, so that they will soon have a natural look about them.

The tall spires of tubular purple flowers are very familiar to most gardeners, and need little description. It is possible to produce populations of pure-white flowers by roguing out all the purple ones (or vice versa, if you dislike the white). They can be distinguished before they flower by the tendency for the white-flowered plants to have green leaf stems, while the purple have purple-streaked ones.

Seed from the wild plants is the best to use; each plant produces millions of seeds, so taking a few seed capsules will make no difference to the wild populations. Seed purchased from seed-merchants is usually of an 'improved' strain, and will look better in an ornamental border.

Foxgloves seem to prefer acid and neutral soils, although they can often be seen growing in pockets of organic material overlying chalk. They will often tolerate quite dry soil. For the initial sowing, just scatter the seed where you want the plants to appear. Subsequently, they are sure to sow themselves in their own favoured positions. (See also page 116.)

Impatiens (touch-me-not)
Even as a mature (I hope) adult, I still cannot resist squeezing the seed pods of *Impatiens noli-tangere* as I walk along a damp country lane, just to feel the pressure of the spring as the pod tries to release its seeds. As it wriggles to get free, the plant feels alive. This is a British native, and with its fresh green leaves and small golden flowers it would be worth adding to your collection of plants if you have a very large garden, but in a small one it could become a nuisance – although not a rampant one.

It is its taller and more vigorous relative, *I. glandulifera*, that is usually seen as a garden plant. This is sometimes referred to as 'policeman's helmet' because of the shape of the pink flower. Growing to up to 180cm (6ft) when it is happy, it originates in the Himalayas; but it has escaped from our gardens and gone rampaging along Britain's rivers, and few banks are free from groves of its tall stems and pink to purple flowers. It is not a plant that is difficult to cope with, and can be controlled in a garden. It looks especially good flowing between tall bushes or in large stands beside a stream or pond. It is a plant only for the larger garden.

In spite of usually being grown in sun, the 'busy Lizzie' type of impatiens that is seen as an indoor plant and increasingly as a bedding plant for containers grows very well in light shade. The luminous flowers lighten up a dark corner especially well, but they do look a bit out of place in the wilder woodland garden.

Impatiens will grow on a variety of soils, but seems to do best in moist ones, especially beside water. Plants can be raised by sowing in pots and then planting out, or by scattering the seed where you want it to grow. Once it is in the right spot, it will continue to self-sow.

Limnanthes (poached-egg flower)
Most will consider this a plant for full sun, but I have grown it for a number of years in a shady position. Its common name is very descriptive of its bright yellow centre surrounded by white. In some ways it might be considered brash, but I love it, and in a shady position I feel it really comes into its own, shining out into the light. I would be happy to see it in odd patches along a path where it could get some light. Growing it with Bowles' golden grass, *Milium effusum* 'Aureum' (page 172), might be good fun. It is a low plant, growing only a few inches, although it is taller in the shade. It vigorously sows itself around and so may need thinning to get the best from each plant.

Limnanthes will grow in any soil. Seed can be sown in pots, or where the plants are to flower; they will self-sow after that, as long as they are happy.

Lunaria (honesty, moonwort)
We have already considered the perennial honesty, *L. rediviva*, in the previous chapter (page 130), but now it is time to look at its more popular relative, *L. annua*. In spite of its Latin name it is, in fact, a biennial. A hummock of coarse leaves is produced in the first year, and during the spring of the second a tall spike bearing bright purple flowers. I always love the freshness that lunarias seem to impart at this time of year. I have them growing in quite dense shade on the edge of a wood, out of which they seem to glow. When the flowers are over they form large flat elliptical seed pods, which, if the outer casings are carefully stripped off, leave a pearly interior. Stems of these casings are much valued in dried decorations. Although one does not often see them used in this way, the flowers, which are sweetly scented, can also be used for cutting.

Even in a small garden, *Liriope muscari* is always worth growing for its autumn flowers.

The curious *Lysichyton americanum* growing in a damper part of a woodland garden.

A good ground-cover plant for the edge of a wood, *Persicaria bistorta* has thick foliage and long-lasting pink flowers.

Polypodium australe 'Wilharris' is a well-behaved, low-growing fern that contrasts well with other plants.

Pleiobastus auricomus, a good, low-growing bamboo, will lighten up any gloomy spot.

Pulmonarias are some of the most colourful woodland plants for the late winter and spring. This is *Pulmonaria saccharata*.

A swathe of colourful *Primula japonica* in a damp spot in a woodland garden.

Rosa rugosa will grow happily on woodland margins and has the benefit of large, coloured hips in the autumn.

Sanguinaria canadensis 'Plena', a sensational plant for light woodland with a leafy soil.

Trillium sessile (now correctly *T. kurabayashii*) has wonderful red flowers and will grow in any good woodland soil.

Not all violets are violet. *V. pensylvanica* has tiny yellow flowers that sparkle up from the woodland floor.

As well as the species, there are several cultivars that can be grown. For a start, there is one with white flowers. There is also one with variegated white and purple flowers, and one that has the normal purple flowers but with variegated leaves. I must confess I prefer the straight species, although in recent times I have grown the variegated-leafed form and, again, this has looked good against a dark background.

Lunarias will grow in any soil, even dryish ones. The initial planting can be from plants grown in pots, or from seed scattered where they are to grow. Leave some stems standing until they have shed their seed, and you will have a succession of plants every year.

Meconopsis (blue poppy)

This genus has already been looked at in detail in the previous chapter (page 131). It is an odd one, because many of its species behave on some occasions as if they are monocarpic – that is, dying after flowering and seeding, and possibly taking several years to complete the cycle so that they are not necessarily annual or biennial – while on other occasions they behave like perennials. This is not the book to look into this phenomenon, but I include it here as a reminder that plants such as *M. horridula*, one of the most beautiful of the blue poppies, should be treated as an annual and fresh seed sown each year. *MM. latifolia* and *napaulensis*, similarly, die after flowering.

Grow all of these in a rich humusy soil, preferably in a peat bed. Sow them from freshly collected seed – seed from seed-merchants often has poor germination rates, and results can be disappointing.

Myosotis (forget-me-not)

Although usually considered sun-lovers, most forget-me-nots will also grow in a degree of shade. They will get more leggy, but this is often compensated for by their climbing up through low shrubs, which allows their wonderful blue flowers to peer out in unexpected places. For those who want to grow things in the shade of their roses, forget-me-nots are rather a cliché, but still effective for all that.

Forget-me-nots will thrive on any soil, and will come readily from seed. Once the first plants have been introduced, they will go on seeding themselves everywhere (but they are easy to remove if you want to). (See also page 133.)

Nicotiana (tobacco plant)

These are not plants that one would normally associate with a woodland garden, and I am not certain that I want to anyway. One that I do grow amongst shrubs – it accidentally (or deliberately) sowed itself there, and I have let it continue doing so – is *N. sylvestris*. The tall (150cm (5ft)) light-green plant has heads of large, white, sweetly scented tubular flowers that show up brilliantly at night. It is wonderful amongst dark shrubs, and is particularly valuable as it flowers late in the year. Several of the others can also be used in shade, but they seem too much like bedding plants to me. At Savill Gardens they have the 'Domino' strain growing in a perfect, even bed right up to the trunk of a large cherry tree; there are very few bedding plants that you can do that with, so I suppose they have some merits if you like that kind of thing.

Nicotianas can be grown in moist soils without much trouble. They can be sown in pots in early spring, and many of the species will self-sow.

Tropaeolum (nasturtium)
Not really a plant for the woodland garden, but in a large garden it might be fun to plant one or two and let them ramp over some bushes that are dull later in the season. The commonest is *T. majus*, but this has several variations, so you are not restricted to the bright colours if you want something a bit more subtle. As well as the flame oranges there are soft apricots, for example. There are also some with foliage splashed with golden variegations, and these do well in the more gloomy spots. As an alternative, there is the small-flowered canary creeper (*T. peregrinum*). The perennial *T. speciosum* makes a very good plant for growing in a light shade over shrubs such as low rhododendrons.

Viola (pansy)
Most of the violas have already been dealt with in chapter 7 (page 147), as they are perennials. Pansies, although they are also perennials, are often treated as annuals. On the whole they are too large-flowered and look too 'cultivated' for our purposes, but they will grow in the shade and may be useful in certain circumstances. They will become very lax, and it is a good thing to grow them through other vegetation such as at the edge of a low bush. Some of the single-coloured varieties may look good in this position, especially if they are winter-flowering forms.

It is hopeless trying to grow pansies in a dry soil. In the winter this should not be such a problem, but for summer flowering make certain that the soil is moisture-retentive. Sow the seed in autumn or spring, and grow the plants on in pots or trays.

9 Bulbous Plants

Bulbs are generally thought of as sun-loving plants, but there are a few that are quite happy in light shade. Many of them finish their flowering cycle in spring, before the leaves have developed on the trees. There are exceptions to this, cyclamen being the most obvious. Some bulbs are slow to increase but most will sow themselves happily, building up large colonies – bluebells (*Hyacinthoides non-scripta*) are a good example.

Start by planting the bulbs in light shade, and let them find their own way into darker positions if they will tolerate them. They will associate with a wide range of plantings. The classic way of using bulbs is to allow them to grow up through other plants, which will take over when the bulbs die back. This is still sensible advice in a small garden, but in a larger one there may be enough space to allocate an area to each.

Below is a selection of the best plants for shady areas.

Allium (onion)

Most onions are bulbs of open areas, but there are a few that will grow in the shade – indeed, they will revel in it. The most obvious are ramsons (*A. ursinum*), which grow in vast sheets in damp hazel and ash woodlands. When satisfied, they can be really rampant, and should only be planted where there is space and where their very strong garlic smell can be tolerated. The flowers are balls of white stars set off against fresh green leaves; there is no doubt that *A. ursinum* is an attractive plant. Another with tendencies to spread like mad is *A. triquetrum*. This is not so attractive, and it also retains a strong onion smell when crushed. The leaves are much narrower, and triangular in section. The drooping flowers are again white, but with a green stripe down the middle of each petal, and the heads are much smaller. This will also colonise shade, although it seems to prefer a lighter one than ramsons. A short yellow-flowered species, *A. moly*, will also tolerate a little shade. All those mentioned so far are spring flowering, but for flowering in late summer *A. amabile*, with rose-pink flowers, can be planted.

All of these alliums can be grown under or between shrubs. The whites are useful for illuminating darker corners. As the first two die back after flowering they can be associated with other plants that take over later – ferns, for example. The first two species prefer a moist soil, while the last two must have a grittier mixture. They all produce plenty of offsets as well as seed, so propagation is no problem at all. (See also page 89.)

Bletilla

B. striata is one of the several orchids that can be grown in woodland gardens. It has loose heads of pinkish-purple flowers held above green, strap-like leaves. It will grow quite happily in shade, but it must have a rich, moist soil. I find that a peat bed with extra manure added to it is perfect. The plant will clump up, and can be divided in early spring if you want to propagate.

Cardiocrinum

This is a genus that requires to be grown in partial or light shade. Its species are unlike any other bulbs that will be mentioned, in that they grow to 2.4m (8ft) or more. They are closely related to the lilies, and until recently were considered to be lily species.

The main one in cultivation is *C. giganteum*. This has white trumpet-shaped flowers, flushed red inside, that point downwards from their great height. The flowers appear in summer, but as the plants begin to die they produce an incredible array of seed pods that are superb for cutting for the house. The leaves are a curious spade shape, diminishing in size as they go up the stem. This is a wonderful plant, but it has two disadvantages: it is monocarpic (it dies after flowering), and it takes eight years or so to grow a new one from seed. Fortunately, it also produces small offsets round the old plant and these can be divided off, but they will still take several years to mature. The answer is to sow some new seed every year, and once the initial wait is up there will always be plants flowering every year. They look most spectacular when growing between, or even overtopping, shrubs, especially when, on suddenly turning a corner, you are confronted with them.

Cardiocrinums are the most hungry of bulbs, and they must be given a rich diet. Before planting, dig a deep hole and fill it with farmyard manure or rich compost.

Chionodoxa (glory of the snow)

From one extreme to another: we are now back at ground level with bulbs that produce flowering stems only 10cm (4in) tall. There are several species, but the one generally seen in gardens is *C. siehei* (often referred to erroneously as *C. luciliae*, which is a completely different species). The 2.5cm (1in) flowers are of an intense blue with a white eye. They appear in late winter and early spring and later scatter plenty of seed, thereby increasing the size of the colony. Each bulb has two strap-like leaves.

Their sudden burst of colour during what is usually still a dull time of the year is most welcome. They will take a light shade, and can be planted under deciduous trees and shrubs. Being short, they should preferably be planted beside a path, but make the most of their beacon-like quality by planting them at a distant point along a path, or under a tree or shrub that will act as a focal point later in the year.

Chionodoxas are not too fussy as to soil but do prefer it to be cool, and therefore a typical woodland soil would be ideal. They will increase themselves without disturbance, but if necessary they can be dug up and divided.

Colchicum (autumn crocus, naked ladies)
Although colchicums are often called autumn crocuses because of their superficial resemblance, in fact they belong to a different family altogether. *Colchicum* is a large genus, but here we are only concerned with a few of the larger plants. The flowers are pink to purple goblets, which shoot straight from the ground in the late autumn, with no foliage in sight (hence their second common name). The dark-green leaves appear in a large cluster in the spring, and last well into the summer.

One of the finest colchicums is the straight *C. speciosum*, which has full petals and such purity of line. It is the largest of the genus, rising to 25cm (10in) or so. It has a fantastic white form, *C.s.* 'Album', that is also well worth growing. *C. autumnale* is probably the species most commonly seen, often in one of its white or double forms. This has a smaller flower and much weaker stems that tend to flop over, particularly in windy or wet weather, and is probably best grown through some other low plant that will give it support. *C. agrippinum* has smaller flowers with narrow petals that have a chequered pattern of pink and a darker pinkish purple. This species requires more sun than the others mentioned. There are many more species for those who want to collect them, but one final one must be noted. This is *C.* 'Waterlily', a spectacular double, which opens up its narrow petals to give a good imitation of a land-bound waterlily.

Most colchicums will take a bit of shade and, I think, look best growing out of fallen leaves under trees or large shrubs. There is no reason, however, for not growing them with or through other plants if you so wish. Colchicums are not at all fussy as to the soil in which they grow, and will tolerate alkaline ones. They can easily be increased by lifting in late summer, and dividing.

Corydalis
Some of the corydalis are bulbous and should, strictly speaking, be dealt with here, but they have already been covered with the others in chapter 7 (see page 114).

Crocus
These spring-flowering bulbs should not require definition for most gardeners, but what may come as a slight surprise to some is that there are also autumn-flowering species. Unfortunately, the latter prefer a warm, open position so are not really suitable for our purposes, unless they are planted in the sunny spots between shrubs. If this is a possibility, then the blue *C. speciosus* is the best one to try.

Spring-flowering crocuses also like the sun, but they can be planted under deciduous trees or shrubs and so make the most of its rays before the leaves appear on the trees, by which time the crocuses will have retired below ground. There is a very large range of species and varieties to choose from – far too many to mention even a fraction here. I must confess a personal liking for the large golden-orange forms that shine out so well in the sunshine. I am not so keen on drifts but I do like the occasional clump, especially if they take me by surprise as I turn a corner or look round a bush. But this is a personal preference, and you should choose what you want. Get one of the large bulb companies' catalogues, make your selection, then give them a try.

Crocuses will grow in a wide range of soils and should present no problems. They multiply quite readily, so once they have died down they can easily be propagated by lifting and dividing up the bulbs.

Cyclamen
These bulbs may be considered the aristocrats of the woodland scene. They appear when most other things have died down, will tolerate quite dry conditions, and will take quite dense shade. They are one of the few plants that I have seen growing under the dense, dry shade of horse chestnut (*Aesculus hippocastanum*) trees.

The wild cyclamen produce much smaller and more dainty flowers than the florists' plants. The most commonly seen is *C. hederifolium*, which flowers from August to November, although its marbled leaves will continue for much longer. Following close on its heels is *C. coum*, which lasts through to January. This has more stubby flowers, often in stronger colours. In turn, this is followed by *C. repandum* which flowers from March to May, and then by *C. purpurascens* which continues the theme through the summer. *C. hederifolium* is by far the hardiest, with *C. coum* not far behind. These are the best to go for, not only because of their hardiness but because of their flowering periods.

I love to see them in haphazard drifts under trees or tall shrubs. Since they retain their leaves after flowering it is difficult to plant them amongst other plants, as the cyclamen, being low-growing, will be deprived of light.

Cyclamen will tolerate quite dry conditions but do best in a leafmould, woodland soil. You can increase them by sowing the seed as soon as it is harvested.

Cypripedium (lady's slipper orchid)

This is one of the most beautiful of the orchids that can be grown outside, but unfortunately it is also one of the most difficult. Since cypripediums need a favoured position, a peat bed is the best place to start. Plant them in a rich mixture of well rotted humus and plenty of grit, to ensure that no excess water hangs around. Position them in dappled shade that gets some sun but still allows a cool root-run.

Having got the position and soil right, the next thing is to choose the plant. *C. calceola pubescens*, which has a yellow flower, is probably the easiest to grow. The most beautiful, however, is *C. reginae*. This has a white flower with a rose-pink 'slipper'.

Cypripediums are virtually impossible for the amateur to propagate, and it is certainly a waste of time trying to sow any seed that may be obtained. Unfortunately the plants are also difficult to obtain commercially, although they are cultivated quite widely by some experienced growers. The best advice to beginners is to gain experience with other orchids before investing time and money in tracking down cypripediums to buy.

Dactylorhiza (spotted orchid)

These are amongst the easiest orchids to grow, and will even self-sow if you are lucky. Most at one time or another belonged to the genus *Orchis*, under which they are sometimes still listed. The easiest, and one of the most natural-looking as it is a British native, is *D. fuchsii*, the spotted orchid. This is a mauvish pink with purple markings. It will grow in quite shady positions, but is usually seen alongside paths and rides where there is just a bit more light. *D. maculata* is a similar species that will also tolerate quite a bit of shade. They both clump up well and can be easily divided. The most dramatic are *DD. elata*, *foliosa* and *majalis*, which have large heads of magenta flowers that are very striking, especially the first two mentioned, as these are tall plants growing to 60cm (2ft) or more, when well suited. They will do well in dappled shade, as anyone who has seen the drifts under the hazel trees at Sissinghurst Castle will know.

These orchids will grow in a moist but well drained woodland soil, with plenty of leafmould; peat-bed conditions will suit them admirably. The only method of propagation is by division; they should never be dug up from the wild. All those listed are available from nurseries.

Eranthis (winter aconite)

These are delightful plants, and I rejoice every year when I see the first stems elbowing their way up through the soil. Once through the surface, the stems straighten and the golden-yellow flowers open up, each surrounded by a ruff of green bracts. These flowers appear in late winter before much else is stirring. When suited, they can seed around to form a great drift, and the shimmering gold in the winter sun is something to behold.

Winter aconites are best grown under deciduous trees, where they catch the sun. If possible they should be left undisturbed, so that the small seedlings can develop, creating a larger colony. The most commonly seen species is *E. hyemalis*. The other two forms occasionally seen are *E. cilicica* and *E.* 'Guinea Gold'. Neither of these is worth the extra expense, unless you have a collecting instinct – although it must be said that the latter is a much larger form than *E. hyemalis*.

Plant the tubers just beneath the surface, in a good leafmould. They can be increased from seed, that should be sown as soon as it is ripe, or by division. Be cautious about buying the dried-up tubers usually offered by garden centres – the success rate with these is very low.

Erythronium (dog's tooth violet)

Yet another genus of marvellous plants. These are not as widely grown as they should be, perhaps because the bulbs sold by garden centres are usually dried out, presenting purchasers with a dishearteningly low success rate. (Buy pot-grown plants from nurseries.) The name 'dog's tooth violet' comes from the shape of the tuber.

The nodding flowers, which have reflexed petals that give them a similar appearance to the Turk's cap lily, are carried in spring. The most commonly seen is *E. dens-canis*. It has purple flowers and very pleasing mottled leaves. Another extremely attractive form is *E.* 'White Beauty' (sometimes referred to as *E. revolutum* 'White Beauty', although it has no connection with that species). The flowers of this plant are a soft creamy yellow with a brown ring around the centre. Another form commonly seen is *E.* 'Pagoda', with pale yellow flowers and mottled leaves. One of 'Pagoda''s parents is *E. tuolumnense*, which has bright yellow flowers well set off against glossy green leaves. There are many more species and forms, if you should become especially interested in them.

Erythroniums can all be grown in a woodland garden; indeed, they prefer a light shade. Starting with one or two plants, you can work them up into small drifts. It is best not to mix the colours, as the effect becomes a bit restless. A peat bed makes an ideal position.

They like a good leafmould soil that will give them a cool, moist root-run. Most multiply quite freely and can be lifted in summer, after they have died back, and divided. They can be grown from seed, but it takes several years to get flowering plants.

Fritillaria (fritillary)
This is a very large genus, of which a surprising number are in cultivation. Although they are mainly grown, often in pots, by experienced specialist growers, there are a handful that can be grown in woodland conditions. The British snake's head fritillary, *F. meleagris*, is a plant of open meadows, but it will grow in a light shade if the soil is not too moist. It has large nodding bells with a chequered purple pattern, which appear in spring. *F. pontica*, a woodland plant happy in light or dappled shade, is reasonably easy to grow. This has smaller bells that are pale green in colour. *F. camtschatcensis*, with its spike of black bells, can look very dramatic. It is a plant that must have a moist but well drained soil, and would be ideal for the peat bed.

   All the fritillaries mentioned must have a cool root-run, but they must not be too wet during the summer months. They can be increased by lifting and dividing in late summer. They will also come from seed, but will take several years to reach flowering size.

Galanthus (snowdrop)
This is yet another of my favourite genera (be warned: bulbs can become addictive). The snowdrop season starts early, if you are a collector, with *G. reginae-olgae*, which flowers in late autumn onwards. For the ordinary gardener the season starts soon after Christmas and continues until the early spring. These delightful white flowers are one of the mainstays of the garden during the winter months. Plant them in odd clumps to catch the eye, or in drifts. Alternatively, grow them through other plants, possibly herbaceous ones that are still below ground, or allow them to emerge through fallen leaf cover.

   G. nivalis is the commonest and, being a British native, one of the best for naturalising. It has a double form, *G.n.* 'Flore Plena', which is equally vigorous. There is quite a number of varieties that are well worth growing. *G.* 'Magnet' has long, thin pedicels (flower stalks), which arch gracefully so that even the slightest breeze sets the flowers nodding. Another favourite is *G.* 'Samuel Arnott'. This has large flowers that smell sweetly when in a sunny position or when brought into a room. It clumps up very quickly and is one of the best snowdrops there is. There are also a few that can be considered as oddities: for instance, *G.* 'Scharlockii', which has leaf-like appendages that stick up like donkey's ears, and *G.n.* 'Lutescens', which has yellow markings instead of green. There are several hundred species and cultivars to choose from if you become addicted, but for general woodland purposes *G. nivalis* itself takes a lot of beating.

Plant out in any good woodland soil, in a deciduous shade. Snowdrops can be increased by dividing, which should be done after flowering and before the leaves die down. The bulbs offered by garden centres are often too desiccated, and result in disappointment. Buy either growing plants in pots, or from nurseries that offer them 'in the green' (while still in growth). This will be a bit more expensive, but at least you will have some living plants and not dead shells.

Hyacinthoides (bluebell)
The Latin generic name of the bluebell has changed several times, but seems at last to have come to rest as *Hyacinthoides*. For woodland purposes it is really the common bluebell, *H. non-scripta*, that is the best. A superficial glance distinguishes no great difference between this and the Spanish bluebell, *H. hispanica*, but on closer inspection you will notice that the Spanish one is a larger, more robust, plant and that the bells hang all round the stem and not just on one side as in the common variety. It spreads just as rapidly, and perhaps this is a cue for a statutory warning. Bluebells can be a real nuisance, once they have been introduced into a garden. The vast sheets you see in woodlands have not come about by politeness and good manners, but by rapid increase from seed and bulblets. Once established, they are very difficult to eradicate, and while at first they may look charming, when their long green leaves have started appearing amongst some of your more choice plants the charm begins to wear a bit thin. So these are really candidates for a large woodland garden, and not for a shady spot in a small one.

Bluebells will grow in any reasonable soil and will take quite a deal of summer shade, as by then they are back below ground. Increase is a simple matter, from seed or by division of the bulbs. Normally, though, they will produce enough and more without the need for active propagation on your part.

Leucojum (snowflake)
Snowflakes are often confused with snowdrops, but to anything other than a superficial glance the differences must be obvious. They have six petals of equal size that make up a wide, nodding bell a bit in the manner of a lampshade, whereas the snowdrop has three large outer petals, with three smaller ones forming a cup on the inside, and the tips of the larger garden snowflakes are touched with green.

The plant that elicits the comparison with a lampshade is *L. vernum*; it is short with tubby flowers, and will do well planted near a path under shrubs or trees or in a peat garden. Its more common relation, *L. aestivum*, is a much taller plant whose flowering stems reach 45cm (18in) or more in good conditions;

it has much smaller flowers and a lot more foliage. Its leaves are narrow and long, making good arching clumps. This species can be planted much further back in the wood, since it can be seen at a distance, and it looks particularly good next to a pond.

Leucojums need a moist, leafmould soil with a cool root-run. They can be lifted after flowering, and easily divided.

Lilium (lily)
Lilies are a big subject to cover in a small space. Vast numbers of them are available from garden centres and specialist nurseries. Most lilies like to have a cool root-run, but are not so fussy about having their heads out in the sun, so they are ideal for planting between shrubs. As well as their wide range of colours and shapes, lilies have the great advantage of being one of the few bulbs that flower during the summer.

There are so many that it is very difficult to know where to start. For simplicity and beauty, the white trumpets, flushed on the outside with pink, of *L. regale* are hard to beat. These have a strong perfume which will invade the whole area around them. *L. szovitsianum* can be the subject of admiration when suddenly glimpsed between two tall bushes, the fragrant yellow flowers well set off against the greenery around and behind them. In good conditions it can grow 2m (7ft) tall. Perhaps more attuned to the woodland scene are the Turk's-cap lilies (*L. martagon*), especially when grown in drifts under trees where shafts of sunlight can suddenly illuminate them. The stems are clothed in whorls of leaves which are attractive in themselves, and these are topped with spires of nodding lilies in pink to purple or, sometimes, white. This is probably the most natural-looking one to grow.

There are many, many more to choose from, and the best thing I can suggest is that you get a catalogue from a specialist nursery and go through it for lilies that appeal. I would avoid some of the larger ones in brasher colours, as these may not be in sympathy with the woodland surroundings.

Lilies generally like a rich, humus-laden soil that has had grit added to it to ensure that it is free-draining. Propagation is a bit complicated, but they can all be grown from seed. Bear in mind, though, that they can take several years to reach flowering size. Many can be lifted after flowering, and divided. Those that produce bulbils in the axils of the leaves can have these sown like seed.

Muscari (grape hyacinth)
This is a genus on which, for a change, I am not so keen. While I like the small, dense spires of blue flowers that they produce in spring, I dislike their habit of seeding everywhere, and their rather lax foliage which seems to take an age to die back and disappear. Neither of these objections is so strong in a woodland

setting, and muscari can be used to good effect to create drifts of blue, preceding bluebells by a month or more. Although spring-flowering, they put up their leaves in the previous autumn. At this stage the foliage is not too bad; it is once the flowers are over that it becomes rank.

Those that are most commonly seen are *M. armeniacum* and *M. neglectum*, the former being a paler blue than the latter. One species that I do like is *M. latifolium* which has a single wide leaf and bicoloured flower spikes, the lower flowers being a dark blue and the upper ones paler. This does need a bit more light than the previous two species. Another that many people like is the fluffy-flowered *M. comosum*, the tassel hyacinth, but unfortunately this really requires a hot, sunny position.

Muscari will grow in any good soil that is not too moist. They can easily be increased by lifting in the summer, and dividing.

Narcissus (daffodil)

Once again we have a genus that is represented by a few species and hundreds of cultivars. Most like a little light shade, and so the choice becomes almost unlimited. In many respects I think simplicity is the keynote when making a selection. I personally like the common wild daffodil (*N. pseudonarcissus*). This might not be as bright and brash as most of the others, but it has that modesty which often separates a wild flower from a highly bred garden flower.

Certainly, if you are contemplating drifts under trees then I think this is the one to go for. As for the larger, cultivated varieties that have been derived from this species, I would be inclined to plant them in isolated clumps where they cannot be seen one from another, so that interest is concentrated on them for a few moments before you move on. Drifts can be created from the larger-flowered varieties, but this is a matter of personal choice. I would, however, advise against buying a large sack of mixed bulbs, as the spotty nature of the resulting planting will not be very pleasing. Once again, with so many to choose from the advice must be to get a comprehensive catalogue and make a personal choice.

Narcissus can be planted in any good garden soil. Once they have died down, they can readily be increased by lifting and dividing.

Nectaroscordum

This genus consists of four species of which two species, or one species and a subspecies, depending on which botanists you elect to follow, are commonly grown. (To further confuse the issue, some botanists still leave them all in *Allium*.) There is, in fact, very little difference between *N. bulgaricum* and *N. siculum*. They are both tall-growing species, reaching 90cm (3ft) or more, with dense heads of nodding flowers in a mixture of pink, green and white. They are certainly decorative, and continue to be so when in seed, as the seed heads rise up like turrets on a fairy-tale castle. However, they have two disadvantages. In the first place they stink something terrible (of rotting onions) when you touch them; and, secondly, they seed everywhere and can become a nuisance unless you have the space to give them their head.

Nectaroscordums are essentially flowers of the sun but will happily take light shade, and look particularly good in tall stands between shrubs. Plant them in any good garden soil. Propagation can be by division after they have died back, or from seed. They provide so many seedlings, though, that there is not much for you to do.

Nomocharis

This unusual genus is closely related to the lilies. Its flowers are extremely beautiful, and do best in light shade. However, these are not the easiest of bulbs to grow, and you might well have many failures before you get conditions right. The reason for including them, in spite of their difficult nature, is that they are very attractive plants.

Nomocharis are quite lily-like in appearance, except that the drooping flowers are much flatter. They all bloom towards the end of summer. The one most commonly seen is *N. saluenensis*, which has a dark purple eye and a paler, spotted pinkish-purple ground. *N. mairei* has much paler, almost white, petals that are heavily spotted, and the three inner segments are fringed. *N. aperta* is pale pink with a very dark purple eye surrounded by purple spots.

They all like a cool, moist root-run and are best planted in a peat bed in light shade. They can be increased from seed. When choosing nomocharis, never buy dried specimens – always purchase them growing in a pot. This is a most delightful genus, and more attempts should be made at growing them well.

Ornithogalum (star of Bethlehem)

This is a very large genus of bulbs, the naming of which has never really been sorted out; but since we are only dabbling on the fringes of the subject, this should not worry us too much. Although many of the species are very much alike, it is still a very attractive genus. I have always been fond of the freshness of the narrow leaves and white (tinged with green), star-like flowers. Most are probably sun-lovers, but there are a couple of common ones that will happily take light shade. *O. umbellatum* is the best-known, flowering in late spring, with each flower held out on a stalk like a candelabrum, and forming a flat sea of flowers. *O. nutans* has similar flowers, but they are held closer to the stalk, forming a spike. The former can be quite invasive when it finds a situation it likes, producing large colonies, so be wary of planting in a small garden near other treasured plants. Sometimes the bulbs can multiply to such an extent that the thick clump seems too exhausted to flower, and they need splitting up if they reach this stage. They are quite happy growing in grass.

Ornithogalums will grow in any good soil, but I would avoid the peat bed, where they could become too invasive. They can most easily be increased by lifting in summer, and dividing.

Scilla (squill)
This is another genus of blue spring flowers, but there is nothing wrong in that. One of the commonest is *S. siberica*, which has bright blue flowers, especially in the form *S.s.* 'Spring Beauty'. There is also a white form, *S.s.* 'Alba'. *S. bifolia* has more open flowers, again in blue, but also with pink and white forms. (Bluebells were once classified in this genus (amongst others) but have now moved to *Hyacinthoides*.)

Scillas do well in light shade, and can be worked up into small drifts that stand out beneath deciduous shrubs. They will grow in any good garden soil and can easily be increased by lifting, after the foliage has died down, and dividing.

Trillium (wake robin)
It is always a toss-up whether to include this in the bulbs or in the perennials; to all intents and purposes it looks more like the latter, although it springs from a bulb-like rhizome. It does not really matter – the thing is, you must grow some trilliums. They are amongst the best of woodlanders; indeed, I first became interested in this type of gardening as a means to growing these fascinating plants.

As the name implies, trilliums have their parts in threes: three leaves, three sepals and three petals. There is still some confusion over the names, but they are gradually settling down. The commonest, and to many people the best, is *T. grandiflorum*, which has pure-white petals set off beautifully by the ruff of green leaves. There is a double form, *T.g.* 'Flore Plena', that to many eyes is even more beautiful. These plants grow to about 30cm (12in) or so.

A taller plant that for many years has been known as *T. sessile* (the true *T. sessile* is a miffy plant in comparison) was thought for a while to be *T. chloropetalum* and is now, we are told, named *T. kurabayashiii*. Once you have waded through all these names, you end up with a most distinctive plant with mottled leaves and rigidly upright petals of a most wonderful rich maroon. These can look superb in drifts, particularly with the sun on them. The true *T. chloropetalum* has very similar flowers, from a yellowish colour to purple. *T. luteum* has similar erect petals, but is much smaller in both stature and flower size. The flowers are yellow and have a fine scent if you bend close enough to smell them.

There are many more species to explore should you wish to go further, but these are the ones to start with.

Trilliums will increase slowly to form drifts, planted either near paths or further into the wood. Most look best if they can be lit up by the occasional shaft of sunlight. They all like a moist woodland soil with plenty of leafmould. Trilliums can be increased from seed, but they take several years to reach flowering size. You can also propagate them by dividing established clumps in autumn or early spring.

10   Grasses, Bamboos and Ferns

This final chapter discusses some of the green plants that constitute the framework of any garden. Their value comes in their shapes and textures, as well as in the numerous shades of green that they supply. Grasses and bamboos can contribute to a wood's sound effects, usually adding a dry rustling to the greener sounds of the leaves and the tapping of the branches. A minor, romantic point perhaps, but there is no reason why the different sounds, as you move from one part of the wood to another, should not be enjoyed as much as the changing sights.

Not many grasses will tolerate too much shade; but there is no reason why clumps, particularly of the larger ones, should not be planted amongst shrubs where they will experience some of the overhead sun. From the design point of view, grasses include plants that have a strong vertical emphasis which contrasts well with most other inhabitants of the woodland garden, as well as some with more arching, rounded shapes. Colours are not always green, but can include gold and silver variegations. On the whole, they are not too fussy about soil conditions. Grasses are still not that common in garden centres, but interest in them is on the increase. Better selections will be found at specialist nurseries. Most can either be divided or sown from seed, in spring.

Bamboos have been all but neglected in gardens in recent times, but there is now a resurgence of interest in these too, which will, perhaps, make them more readily available. There is an increasing number of specialist nurseries which offer not only a large range of plants but also advice that would not be forthcoming from the average garden centre. Bamboos can be a bit of a pest, as some are decidedly invasive, making them plants for large woodland gardens. Some, however, are well behaved, and can be introduced into the smaller garden. I feel that large blocks of bamboo can look alien in the landscape, and that they should be used with care. They all like a woodland setting with dappled shade. They rarely flower and therefore sowing from seed is impractical; the main method of increase is by division in spring.

Ferns can become addictive. So far I have resisted the temptation to collect them, although I do have several different types dotted around the garden, including the dreaded bracken which wanders in from an adjacent field. Fern freaks tend to see much more in their ferns than do the rest of us, but without necessarily delving into the minutiae most of us appreciate their general shapes and appearances. Ferns are attractive throughout their year's cycle, from unfurling until they turn brown (assuming that they are not evergreen ones). The feathery green fronds lend a coolness and delicacy to the scene that contrasts well with bolder shapes, such as that of hostas. They are very useful next to plants that die back early in the year at the time when the ferns are still unfolding, because they will expand to cover the vacant ground or the dying vegetation. No woodland garden should be without a few, either as single dramatic clumps or in drifts.

Propagation is not so straightforward as with some other plants in this book. Certainly, many can be divided in autumn or spring, which presents no particular problem, but most can also be grown from spore – which is where the difference lies. Spore cannot be dealt with in the same way as seed, as it has a much more complicated life cycle which involves growing an intermediate plant before the fern is recreated. Many will self-sow, thus presenting no problem; but if you want to go into the process of growing your own, I strongly recommend that you obtain a book on the subject because, although not a difficult task, it is far too complicated to explain here. Most ferns prefer a moist soil in shade, but many will grow in surprisingly dry situations.

The number of grasses, bamboos and ferns is legion, but I have selected a few of my favourites and present them here with brief descriptions.

Adiantum
Fern. This is a large genus of which only two species are generally grown. *A. pedatum* is a most beautiful plant. It grows to about 45cm (18in) and has thin black stems with delicate leaflets. There are dwarf forms, which would do best on a peat bed. It is a slowly increasing plant. *A. venustum* is very similar, but is only about half the size of its relative. They both prefer a reasonably protected site.

Arundinaria
Bamboo. This is a genus of about fifty species, of which several are available. Unfortunately the nomenclature is far from clear, as some authorities have split the whole genus up under new names, while others still retain some of it. *A. amabilis* is a fine bamboo that is often used for making fishing rods and for other commercial purposes. It forms a dense clump of straight stems that rise up to 10m (33ft), if well suited, but it is not always hardy so should only be grown in the warmer areas. The only other one I wish to mention is *A. spathacea*,

which forms a tight clump of gracefully arching stems covered in small leaves. This needs to be planted in a position where it catches the breeze (but not strong winds), so that its graceful movements are emphasised. It likes a moist soil, so would do well near water.

Asplenium
Fern. *A. scolopendrium* is one of the best ferns in the genus, but has been moved to *Phyllitis*. This does leave, however, *A. trichomanes*, the maidenhair spleenwort, a dainty plant of no more than 12.5cm (5in) or so that grows on shady walls. It is a British native and will quickly colonise a damp wall, which can be ideal if you are lucky enough to have such a structure passing through your woodland garden.

Athyrium (lady fern)
Fern. *A. filix-femina* is a splendid British native plant. It has light-green fronds with a delicate, lacy appearance. It grows up to about 90cm (3ft) in good conditions, which include a moisture-retentive soil, although it will do reasonably well in quite a dry position. It will take a surprising amount of shade, but it would be best to plant it in a more dappled position and let it sow itself into the deeper shade if this is to its liking. *A. filix-femina* has several distinctive forms, but in a wild woodland garden the species itself is to be preferred. There are also other species of *Athyrium* to explore, if you so wish.

Blechnum (hard fern)
Fern. *B. spicant* is the British native hard fern. It likes to grow in moist positions where the atmosphere, as well as the soil, is damp. The fronds have darkish stems and simple leaflets on either side that give the impression of the bones of a flat fish after the flesh has been removed. They are a shiny green and reach a height of about 75cm (30in), making it a very attractive plant for a woodland setting. *B. tabulare* is much larger, reaching 90cm (3ft) in height. This is a spreading species and will soon make a colony; in drifts is perhaps the best way to see it. It dislikes alkaline soils.

Carex
Sedge. The sedges are a very large genus (some authorities list two thousand species), but I am going to be very selective. The one I like most in a woodland setting is the weeping sedge (*C. pendula*), which can often be seen in wetter spots in native woods. The broad leaves make a large drooping hummock about 45cm (18in) high, from which emerge long, arching stems carrying the sedge's flowering head, which hangs like fish on a line. The boldness and simplicity of

the plant can be quite stunning. It will take quite a deal of shade, but it must have moist conditions.

Cystopteris (bladder fern)
Fern. One of the British natives, *C. fragilis*, brittle bladder fern, is especially attractive, with dark, brittle stalks and delicately cut pinnae (leaflets). It is well worth attempting to grow this 30cm (12in) plant in a wall or amongst rocks, if you have such a feature in your wood.

Dennstaedtia
Fern. *D. punctilobula* is invasive, and should only be grown in the larger woodland gardens where it can be allowed to form a large attractive colony as a background to some other planting. In spite of its tendency to spread, it is a pretty fern with light-green fronds.

Dryopteris (male fern, buckler fern)
Fern. *D. filix-mas*, the male fern, is a native plant that is likely to find its own way into your wood without your having to introduce it. If it is not there, it is well worth putting in a plant and letting it seed around. It is particularly attractive at the time that each frond unfurls. Less dainty than the lady fern, it is still very pleasing, and forms clumps 90cm (3ft) or more tall. Although it prefers a moist soil, it will take to dry conditions and will flourish in quite deep shade. There are many forms of it in cultivation. Another native is *D. dilatata*, the broad buckler fern. This has wider fronds and is more segmented than the male fern. A magnificent giant amongst ferns is *D. wallichiana* from Japan, which will grow up to 1.5m (5ft).

Glyceria
Grass. Of the several members of this genus in cultivation, *G. maxima* 'Variegata' is the only one I wish to mention. *G. maxima* itself is a coarse green grass that runs around and should be ignored. Its variegated form, however, is a very good plant that is not as footloose as the type and makes a good clump in a moist position, preferably beside water.

Gymnocarpium (oak fern)
Fern. The British oak fern, *G. dryopteris*, is not one of the big stately ones, but a small one (up to 30cm (12in)) that grows in shady places, especially on stream banks and rocky outcrops. It has a fresh green appearance with a dark wiry stem and delicate leaflets, which makes it well worth growing in any garden. It spreads slowly, so is not a nuisance even in the smallest garden.

Matteuccia (ostrich feather fern)
Fern. *M. struthiopteris* is a very distinctive fern with an upright growth like a narrow shuttlecock. It grows to about 90cm (3ft), and has fronds of a fresh green. There is a tendency for it to put out underground runners, so that new plants crop up at intervals until a drift is established. They look fine in this context, but lose part of their upright charm.

Melica (melick)
Grass. Since childhood I have been fascinated by wood melick (*M. uniflora*). I am not certain why, but I think it has something to do with running the flower and seed heads through one's fingers. Be that as it may, it is a good grass (growing up to 60cm (2ft)) for planting in a wood. It runs underground and will soon make loose colonies.

Milium
Grass. Here my favour falls on Bowles' golden grass (*M. effusum* 'Aureum'), which is a plant that few gardens can afford to be without. It is about 60cm (2ft) high with blades and stems of a soft golden yellow which blend in extremely well with so many colour schemes. Plant it in clumps or drifts, depending on the situation. It does not run, but seeds itself around in an innocent kind of way.

Miscanthus
Grass. Generally tall, these grasses will make a wonderful contrast when planted as single clumps between shrubs. The various forms of *M. sinensis* are amongst my favourites. They have upright stems with floating leaves and loose, silky flower heads that blow in the wind, *M.s.* 'Silberfeder' being the best. *M.s.* 'Zebrinus', tiger grass, has curious variegations in the form of gold bands painted *across* the stems. These are all about 180cm (6ft) or so, but coming in at 270cm (9ft) is *M. sacchariflorus*, which makes very distinctive large clumps.

Onoclea
Fern. *O. sensibilis*, the American oak fern, has large fronds with broad, flat, pale-green segments. It is quite distinct, particularly in autumn when it turns a wonderful russet brown. It is invasive, and should only be planted where it has room to roam. Damp soil is preferred, but it will happily colonise under trees.

Osmunda (royal fern)
Fern. *O. regalis* is one of the tallest of our native ferns. It has very large green sterile fronds through which rise the erect brown fertile ones, looking for all the world like the dried seed heads of a large dock. The plant reaches 150cm

(5ft) or more when well satisfied, in moist conditions. It grows especially well (and looks good) beside water.

Phyllitis (hart's tongue fern)
Fern. *P. scolopendrium* (formerly *Asplenium scolopendrium*) is a plant without the usual ferny fronds, but has instead a plain, wide strap-like frond with an undulating edge. These dark-green leaves grow up to about 60cm (2ft) in length. It is a particularly beautiful fern, which retains its foliage during winter. The fronds make it a good foil for plants with a more delicate foliage. It should be planted in a moist soil, in a shady position.

Phylostachys
Bamboo. A large genus, of which quite a number of species are in cultivation. The commonest is probably *P. nigra*, which has distinctive black stems that arch gracefully and form dense clumps. There are several named forms. Another popular variety is *P. bambusoides*, which is grown mainly for its height – it will reach 20m (66ft) in the wild but less than a third of that in the most favourable conditions in Britain. Again, there are several forms.

Pleioblastus
Bamboo. Another genus of which quite a few species are cultivated. The two most common are *P. humulis* and *P. pygmaeus*. The first is about 150cm (5ft) tall, and the second much shorter at about 45cm (18in). What they have in common is that both travel at speed, swiftly making a large colony. These are plants for only the largest of woodland gardens where it does not matter if bamboos get a bit out of hand – indeed, it might even be encouraged.

Poa
Grass. *P. nemoralis*, wood meadow-grass, is one of the few lawn grasses that will succeed in light shade conditions. Use it on paths or other shady areas that require a grass cover. It can be bought in some varieties of lawn mixes.

Polypodium (polypody)
Fern. *P. vulgare* is the common polypody of the British countryside, and will make a natural resident for a woodland garden. The fronds are quite narrow, deeply cut, and shaped a bit like a long spear-head. Polypodies have the great advantage of growing in quite dry places and therefore are admirable for use on walls or banks. They will even grow on trees, in some areas. Another that is worth acquiring is *P. australe* and its various cultivars.

Polystichum (shield fern)

Fern. Except for bamboos, I have tried to stick mainly to native plants in this chapter, because they will be most at home in the woodland garden. The soft shield fern (*P. setiferum*) is no exception, growing throughout the British Isles, even in quite dry places, which is a bonus. The fronds are particularly interesting when they first unfurl, but they have a freshness and poise that make them most welcome at any time, especially as they last well into winter. They are quite large ferns, reaching up to 120cm (4ft). As one would expect, there is quite a number of cultivated forms available. Another native species is the hard shield fern (*P. aculeatum*). This has much narrower fronds with a shiny surface that makes them one of the most attractive species to grow.

Sasaella

Bamboo. This is a small genus, of which the commonest species is *S. ramosa* (previously *Arundinaria vagans*). This species has short canes reaching only about 1m (3.3ft). It is a rapid spreader which will soon form large colonies – so it is not a plant for the small garden. In a larger woodland setting it can make a good foil to the rest of the vegetation. It will take quite deep shade, often in places where nothing else will grow.

Sinarundinaria

Bamboo. A genus of but a single species, that is a refugee from *Arundinaria*. *S. nitida* is a very attractive bamboo, with canes that reach up to about 3m (10ft) or so. It has narrow leaves and forms dense clumps. It needs protection from cold winds, but otherwise can be grown anywhere in a woodland garden, either between shrubs or under trees.

Appendix: Suppliers of Plants and Seed

While the stock of garden centres is extending in range, it is well short of what most serious gardeners require. To make matters worse, some of it is of poor quality and relatively expensive. Greater satisfaction can often be obtained by going to specialist nurseries, where not only is there a wider range of plants but the prices are usually much lower (fewer overheads), and best of all there is often somebody who will be willing to talk to you about plants. Next to growing plants, nurserymen love to talk about them, and much knowledge and experience can be picked up in this way. Remember, though, that they have a living to make and do not keep them talking all day, especially in the spring when there is a great deal of work to be done.

Many nurseries still operate a mail order service, in spite of the increased costs. *The Plant Finder*, obtainable through most bookshops, will help you locate nearly all the plants that are available and, as far as I am aware, virtually all those mentioned in this book. Although extremely useful, it is only a finding list, and it is still advisable to get hold of as many nursery catalogues as possible, as they contain a wealth of descriptions as well as cultural information. There is nothing more delightful than thumbing through catalogues on a cold winter's night, and dreaming of what they hold in promise.

Below are listed a few recommended suppliers, but there may well be others who are equally good but closer to hand; consult the maps in *The Plant Finder*.

Also listed is a number of seed suppliers. Along with seed-merchants, there are a few societies which run seed exchanges for their members. Their lists contain numerous unusual plants that are not often available from any other source. You must belong to the society in order to get the seed, but there are many other benefits which will make it worth while joining.

PLANTS

Axeltree Nursery, Starvecrow Lane, Peasmarsh, Rye, East Sussex TN31 6XL. (A good collection of perennial plants and some shrubs. They specialise in *Geranium*.)

Jaques Amand Ltd, The Nurseries, 145 Clamp Hill, Stanmore, Middlesex HA7 3JS. (A wide range of bulbs, including lilies.)

Bamboo Nursery, Kinsgate Cottage, Wittersham, Tenterden, Kent TN30 7NS. (Bamboos.)

Blackthorn Nursery, Alresford, Hampshire SO24 0NL. (Daphnes and helle-bores, as well as many other unusual plants.)

Blooms of Bressingham, Diss, Norfolk IP22 2AB. (A general range of plants.)

Goldbrook Plants, Hoxne, Eye, Suffolk IP21 5AN. (A very large range of hostas.)

Green Farm Plants, Bentley, Farnham, Surrey GU10 5JX. (A good range of unusual shrubs and perennials.)

Hoecroft Plants, Fosse Lane, Welton, Midsomer Norton, Avon BA3 2UZ. (A wonderful range of grasses; also, variegated and coloured-leafed plants.)

Madrona Nursery, Tara Lodge, Harden Road, East Rype, Lydd, Kent TN29 9LT. (A good range of unusual shrubs and trees.)

Savill Garden, Great Park, Windsor, Berkshire SL4 2HT. (A good source near London of trees and shrubs, including unusual ones.)

Starborough Nursery, Starborough Road, Marsh Green, Edenbridge, Kent TN8 5RB. (A very good collection of trees and shrubs.)

Stone Lane Gardens, Stone Farm, Chagford, Devon TQ13 8JU. (A large range of trees and shrubs, especially of birches and alders.)

Tile Barn Nursery, Standen Street, Iden Green, Benenden, Kent TN17 4LB. (A nursery specialising in species cyclamen.)

Unusual Plants, Beth Chatto Gardens, Elmstead Market, Colchester, Essex CO7 7DB. (A wide range of perennial plants for shady areas.)

Wallace & Barr, The Nurseries, Marden, Kent TN12 9BP. (A large selection of bulbs, including lilies.)

Washfield Nursery, Horn's Road, Hawkhurst, Kent TN18 4QU. (A wide selection of perennial plants, including hellebores and snowdrops.)

SEED

John Chambers, 15 Westleigh Road, Barton Seagrave, Kettering, Northants NN15 5AJB. (An extensive list of wild-flower seed.)

Chiltern Seeds, Bortree Stile, Ulverston, Cumbria LA12 7PB. (A wide range of perennials and shrubs, many unusual.)

Hardy Plant Society (Secretary), Garden Cottage, 214 Ruxley Lane, West Ewell, Surrey KT17 9EU. (A large seed exchange covering a wide range of perennial plants. Seed can be supplied only to members.)

Royal Horticultural Society (Secretary), Vincent Square, London SW1P 2PE. (A large seed exchange covering perennials, trees and shrubs. Seed available only to members.)

Suttons Seeds Ltd, Hele Road, Torquay, Devon TQ2 7QJ (General ornamental plants.)

Thompson & Morgan, London Road, Ipswich, IP2 0BA. (General ornamental plants.)

Wildseeds, Branas Llandderfel, Gwynedd LL23 7RF. (Wild-flower seed.)

Bibliography

Berrisford, Judith. *The Wild Garden*. Faber & Faber, 1966.

Bird, Richard. *Flowering Trees and Shrubs*. Ward Lock, 1989.

Brown, George E. *Shade Plants for Garden and Woodland*. Faber & Faber, 1980.

Davis, Brian. *The Gardener's Illustrated Encyclopedia of Trees and Shrubs*. Viking, 1987.

Evans, Alfred. *The Peat Garden and its Plants*. Dent, 1974.

Fish, Margery. *Gardening in the Shade*. Collingridge, 1964.

Jekyll, Gertrude. *Wood and Garden*. Longman Green, 1899.

Kelly, John. *Ferns in Your Garden*. Souvenir Press, 1991.

Lloyd, Christopher. *Foliage Plants*. Collins, 1973.

Mathew, Brian. *The Year-Round Bulb Garden*. Souvenir Press, 1986.

Robinson, William. *The Wild Garden*. John Murray, 1870.

Thomas, Graham Stuart. *Perennial Garden Plants*. 3rd ed. Dent, 1990.

Index

Page numbers in *italic* refer to the black and white illustrations. Entries marked with an asterisk are illustrated in the colour plates